CHICAGO QUARTERLY REVIEW

D1528382

Volume 33

AN ANTHOLOGY OF BLACK AMERICAN LITERATURE
GUEST EDITED BY CHARLES JOHNSON

2021

GUEST EDITOR
Charles Johnson

SENIOR EDITORS
S. Afzal Haider, Elizabeth McKenzie

MANAGING EDITORS
Sean Chen-Haider, Gary Houston

FICTION EDITOR
John Blades

POETRY EDITOR
Jake Young

ASSOCIATE EDITOR
Mona Moraru

CONTRIBUTING EDITORS
Jennifer Signe Ratcliff, Jim Stacey,
Umberto Tosi

GRAPHIC DESIGNER
Alvaro Villanueva, Bookish Design

EDITORIAL STAFF
Chuck Kramer

INTERN
Stuart Woodhams

BOARD OF DIRECTORS
Lois Barliant, Peter Ferry, S. Afzal Haider,
Anna Mueller Hozian, Richard Huffman,
Elizabeth McKenzie, Kathryn Vanden Berk

Cover art by Jamiel Law

The Chicago Quarterly Review is published by The Chicago Quarterly Review 501(c)3 in Evanston, Illinois. Unsolicited submissions are welcome through our submissions manager at Submittable. To find out more about us, please visit www. chicagoquarterlyreview.com.

PROUD MEMBER

[clmp]

COMMUNITY OF LITERARY MAGAZINES & PRESSES
W W W . C L M P . O R G

TABLE OF CONTENTS

POETRY

ART

EDITOR'S NOTE

These have been difficult years—2020 and 2021—for all of us. We have endured, and continue to muddle through, crises thick and threefold. Through layers of suffering that include an ongoing, mutating global coronavirus pandemic that has, at the time of this writing, caused over five hundred thousand deaths in America alone. Added to which, we endured a contentious presidential election that divided Americans in ways we have not seen since the 1960s and perhaps the Civil War, leading to an assault on the nation's Capitol on January 6, which resulted in five deaths. And death for black Americans at the hands of police officers emerged as the central theme of the Black Lives Matter movement, triggered by the killings of George Floyd and others, which drew international attention to centuries of racism and inequality in the United States and around the world.

Yet pandemics, racism, and political corruption are not new to human experience. Deaths, plagues, impermanence, and social conflicts have been with us since the beginning of human history. We can expect such experiences in the future. Just as we can expect our writers and artists to continue creating during good times and bad, "singing the world," to borrow a phrase from philosopher Maurice Merleau-Ponty, especially during troubled times, when we need the gifts of their imagination and insights to help us understand, heal, adapt, and gain the courage to live, grow, prosper, and love.

So one has to ask, how did our black storytellers, poets, essayists, and artists sing the world in the last year and a half? What kinds of worlds do black creators sing in the twenty-first century?

Moving as a phenomenologist would through the contributions of twenty-seven poets, storytellers, essayists, and artists in this special edition of *Chicago Quarterly Review*, I see not a single, monolithic black experience of our world, but instead a rich, thought-provoking, and very human diversity of profiles on our lived experiences that defies oversimplification, easy ideological slogans, and sociological clichés. When talented writers like Tibetan Buddhist teacher and spiritual icon Jan Willis, John McCluskey, Jr., Delia C. Pitts, and Cyrus Cassells conjure what we think we know about the collective black past, making visible what hitherto had been invisible, they enrich a reader's thoughts about

Booker T. Washington and W. E. B. Du Bois, the civil rights movement, and the quest for liberation and justice. Yet they show how the historical imagination need not be humorless. In the project of historical reimagining, reinterpretation, or signifying, it is possible for a writer like David Nicholson to play riffs on white pop culture artifacts—*Huckleberry Finn, Gone with the Wind, Casablanca*—that feature black people, performing imaginative variations that allow these famous characters to speak their long-suppressed truths. Or one might whimsically signify on Shakespeare in the style of celebrated poet Rita Dove.

At times a reader sees a familiar eidos or leitmotif of individual or group suffering in the poem by David Henderson brooding on the death of Eric Garner, on the certainty of aging and life's disappointments as told by arts activist E. Ethelbert Miller, in veteran actor (*Network*) Arthur Burghardt's musing on life's meaning in a bar, or in Rachel Eliza Griffith's tale of a woman lost in tragedy. But conversely, one hears exuberant joy in the gift of our all-too-brief lives in poet Peter J. Harris's spirited explanation of his Black Man of Happiness Project, which does not deny the reality of oppression. Rather, it celebrates with unabashed happiness and thanksgiving the often forgotten or ignored dignity, courage, resilience, and quotidian heroism of our black predecessors, whose daily sacrifices made our lives in the present undeniably freer than their own. One such wise elder, interviewed in this issue by John McCluskey, Jr., is jazz pianist, composer, band leader, and teacher Ahmad Jamal.

There is a healthy experiential counterpoint in the worlds embodied in these words. Time and again this complexity forces a reader to abandon preconceived notions about what it means to be an American. And black. We see this in the riveting immigrant's journey of *Black Scholar* editor in chief Louis Chude-Sokei, from Biafra to Inglewood, California. It's equally there, this complexity, in novelist Jeffery Allen's remembrance of Stanley Crouch, the nonpareil, combative, common-sense culture critic whose brutal honesty we sorely miss in our present moment of racial confusion and turmoil.

Crouch, I believe, would have appreciated the clear-eyed acuity some of this issue's writers bring to addressing the notes of purposelessness in black lives: the minefields awaiting our children who must cross dangerous terrain in their own communities, and sometimes in their families. Playwright Tsehaye Geralyn Hébert traces a mother's pain over lives tragically cut short by black-on-black violence in Chicago, while the prolific Afrofuturist sci-fi author and accomplished martial artist Steven Barnes reveals how he, as a sensitive, imaginative boy, found the strength to not back down from bullies who were on a trajectory toward early death. Much the same rite of passage appears in the young life of artist-writer Clifford Thompson, creating a sense for how the discipline of martial art training often helps talented but not necessarily athletic young black males who are shy and nerdy in their early teens. Such a discipline strengthens their character, their values, their independence, the acceptance of themselves, and the devotion necessary for the demands of their art. The minefields these young men must negotiate can be as close to home as when a security guard in my story must face an almost impossible moral dilemma during the worst days of the COVID-19 pandemic.

The essayist Jerald Walker, whose recent book *How to Make a Slave* was short-listed for last year's National Book Award, muses on the dilemma of cultural appropriation and, by doing so, invokes not just a black experience seldom described, but also the thoroughly profound American truth of how our lives are integrated in a multiracial tissue of cross-racial and cross-cultural influences. Put another way, integration, as Martin Luther King Jr. knew, is seen as the lifeblood of being. This is a sensitivity for the cultural and racial "one, and yet many" that characterizes black American life (and all life), an observation made long ago by the great novelist Ralph Ellison. An appreciation for that shrewd perception, as well as for the highly sophisticated lives of well-educated, talented, and consummately professional black people, is bodied forth in an excerpt from the second novel of award-winning novelist Sharyn Skeeter, a Tibetan Buddhist practitioner, who was once an editor on the original staff of *Essence* and editor in chief of *Black Elegance* magazine. This is a valuable ontological clarification of the way our lives exhibit integration in the very depths and DNA of our being. (In his book *In My Father's House*, Kwame Anthony Appiah reminded us that "we are all already contaminated by each other.") Such a truth by itself is worth the price of admission to this special issue on black literature.

But of course, there is more here to delight readers. Much more. The work of distinguished poet and painter Clarence Major, who for more than half a century has delivered innovative works of fiction to our literature, brightens these pages. Masterful contributions by poets Mona Lisa Saloy, Yesenia Montilla, celeste doaks, Aaron Coleman, and E. Hughes and memorable nonfiction by Le Van D. Hawkins are also here.

The editors of this special issue deserve special thanks, first to *CQR* founder and novelist Syed Afzal Haider (*To Be with Her* and *Life of Ganesh*). I must also express my gratitude to two of *CQR*'s gifted editors: novelist Elizabeth McKenzie (*Stop That Girl*, *MacGregor Tells the World*, and *The Portable Veblen*) and journalist and actor (*Fargo*, *Watchmen*, and *Proof*) Gary

Houston. This issue would not have been possible without the skill, sweat, and sacrifice they devoted to it.

For me, it has been a pleasure and privilege to experience this cornucopia of creativity by some of the best artists at work in America today. It is my hope that readers will feel the same.

—Charles Johnson

REMEMBERING STANLEY
Jeffery Renard Allen

I n early 2000, the *New York Times Book Review* reviewed first novels by three black writers, Zadie Smith, Stanley Crouch, and myself, three black writers in one issue, a cause for celebration. Zadie and I had glowing reviews, but Stanley's reviewer trashed his book. Later that week, I received a voice message left on my answering device. "Jeffery Renard Allen, this is Stanley Crouch." Then he said something about how

Stanley Crouch at Lincoln Center, 2013
Photo by Brad Barket, Getty Images

I had written an extraordinary novel, as good as *Invisible Man*, and that I would get the National Book Award and a "bunch of other shit," and how he, Danzy Senna, and I were the three greatest living "Negro" novelists and that being the case, "we should first do a reading series in NYC where we would read every week somewhere, then perhaps go on a national tour so people come and hear what we are doing since too many people these days don't read, they just pretend to or they read dumb shit, which is one reason why everything is so fucked up, so we would be doing these dumb motherfuckers an invaluable service because we could read every week somewhere and these clueless politically correct types could come listen and be blown away by our shit, then they would know the good shit, which would in turn teach all the other Negro novelists that they need to stop writing that stupid-ass P.O.C. shit and write about the eternal verities. Wise up and start writing some good shit, the great American novel rooted in the greats, namely, *Moby-Dick*, Dostoevsky, Faulkner, and *Invisible Man*, and also jazz, which is the highest articulation of Negro excellence, none of that 'here today gone tomorrow' shit that stupid people praise and that involves no craft, especially stupid white people and these so-called Black Radicals who you can tell never read Ellison, only dumb shit like Marx and Amiri Baraka, who has wasted his talent believing dumb shit."

He left a number where I could call him back.

I didn't know it then, but Stanley Crouch was seeking to champion me as he had tried to champion other black ("Negro") writers. Indeed, recently, John Edgar Wideman told me that he had received a similar phone call from Stanley back in the seventies. And Charles Johnson offered a similar report: "In 1982, I got a phone call from Stanley, who wanted to talk with me before he reviewed my second novel, *Oxherding Tale*, for the *Village Voice*. We'd never met until that moment. That novel was a book no one wanted. Editors were afraid of it or couldn't understand it, and even my literary mentor, John Gardner, who was Christian, was uncomfortable with its interface between slavery, Buddhism, and Eastern philosophy. It was rejected two dozen times, though I poured everything I had at the time into it for five years. Originally, it was published by Indiana University Press. It was the book I personally *had* to do. If I'd not published it, I would have had no interest whatsoever in writing anything else, and I can say with no hesitation that it has been the foundation for everything else I've done since 1982. Stanley's magnificent two-page review (which is in *Notes of a Hanging Judge*) led to *Oxherding Tale* . . . being leased by Grove Press for a paperback edition, and that kept it available to readers and literary scholars for decades."

At the time Stanley left a message for me, all I knew is that I needed to return his call. I figured I should first read his novel, so I bought a copy. The negative review had been on point. (My agent put it succinctly, "You're a novelist and he isn't.") What would I say to Stanley?

I gave him a call. We made some casual conversation with him playing the role of mentor and advisor. "Hey, don't let teaching get in the way of your writing. Otherwise you will be known as a teacher who writes books some of the time." (I failed to heed his advice.) Somehow it came up that I had been a student of Lore Segal and that we remain close friends. "That explains a lot," he said. For he said that she'd written a great novel, *Her First American*. A great novel indeed. It tells the story of an interracial relationship, a theme that I would discover was of great interest to Stanley, along with passing, hence his admiration for Danzy Senna's *Caucasia*.

He started reading passages of *Rails Under My Back* and explaining what I was doing. "See, there you're . . ." I mostly stayed silent through it all, thanking him from time to time for his compliments. Then he started talking about his own novel, waxing on his choice of devices—the "tropes" and "triplets"—and laying out the reasons for why he'd chosen to write a book about a white woman with a big derriere.

Now I understood that Stanley didn't think like a fiction writer, didn't know that he couldn't approach fiction in the same way that he approached nonfiction, criticism. A fiction writer has to be loose, like an athlete who has warmed up before a competition. You prepare but you never impose.

Then Stanley started talking about another novel he was working on. The pattern was set. For years to come, he would call me each Saturday and read me sections of bad novels in progress, the worst being the one about a character called SabreTooth Pootiebutt; correction, the one featuring African American porn star Sean Michaels. "The other day I was watching Sean Michaels in this porn movie and saw something I've never seen before . . . Man, that's some extraordinary shit. I'm going to put that in my novel." To keep up with Stanley, I felt compelled to share with him what I knew about porn. So one Saturday I told him that there is an entire genre of racist fetish involving white men abusing black women. The next time we talked, he chuckled. "Hey, Jeff. Thanks for telling me about Ghetto Gaggers. I'm going to put that in my book."

During those years, I had to put up with Stanley trashing two of my favorite writers, Toni Morrison and John Edgar Wideman. He believed that Morrison had stolen from Leon Forrest, a writer she edited and one that he championed. Claimed that Leon knew it. To Stanley, Danzy Senna was a better writer than Morrison, was one of the few women novelists of today worth reading because she didn't write through the lens of that "feminist bullshit." As for John Wideman, "Man, whatever that shit he is writing doesn't make sense, pure gobbledygook. Have you ever read one of his novels? Could you finish it? I can't finish one either. Now what he needs to do is write a book about his son in prison. I don't see why he won't write that book."

Stanley's notion of art and of greatness was too narrowly defined. He wrote a great book about Charlie Parker, *Kansas City Lightning*, that had a fatal flaw, his belief that Parker's genius could be explained, that this genius came from geography, upbringing, hard work, and other identifiable factors. "The skills that Charlie Parker brought to such visceral prominence on those nights at the Savoy were the result of a tenacious ambition that first took shape in the latter-day Wild West known as Kansas City" (42). Stanley believed that Clint Eastwood's film *Bird* didn't show Parker's genius, but he failed to understand that sociology can't "show" genius, explain it, define it.

For Stanley, both Parker and Ralph Ellison, the "Oklahoma City Kid," embodied the spirit of the "Wild West." He starts his eulogy for Ellison this way: "When Ralph Ellison saddled up the pony of death and took that long, lonesome ride into eternity . . . the quality of American civilization was markedly diminished. He had always traveled on the ridge above the most petty definitions of race" (*All-American Skin Game*, 86). He continues in this vein: "I sometimes thought of him as riding high into the expanses of the American experience, able to drink the tart water of the cactus, smooth his way through the Indian nations, drink and gamble all night long, lie before the fire with a book, distinguish the calls of the birds and the animals from the signals of the enemy, gallop wild and wooly into the big city with a new swing . . . , then bring order to the pages of his work with an electrified magic pen that was also a conductor's wand" (86).

Here, Stanley sounds like a precocious teenager trying to impress his English teacher. Metaphor does not make the world. Where in Proust the extended metaphor gives shape to the world, showing it from several angles at once, in Crouch the extended metaphor is often a rhetorical strategy, mere image, idea. Stanley could not loosen up and let the world be.

I find this surprising since Stanley started out as a loose writer. Here is how he begins the introduction to his first book, the verse collection *Ain't No Ambulances for no Nigguhs Tonight*, poems that were mostly penned in 1968, three years after the Watts riots, which Stanley knew firsthand:

> As I look at this book now, as I think about it, it is about me when I'm on the real, on the right side. It's also me when I'm crazy, when I'm trying to put some sort of frame on a world that will slide out of any frame, that will not be locked down my way or anybody else's. Yes, there will be shapes, there will be structures, but there is something in this world so free, so purely warm and compassionate that it will have nothing to do with that other. It will continually be where you wouldn't expect it to be, as wild flowers on mountain tops blooming bright in the cold, blooming *bright* in the cold. (11)

Stanley's propensity for metaphor is evident everywhere in the collection:

> Love is the body of the bird
> and we are its wings
> full of bullet holes
> weighed down with stones
> the perpetual new movement
> lashed, of that poem,
> the swish of that hymn against the air
> lashed by the metal standing army of this cage
> (heavy artillery brought down the bird
> it hit the snow like a shell
> and railed ice in spattered slaps in the air. (20)

Here, Stanley is loose as in his best writing, his music criticism, jazz writing. However, Stanley writing *about* jazz (and the blues) is another story. Jazz (and the blues) always become existential philosophy: "Jazz teaches us how to convert the pulp frog into the prince with the swing of Louis Armstrong. Jazz is not only about transforming pulp frogs, it is also about slaying the dragon and making cuisine out of his corpse. When that dragon is our industrial world, we have to face its menace and slay the temptations of the cynical and defeatist; we have to use the blasts of dragon fire to smelt the durable industrial lyricism that arrives through that perfect symbol of human being and machine: the musician putting personal and collective human meaning through the machinery of an instrument, swinging the blues to be here, swinging the blues to be there, swinging the blues to be everywhere" (*All-American Skin Game*, xv).

That is a lot for a song or a performance to bear. (Pity any musician who would make such claims for his music.)

But Stanley was a great writer about jazz when he kept it specific, *real*. He knew the world of jazz, the people, the musicians. He had plenty of revealing anecdotes and stories—about Billie Holiday, Miles, Max Roach, Jackie McLean, Cassandra Wilson, Wynton, others—that were either his firsthand experiences or accounts he'd gotten from the horse's mouth but that he never put down on paper.

I was surprised to discover that Stanley had actually produced a record album by the great saxophonist Joe Henderson. I asked him, "What was that like?"

"Man, if Joe could have taken all the money, he would have."

Since Stanley got so much right about jazz, I never understood his position on Miles Davis. He accused Miles and Quincy Troupe of plagiarism in Miles's autobiography. One Saturday, he read me a passage from the book. "See, this is the passage Quincy plagiarized." Then he read me a similar passage from the "original" source. Then he read a second passage from Miles's autobiography. "Quincy stole that." And so on.

Recently I spoke to Quincy about this matter. Quincy believes that Stanley's distaste for Miles stems from an incident in a club where Stanley attempted to introduce himself to Miles, only for the latter to rebuff him, curse him out and insult him.

Stanley also accused Miles of lying in the autobiography. "Miles is lying in his book when he says he slapped John Coltrane. Coltrane didn't take no shit from nobody." And he refused to believe that Miles had punched Charlie Parker. In Stanley's universe, Bird, the Kansas City outlaw, and Ellison were invincible.

Once I recounted an incident that happened when Ellison was teaching at Columbia University in the late sixties, which I'd gotten from a reliable source. A young blood approached Ellison at the end of class and informed Ellison that he wouldn't be attending for the remainder of the semester because he would be busy with the Revolution. He expected an A for his final grade. Ellison told him no. The student slapped Ellison.

"I know that's a lie," Stanley said. "Ellison carried a straight razor tied to a string under his shirt."

Stanley knew a thing or two about slapping the shit out of people. Back in 2000, he encountered Dale Peck inside a Manhattan restaurant and slapped him. Famous for "hatchet jobs," Dale had written a negative review of Stanley's novel. I never spoke about the incident with Stanley. (He would have described it as "pimp-slapped.") And I was never convinced that this incident involved a true display of anger, of outrage. Instead I thought, "Stanley knows who he can hit." Violence as New York theatricality. Around the same time, Richard Ford spit on Colson Whitehead at a literary party in New York because Colson had written a bad review of his novel. (Had Stanley started a trend?) I had a similar reaction, "Ford knows who he can spit on."

I often heard Stanley talk about what he would do to Amiri Baraka if afforded the opportunity. That said, knowing how Stanley knew jazz, in time I came to believe that his beef with Amiri stemmed from artistic competition, one-upmanship. Each wanted to be recognized as the best jazz writer. They represented two styles, Stanley coming from the line of Albert Murray. In an interview, Stanley recounted how he, John Wideman, James Alan McPherson, and Michael Harper would go to Albert Murray's Harlem apartment. "Yeah, we would show up at Ralph Ellison's house, but his wife wouldn't let us in. She said Ralph was working. So we'd go to Murray's house." (For the record, John Wideman remembers it differently.)

Later I would hear stories about Stanley the alcoholic, not the Stanley I knew. The most comic and pathetic incident took place circa *Notes of a Hanging Judge*, when Stanley and a number of other African American writers were invited to a summit to discuss the merits or lack thereof of hip hop. Event done and zipper undone, Stanley went about the room peeing into one champagne bucket after another.

Stanley knew something about everything and often had his own interesting and unique take on a particular issue, which didn't fit into neat political categories, his own way of seeing. He believed that mediocre black people are often put in positions of power to deny access to intelligent and deserving black people. He lamented the fact that an "extraordinary woman" like Serena Williams experienced difficulties in love and had to resort to dating a "corny" guy like Common. No fan of the rope-a-dope, he thought Muhammad Ali was the "dope" for taking all those punches to the head. When I asked him why he stopped believing in Black Power, he answered, "My mom taught me better." In his eyes, George Zimmerman was an "asshole" who deserved to go to jail, but he felt that the Black Lives Matter movement should focus on black-on-black violence, which claims the lives of black people in far greater numbers than racist cops and killers. "They need to protest the occupying fascist armies within lower-class black communities." After Barack Obama was elected in 2008, he told me that Obama would be a great president if he studied Ralph Ellison's books of essays. This was Stanley.

As Charles Johnson said to me in an interview, Stanley was a "fighter and a truth-teller—call him our H. L. Mencken—whose voice I think we sorely need at this tortured moment in American history." I second that. We need his mixture of radicalism and conservatism. "Man, we try to tell these Negroes the truth but then they scrunch up their face and say, 'Stanley, you can't say that. And Stanley you can't say this.'" Stanley lays out that truth as he sees it in his introduction to *The All-American Skin Game*. According to Stanley, Ellison understood that black and white people in America share an interconnected fate, that he "knew that we all, in our failures as well as our victories, speak for each other" (xii).

Ellison, Murray, and Crouch all had an unshakeable faith in American democracy and were believers in American exceptionalism. Where writers like Hawthorne, Henry James, Twain, Hemingway, Fitzgerald, and Faulkner saw a nation doomed by its innocence (naivety) and its refusal to come to terms with the original sins of genocide and slavery, Ellison, Murray, and Crouch perpetuated the myth that the US is the greatest country in human history. In *The All-American Skin Game*, Stanley writes, "I don't doubt the humanity of Africans nor the humanity of any people"—Well, thank you, Stanley; how nice of you—"but . . . my recognition of the universal and boundless potential for good, for evil . . . doesn't change the fact that everything truly important to me is the result of American democracy and the European ideas that were expanded and refined in order to adjust to the intricacies of human experience, action, conflict, and ambition within these United States" (xiii). Stanley could not tolerate other visions, interpretations, of America and the world. And he had little appreciation for American artists who viewed race differently from him.

For example, because of his belief in American exceptionalism, Stanley could not see the genius of *Menace II Society*, a darkly comic film. You get no sense of the film's tone in Stanley's review: "In effect, the Hughes brothers have succeeded in making a film about the way the urban problems presented by the classic gangster tale have evolved over the last sixty years. It is about the mortal wounds of corruption, as all gangster films of serious import must be—corruption of the individual, the family, the community. The classic gangster is a man of arrogance who substitutes bold, unsqueamish action for patience and discipline; he doesn't ask, he takes. Existing in a tar bucket of the soul, he discovers that the illegal appetites of masses of people will enable him to become rich on the express train, not the local; all he has to do is keep up his nerve and limit his loyalty to those willing to die with him and for him, and he can rise above the limitations of class or the alienation of an immigrant background. In the old films, the way up for the Italian or Irish gangster was through selling illegal booze; in our time, for the lower-class black gangster, drugs up the bucks" (*All-American Skin Game*, 215).

If a reader encountered the film only in the pages of Stanley's review, he would expect the earnest, social realist exposé typical in early nineties blaxploitation. Stanley writes, "To 'act like a bitch' is to lose all respect, to be relegated to the sub-position of a 'ho.' As for education, there is only the lore of the streets—adults giving children liquor, showing them how to hustle, cursing in front of them, murdering as they look on. Beyond that, there is the blast of rap recordings and the images arriving from television. Books exist neither for learning nor pleasure. Reflection is foreign to this world of shadows, and the gangster, as always, is the man of action gone terribly astray" (216).

The larger point Stanley misses is that the film is an indictment of America, one that argues that American democracy is a lie. The film offers the idea that the powers that be introduced drugs (heroin) to South-Central Los Angeles after the Watts riots in a deliberate effort to pacify black people, to douse black anger. Interestingly enough, the Hughes brothers started shooting the film only a few months after the LA riots. They do not share Stanley's hopeful vision of American democracy. Instead, their character Caine, like all black people in America, bears the stigma of Cain, or race, a notion that Jean Toomer explores in his brilliant 1923 novel *Cane*. Unlike Stanley, the Hughes brothers do not see the "central issue of our time" as one of "maintaining democratic morale."

Stanley's fiction starts from such an optimistic position. In 2014, Stanley sent me a collection of stories, *A Clothed Woman and All That Jazz*, and asked me to peruse it and give him my opinion. Caught between a rock and a hard place, I could never bring myself to open the file, only waited a week or two and shot him back an email saying that he'd written a great book of fiction in the spirit of Ellison, what I knew he wanted to hear. I don't think he believed me.

Truth to tell, I often found Stanley's positions perplexing or troubling and suspected at times that he was performing. Could I believe him? More than one person told me I could not trust him. They were wrong.

The year before he sent me the story collection, Stanley had agreed to come to a literary and jazz festival I helped organize in East Africa. Frankly, I was surprised that he had any interest in coming to the continent given his position on Africa and Africans. More than once he'd said that Africans had made not a single important contribution to the world in arts, culture, science, or technology. Be that as it may, he agreed to come to the festival. The organizers gave me $5,000 to pay him up front, his honorarium.

However, at a certain point he felt that the organizers were harassing and disrespecting him. He told me to tell them, "Thanks for the money." We did the festival without him. Not surprisingly, come festival's end, the organizers started disrespecting me, claiming that they were experiencing a "cash flow problem" and couldn't pay me the $8,000 they still owed me in salary. They demanded that I get Stanley to pay me the $5,000 he'd received.

I called Stanley. I explained my dilemma.

"Yeah, Jeff, they've done that to people before. In fact, they do it all the time." As I would learn, his reading of the situation had proved to be right.

He told me that he didn't have the money but would later in the week, on Friday. That Friday, as promised, he met with me and paid me the $5,000 in cash. His coming through for me that way put an end of any doubts I had about Stanley the man, Stanley the talker, and Stanley the writer.

Whatever his problematic positions, he was a man of great integrity. How better the world would be if we had more like him. ∎

WORKS CITED

Crouch, Stanley. *Ain't No Ambulances for No Nigguhs Tonight.* New York: Richard W. Baron, 1972.

———. *The All-American Skin Game, or, The Decoy of Race.* New York: Vintage, 1997.

———. *Kansas City Lightning: The Rise and Times of Charlie Parker.* New York: HarperCollins, 2013.

TOMB OF THE UNKNOWN SOLDIER
Arthur Burghardt

My

Daughter

In cold winter drought

Wished me dead:

Now she weeps

Hot floods

In my spring

Post-mortem.

Pity

The trefoiled clover:

Gentle wet love

A granite green

Mist richly shawled

For the poor grave

Grown around

Me.

HAPPY HOUR MANHATTAN
Arthur Burghardt

inside, shaded afternoon of life,
outside, going again to dusk,
then the long comatose night
of too short day of gray
overcast's browning yellow fogs,
as ruddy oily faces meld by noon;
then swim bounce by a stupor in time,
claim a jigger glass of swizzle sticks
on little napkin pads spotted with crumbs
and clusters of broken toothpicks,
bloodied at ends by pieces of my gums.

remove the chicken wing
slices from between offset
off white teeth growing
darker from the brown
stains of acid gin and nicotine,
the color of the stained wood
of a corner booze dispenser;
the leather toes hook upward
in constant spasm against the brass rail
below the wood lip of its bar;
at six of the clock the noise n din begin,
so gulp a feather of the cock's tail
that rocked the world the night before
to quell the basal noise within.

In God We Trust All Others Must Pay Cash!

from the sign *look up gaze* upon this blur
of face that grows older by moments
in the *lucky strike* smoked reflection;
but the more I drink the younger
does my wan Afro visage look to be
in that mirror behind the honeycomb
of bottles and empty glasses loudly

resonating with juke's bass speaker boom;
stacks of smoky glints of mirrored
bottles n glass compel another throbbing
at temples of my head behind red dimmed
bloodshot eyes in the ever dimmed room.

mine eyes, skeins of gin cataracts
look clear in the double malt distance
and younger with each downed shot;
will this face leave any trace behind
that this veneers a mind, a life;
was this life just an obsessive's dream,
an abscess sore on the living mind,
more than an amusing swirl
of urine and *wild turkey* down,
down into the trap of the cracked
toilet bowl?

around its brownish white porcelain base
the bloodied food of someone's innards
mould on black and white octagons,
the ceramic tile of the john, this place,
an agar plate under an alien macroscope,
this stuff, peptic acid of one's scrambled
insides slide hither, digest the old grout
yonder on the worn patched *pissoir* floor;
mebbe mine this yellow gore of an earlier visit:
so with throbbing blur push past out
this men's room splintered door,
for a teetering mind can't re—member
what's been shriven n dis—membered.

                    In God We Trust All Others Must Pay Cash!

step through, close your eyes
capture a lightning bug in a jar,
hot dogs crackle at a hickory fire;
shades fade up of playing on swings,
capture fevered voices' echoes' desire,
lust to re - live spent childhood's wings,
skip swim romp climb roll catch caress,
be bored by an *ennui* of precious little things!

would I rather die to stop mind's backward crane,
torturous constant ebb of old dreams in refrain:
shades of mom's looks, breaths of papa's sighs,
dizzying smells of elms holly pecan trees,
stretching over cherry apple cinnamon pies
cooling on country sills in clean warm breeze?

eyes jolt open just before a beery tavern faint
return instead to noise stink n clink,
feel a bubbling abdomen burning;
instead capture intestines churning,
in sink n tumble of bloated organs turning;
reflex circuits check in with a floating head,
as drunken muses intrude to smirk, laugh;
is this what it's like just before you're dead?

finally toast happy hour as an assail at dusk
of useless ante-mortem thoughts pop, leer:

like herding feral cats,
like a one handed capture of gnats,
like confining worms, repelling germs,
like seeing ants crawl behind the lids,
watching the aging gnarl of your fingers,
smelling lingers on them of ether, sex,
old joys n sighs, behold the bar sign be the last
you see behind fogs of slowly blinded eyes.

In God We Trust All Others Must Pay Cash!

RUDY
Steven Barnes

> When someone with the authority of a teacher, say, describes
> the world and you are not in it, there is a moment of psychic dis-
> equilibrium, as if you looked into a mirror and saw nothing. Yet
> you know you exist and others like you, that this is a game with
> mirrors. It takes some strength of soul—and not just individual
> strength, but collective understanding—to resist this void, this
> nonbeing, into which you are thrust, and to stand up, demanding
> to be seen and heard.
>
> —Adrienne Rich

When I was a first grader at Alta Loma Elementary School, a teacher tore my world apart simply by putting me in the slow reading group because of my skin color. And it was my fellow students who saved me, with love and companionship. Adults were fools, we knew. Kids ruled. They gave me a place to hide while I tried to figure out what I was to do. This early introduction to the realities of racism was not wholly without a silver lining: it was my first clue that the world was not what adults said it was. They were wrong about me, so I knew they were wrong about other things as well. Such a realization was frightening . . . and liberating.

Later, another teacher believed in me . . . and another student tore my world to pieces.

But the fascinating thing is that I'm not sure what actions, by teacher or student, positive or negative, made the most difference in my life. I just don't know.

* * *

Out of the millions of minutes in the average lifetime, there are those that are pivotal and live on in our memories. And of all the dozens of teachers you have in a grade-school education, there are just a handful you remember. One of mine was Mrs. Elaine Otterness, who was the first adult who believed I could be a writer. She read my *Man from U.N.C.L.E.* pastiches (very thinly veiled as "Bill Conway, Agent of OCTOPUS") and, while confessing that she preferred *I Spy*, saw something to praise in my early work, even as other teachers, as late as college, mocked me for my untethered imagination. Yes, she must have laughed at the plastic jelly-bots that wiggled through sewers to attack OCTOPUS headquarters by self-assembly with magnetic joints. But maybe she saw something . . . and the fact that thirty years later that very scene made it into my Star Wars novel *The Cestus Deception* validated her trust. I was crazy . . . but maybe, just maybe, could make that insanity work for me in the adult world.

Her kindness and interest have stayed with me a half century later, as does the fact that the last time I saw her was just after Christmas vacation, smiling, looking much like the actress Sandy Dennis. She seemed strained, and when she told me her husband had died over Christmas after losing a battle with cancer, it blew my mind. She had to have known for months, and never gave a clue. All the time she cheered me on, all of the caring . . . now took on new significance seeing she had been walking through the valley of the shadow. "Write, Steve," she'd told me. "Never let anyone steal your dreams. Life is shorter than you think."

Damn. She'd said that to me before Christmas vacation. But in the New Year, she shared the reason for her clarity. She didn't return after summer vacation, and I never saw or heard of her again.

Just possibly, she gave me permission to live. What she never knew, what I never told her, was that at another moment, something she did led to the small, gentle, bespectacled and potbellied boy discovering that he had to learn how to die. And how to kill.

Strange, but true. Life is like that.

* * *

The writing aspect of my life is simple. I wrote stories and was delirious to discover that people liked them. My mother was afraid of my career ambitions, probably based on the fact that Dad was a singer—often gospel, with groups like Wings Over Jordan, but also secular, as with Nat King Cole (he was on backup on "Ramblin' Rose")—but had ultimately failed in his career, and it had damaged their marriage. As a result, I grew up without a father, uncles or brothers, raised by my mother and sister, and had no real idea how to be a man. I escaped into books, and in that world I was a mighty barbarian like Conan, or a brawling scientist adventurer like Doc Savage, or a romantic primal man like Tarzan. If there was a problem, it was that black people, if they existed at all in these exotic tales, were barbarians at best, servile or cannibalistic monsters at worst. Robert E. Howard would have his heroes enter a town and be "repulsed by the stench of Negroes" and Edgar Rice Burroughs, in his *Jungle Tales of Tarzan*, made the racist underpinnings of the jungle king explicit: "white men have imagination, black men have little, animals have none."

Horrific insults, but as I later told a college class, I "sold my melanin on the altar of my testosterone."

In some ugly ways I just wasn't a man, and both the girls and boys let me know I didn't measure up. It left me in a no-man's-land, and I hoped I could slip through without ever being challenged. The writing was actually useful here: I would tell stories to the football team as they had lunch, and used the Scheherazade technique, telling them only half a story at a time so that they needed me to live long enough to finish the story the next day. More than one would-be bully found himself dealing with a beefy pair of linemen, snarling, "Leave the little brother alone!"

I may not have been large, or hip, but I was a storyteller. I could tell stories of courageous people, even if I couldn't fight my own battles and demons.

Until one day, thanks to Mrs. Otterness . . . I had no choice.

* * *

I was pretty badly bullied. A smart-mouth without the muscle to back it up, or legs fast enough to outrun the insulted, I took a lot of thrashings. The worst of my tormentors was a kid named Rudy. I'd known this little thug since kindergarten. He was shorter than me but built like a wedge and radiated an aura of barely leashed violence. I wasn't enough of a threat to be his enemy and generally tried to stay out of his way. I was in fourth grade when he pulled out a pair of brass knuckles on me in the lavatory and took my lunch money. Great.

Well, he and his brother, Oliver, and friends were even bigger thugs when we graduated to Mount Vernon Junior High School. Rudy was terrifying and fascinating. Seemed afraid of nothing and no one and claimed to be having S.E.X., which was some strange and arcane activity beyond my ken. I'd tiptoe up to the edge of lunchtime groups he regaled with his erotic adventures. Yeah, he was probably lying, or at least exaggerating . . . but he was a member of a different tribe, and in some way I longed to be a part of it, and knew I never would.

And one day, maybe in eighth grade, Mrs. Otterness sent me to the main office to get some mimeo sheets.

I got down there, and Rudy was sitting in the office, glowering. Apparently he'd gotten into trouble yet again and was waiting to be dealt with by Miss Thompson, the vice principal. I barely looked at him as

I walked into the office, but somehow he got it into his head that I had narced on him, turned him in for whatever thuggery or theft he was currently in dutch for.

And he swore that, after school, he was going to kick my ass.

Can I even clearly remember the dread, the fear that followed me the rest of the day? My horrified glances at a clock that seemed to race toward three o'clock, rather than crawling at its usual snail's pace? I doubt it, but no prisoner awaiting execution could ever have wished more fervently for time to freeze in place.

And he made good on the promise. He and his brother and friends followed me all the way down Washington Boulevard, hitting and spitting and cursing at me, daring me to stop and fight.

At five-to-one odds.

Hell, Rudy was bad enough by himself! But as I walked, something was breaking inside my head. Some essential sense of self was dying. I simply couldn't continue like this, humiliated, diminished, emasculated. But I couldn't get beaten more, either. I couldn't win, and I couldn't go on. It was a nightmare scenario for a timid and insecure kid.

I felt myself dying inside. All of the abuse, all of the daily reminders that I was undesired, alone, strange, weak . . . something collapsed within me. I knew that if I didn't do something, and right then, that I would lose some essential part of my being. Something I could not afford to lose. Something I would rather die than lose.

But I could not beat him. And even if I did, his friends would finish the job. But I couldn't let the humiliation continue.

Something snapped in my head. I put my books down and walked out into the middle of Washington Boulevard, standing on the double yellow line with trucks and cars whizzing past me on both sides. I looked at him, and in the coldest voice I had ever heard, said: "Come out here and do that."

I was going to push him in front of a truck. I was going to kill him, or die in the attempt. He looked in my eyes and all the bullshit went away. He KNEW that he was looking at serious injury, or death. Playtime was over. He blinked first. Turned to his companions, and said five words I remember fifty years later: "Aw man, this nigger's crazy."

And they walked away . . . and never bothered me again.

* * *

That day was the beginning of my search. I believed that there was an answer. That there was a way for me to find peace. Joy. Tribe. That I was not the ugly, twisted thing that I had been told I was. I had spun into the abyss and realized that there was nothing there but death, and was happy to find it. Death was better than losing my soul.

* * *

I feel so sad for the boy I was. What was he, twelve? To learn a lesson that grim, at such an early age. So alone. To feel no protection, no welcome, from anything, anywhere. To be driven within himself, searching for decades to find some truth, some rock on which to stand.

And yet, ultimately, fear pointed the way. Death pointed the way. There are limited options in a Newtonian universe. There is fear, and there is love. There is death, and there is life. There are lies, and there is truth.

I feel sorry for that boy. But that boy does not feel sorry for me. He is proud of what I've made of myself. He knows that I've failed at so very many things, but is proud that I've picked myself up and kept going. And he knows I love him, more than life itself.

He is my integrity. My soul. He was there before I was born and will be there when my flesh has turned to dust. I decided that day I would die to protect him.

And the only moments of failure, of cowardice, of dishonesty I have experienced in my life are when I have forgotten his face. When I have left him standing in the street, trucks whizzing past on either side, with tears streaming down his cheeks.

* * *

Years passed, and the martial arts beckoned. The wellsprings of pain and fear were deep, and it took me seventeen years to earn my first black belt, but after that, progress was more rapid, and two more belts, as well as high rank, followed.

I wondered what would happen if I ever encountered one of my tormentors again, especially Rudy. And at my twentieth high school reunion, I found out. It was held at the Ambassador Hotel. I went just thinking to see old friends, and did. But one of them was a guy named Anthony, who had gone to junior high and elementary school with us, who had lived in the old neighborhood. And as we discussed old times, the name "Rudy" came to mind. I asked Anthony if he knew what had ever happened to him.

Anthony grimaced. Rudy had indeed continued and accelerated his criminal tendencies and eventually had conducted a series of petty robberies, culminating in a gas station holdup . . . at which he had been shot and killed.

My mouth opened and closed. A rush of complex emotions flooded through me. I think what I'd have wanted to say to him was not "Let's go outside" but rather: *Thank you.*

I'd become who I was, a best-selling, award-winning novelist, because of people like Mrs. Otterness. And was an accomplished martial artist because of boys like Rudy. The world, I knew from an early age, was a place that rewarded dreams but hated dreamers . . . unless they were strong enough. Because I had feared for my body and heart, I had made my mind strong, and that strength had served me in life, countless times.

Mine was the path of the writer . . . and the warrior. Pen and sword in accord, as my training partner, Jeff Learned, said, many years ago.

My absent father had not made me strong. Boys like Rudy had. Adults like my first-grade teacher had. Whatever I was, I owed to everyone who had shaped my heart, for good or ill.

I would have said thank you to Rudy. But it was too late. So I'll say it here, put it out into the universe.

I more than forgive you, Rudy. I thank you. And I'm sorry life didn't work out for you. But whether or not it was the furthest thing from your mind . . .

You did good.

In your way, you were as important as Mrs. Otterness, wherever she is. And wherever you are . . .

You probably bore me no real ill feelings, were just dealing with your own demons. I was just collateral damage. Or would have been, were it not for the writing, which kept my heart alive, and the martial arts, which taught me, after many years, the power of that space I found spontaneously, accidentally, in the middle of Washington Boulevard.

It was the Way of the Warrior: *We all must die. All we can do is choose the way we will live, and what we are willing to die for.* You pushed me to clarity, Rudy, and saw in my eyes your own death. I searched half my life to find that space, only to discover it had been within me all the time.

But there is also the Way of the Artist: *We all must die. So sing your song, speak your truth, be what you were meant to be, in the time that you have, with all of your heart.* You opened THAT door, Mrs. Otterness. You gave to us even in the midst of your grief and loss. You knew you were losing the love of your life . . . even as you taught us to live for something we love. You saw that song within me, even when no one else could.

I love you both. ■

PTSD (YOUR MULTIPLE EPISODES)
Cyrus Cassells

Warning: here comes the place
Where they broke your insurgent hands,

Your mutinous heart,
Where they burgled you,

Detained you,
Shot holes in the walls & windows—

*

Where they bound & gagged you, ardent protestor,
With your own dissenting hair—

*

Here comes the demeaning dunce-cap,
The pill-white, punishing psych ward,

& please-let-me-out-please dungeon,
Despot-blessed straightjackets

& stifling Pilgrim-era stocks,
The cruel hand on the Catherine wheel—

*

O shell-shocked veteran, truce-seeking ace
Did you think that harpy-harsh

Volley & gas, that limitless battlefield
& engulfing no-man's land,

That barbed-wired locus could stay
Completely faraway—forgotten?

*

Your frantic, full-frontal film
With its cutaway to flames—

*

Here comes your woeful white night,
Your hard-to-witness Waterloo,

All mayhem & moon-driven werewolves,
Survivor, your razor-sick score

*

Of shark-like kings & vampire conquistadors,
Of soul-crushing Cossacks—

*

Your black-&-blue, full-speed blender.
Your havoc of night beat police beams

& bigoted APBs,
Your winged-monkey medley

Of reliable hurricanes & pogroms,
&, of course, those stern,

Never-gone-for-long Southern trees
Billie Holiday sang about.

DOSAGE
Cyrus Cassells

Since you ask,
It's always a firehosing summer

In the unrelenting Dixie
Of the antebellum mind

(Bell as in belligerent!):
Drawn, not quite rusted swords,

Cobwebbed oaths
& querulous cannon-fire

Of the intractable Confederacy,
Smudged postcards from the plantation

Picnic-cum-lynching,
Punishing stars & barricading stripes

Arriving as a plebeian barrage
Of handcuffs, rubber bullets,

& cop-lobbed canisters of tear gas—
Open wide!

Here's your daily dosage
Of breathlessness & Black body counts,

Rakish chokeholds,
& blue-serge knees to the neck—

Which only the Dashcams' abraded oracles
Bother to reveal—

Admits one repentant Southern belle
After viewing the infamous footage:

I do declare,
When poor, luckless Mr. Floyd

Cried out for his mama,
It broke my barbecue & hush puppy heart!

It broke the proverbial camel's back—
O my country-'tis-of-thee,

How shall we the people cure
This outrageous injustice?

Dear Mademoiselle Late To The Table,
Speaking of can-do doses & cures,

There's a deadsure virus on the loose,
So what's the perfect ratio

Between household cleaner
& human blood—

The right as rain (or heaven-sent manna) dose
Of "controversial" hydroxychloroquine?

Shorty the never-fail bootlegger insists:
It's all about mixing the moonshine,

The backwoods hooch just right
Without killing the clients!

The secret's in the sauce. . .

July 26, 2020

EVERYONE HERE SPEAKS POPPYCOCK
Cyrus Cassells

And I would shut my gossip-addled ears
(I was Hitler's secretary

And he was a sweet boss!)
For everyone here speaks laughable

Poppycock *(Say, that Fred Douglass is doing*
An amazing job!)

Or infallible *ennui*—fanciful
As an imp's florid pig-Latin,

And I would close my eyes
But this is Creation: *look, look,*

This midway lined with a squalor
Of fire-eaters, two-headed calves, pornographers

Devoted to the maudlin, funeral chasers,
Slashing pimps, like lowercase gods,

Mystic elephant men, replete
With marred, radioactive lips, hawking

Crack! Fentanyl! OxyContin! Magazine!—
Magazine whose pages are narcotic,

Whose runaway articles are all
Drug-riddled downfall and despair:

Is that you, beloved,
Or the OxyContin talking?

But now I swerve straightaway
To Sir Avarice in his silk carapace, bolo-cool

Prince of the bottom line, purring
Let me hand you the demographics . . .

All these, all these elaborate
Infrastructures, spreadsheets,

To-do lists, multiplication tables,
Multi-colored charts of new-minted

Campaigns, poverties, and plagues . . .
Dear ready-for-your-close-up prince,

Born under lethal silencers, raised
In the reign of the salacious eye-wash,

Dear jury of ash and indifference,
There is an unsettling hole in Exhibit A,

So help me, a sullied corridor,
And our real selves

Dash through it—like speeding-to-the-goal
Greyhounds or in-a-dead-run deer—

O prince of collapsing force fields, hurry
The bonanza of your deep-drinking gaze,

Your undeterred hand—
Scepter, laser, potent flower—

That might still bless and transfigure
The detained boy of the holy,

Threadbare flesh, the ensnared boy
Eliciting our eyes,

Little bird, little oil-soaked bird,
The fury of ruffian holding cells,

Borderland skeletons, and festering rooms,
Burgeoning, burgeoning,

The manacled women and trammeled men, the caged,
Empty-bellied children still eliciting

Our blank or annihilating eyes—

THE KNOW-NOTHINGS (PEOPLE SAY A LOT WHEN THEY WANT THE JOB)

Cyrus Cassells

Corruption with a magnificent capital C
Forever pouts to put on a show:

It fondles Mommy's pretty paste
And pretends it's irreplaceable diamonds;

Like the Flintstones, it wakes, rises, and breathes
In plain ole ordinary Bedrock

But imagines it resides
In the chicest part of Beverly Hills—

Relevant degrees? Expertise?
Fast-track appointee, you confess,

In your crocheted *comme il faut* purse,
You harbor only stale

After-supper mints, Handi-Wipes,
Monopoly play money,

A bedraggled but beloved teddy bear,
Foam dice, miniature boxing gloves,

And a crumpled high school diploma:
No terminal degrees?

Not a problem!
Not in these throwaway days of *Scout's honor!*

I swear on a stack of Bibles!—
Followed lickety-split

By *On second thought* . . .
In Secretary Crass-Cum-Unqualified's complicit,

Counting-house peepers or pearl-clad Lady Devos's
Two-plus-two-equals-a-million mindset

(They of the Royal Order of the Benighted),
Nepotism with an impressive N is practically

The oldest profession:
Like a juicy, galvanizing secret,

Corruption's gaudy lawlessness and tawdry logic
Beg to be given away—

Trick questions: when did omnipotent real estate
Become a religion?

Shelter become like fine wine?
When was the Constitution voided?

Conclusion: to transcribe and assess
All the semi-despot's 24/7 lies and non-sequiturs,

To do a hefty percentage of the task
Of supplanting democracy and demanding

Strict Obedience with a blazing capital S and O,
Why depend on actual leadership,

When you can order dissembling,
Know-nothing trolls, abetting judges

(Null as storefront mannequins)
And wide-eyed sycophants,

Plus blatant, never-miss-a-trick elves
To serve, all systems go,

As hastily rigged boogoloo bombs
Or hellbent human wrecking balls . . .

DOCTOR KING'S QUEENS
Cyrus Cassells

An excerpt from *My Gingerbread Shakespeare*, a recently completed
novel about the life of a fictional Harlem Renaissance poet,
Maceo Hartnell Mitchell. (This section is narrated by Maceo's
great love, Duncan Thaddeus Metcalfe, a famous actor and
singer, known affectionately in the press as "Dark Gable")

Dear fans, it wasn't the roiling Deep South—fed-up Montgom-
ery or rebelling Birmingham—but the heart of "genteel,"
tobacco-rich Carolina, where an old colored follower of the
Movement, I mean *really* old, had bit the dust while in redneck cop
custody. The hot-potato spot where the deviltry went down was Pecora, birthplace of revered Harlem poet Maceo Mitchell. The unlucky
picketer, known to have rallied area Negroes in favor of civil rights,
was some kin to the poet, so his sister, Delaine, and the local chapter of
SNCC at Pecora State requested "Dark Gable" sing at Mr. F. D. Kinnison's funeral, since the deceased organizer, bless his "disrespectful to
Dixie" soul, was a longtime admirer. I said "genteel" Carolina, but of
course, the prime feature of my old sweetie pie Maceo's no longer sleepy
hometown (a Confederate stronghold that rampaging General Sherman
once set ablaze) was the galling slave auction place, the brick behemoth
at its stubborn-as-hell center, and, no new shakes to any Negro fast on
his menaced feet, a bullyboy sign on Pecora's outskirts that trumpeted
"This is Klan Country."

I hadn't soloed for a while, let alone stood on a stage since Bayard
Rustin's miraculous March on Washington. I certainly wasn't any match
for show-stopping Mahalia Jackson in a feathery Easter "crown" (a gospel
muse for the growing Movement if there ever was one) or even my old
fit-as-can-be vocal-champ self. Alas, my beloved baritone was no longer
"the marvelous melter of resistance" that it had been back in my heyday,
but my heartfelt version of "Were You There" moved the sorrowing
congregation anyway, especially when I put some oomph behind the
words of the haunting question, "Were you there when they nailed him
to the tree?"

In low-key Charlie Chan mode, I did a little snooping around Pecora
concerning the elderly but defiant man in the alderwood casket and found

out a hell of a lot more than I'd bargained for. Willing to play court jester (but never toadying Sambo), Maceo's kin was rumored, on a few occasions, to have stuck out his long, pink tongue (like his own personal, on-command genie!) to floor huffing-and-puffing sheriffs. One of Bayard Rustin's "angelic troublemakers," "Doc Kinnison" also relished announcing at every mass arrest, in a theatrical yet dignified voice, "Brothers and sisters, it's a beautiful day to go to jail."

Well, our hero was marching along with some activists, unified against the town's habitual Jim Crow trickery and Klan chumminess, when he was nabbed and his un-bowing head treated like a West Village beatnik's bongo. Outraged onlookers claimed Kinnison was trying to shield a sign-carrying picketer from a merciless blow when the hot-under-the-collar cops decided he'd do just fine instead.

A Howard grad, "FD" was on the poli-sci faculty at Pecora State for a long stretch (nearly half a century!) and even managed to coax a couple of high-minded Negro kids to gallop off to the aid of that old underdog, Republican Spain. Kinnison retired the year after Truman bombed the Japs (it seems the former professor emeritus protested that, too); right on time, as he probably wouldn't have survived the Red Scare. A dedicated disciple of Charles Atlas, and later, a follower of that exemplar of exercise, Jack LaLanne, FD wasn't just any old "feet don't fail me now" geezer; besides his keen political smarts, he was in top shape for his advanced age. Maybe that's what inspired laughing cops to pound his superannuated but still hotshot body to a pulp.

I discovered from a handy spy that, in a sneaky about-face from his pipe-sporting, sweater-wearing prof side, Doc Kinnison was also a pretty steady visitor to the Hi-Hat, a favorite homo watering hole in Pecora, where he was whispered, by lively, knowing patrons, to be in possession of the largest instrument in the local area, and, children, I don't mean a jazzman's cumbersome bass or a big brass tuba! Apparently his skills as a sought-after nighttime educator were much in demand; even some of the younger "initiates" were said to have been all systems go for his "coaching," though I'm sure that, like some crafty actress, he kept his actual age an enigma. Cuffed one evening in a leafy riverside park, he did have one charge for "public perversion" (not unlike Bayard's one spectacular slip-up in the back seat of a parked car with a pair of young gents, the "wayward incident" that nearly put the kibosh on his career), a scandalizing charge against Doc Kinnison that got magically watered down in its severity, so Maceo's "king-sized" kin must have inspired some late-night devotee, some undercover ally with a little legal clout. Of course, by then, FD was too far along in age for a lickety-split firing from Pecora State, or to care a whit about any Nosy Parker's prickly opinion.

The more I dug up about the unusual oldster, the more I felt like tipping my finest porkpie hat to him; yes, I was mighty pleased to play the warbling angel at Dr. Frederick Douglass Kinnison's funeral.

* * *

Truth to tell, it was the mighty lion in Martin that made me enlist, the gusts in his can-do voice, able to whisk you to a sacred mountain peak or plunge you to the very depths of your Negro pain—the gospel lion in him that made me link hands with other colored brothers and sisters striving to be more than second-class: oh you best believe, Martin was the Movement's immovable tree, and we were the many ornaments, ready to shine. If I live to be five hundred years old, I swear I'll never forget the sea of dark-skinned folks (from the numbers runner on the corner to Negro stars like myself) crowding the DC Mall that impossibly joyous summer day, as I stepped onstage, at Bayard Rustin's insistence.

Instead of all-out singing or fancy speechifying, I chose to read Maceo's breathtaking "Message to America from a Sundown Town"—an old poem, yes, but an almost perfect bull's-eye for the occasion. Ah, Maceo, the poet with a thousand pockets, and not even fast-moving Mace knows what's in them all! At Lincoln's giant marble feet, Bayard, the mastermind of the whole miracle protest, chuckled a little and whispered, "Still carrying that Maceo torch, I see." I'd known Mr. Rustin, brash mockingbird and born rabble-rouser, since his crooner days in Harlem. Confident, buoyant without fail, the lanky musician I'd first caught wind of back in the thirties had grown into an activist with balls, a bold-as-you-please proponent of rousing Gandhi's tactics and one of the Movement's right-hand men. On that mind-blowing march, we were all of us battle-ready privates in Bayard's fast-growing army, in his giant *Hell, no!* to unjust Jim Crow.

High on the list of cool things I cottoned to about Mr. Rustin was his dignified refusal to mask his hankering for men, to give in to disapproving churchgoers' smears, and I loved his shameless Quaker ass for it. Leave it to always-naughty Killian Costen Foster, that old cellars and Chitlin' Circuit tease and legendary flirt, now a more or less respectable entertainer and show-offy host of a supper club ("Why, DT Sweetie, chile, I haven't seen you in a 'coon's age'!!"), to start referring to the "Negro bachelors" in the Movement as "Doctor King's Queens," and when I shared that little bit of sauciness with Bayard, he let out a hearty laugh. Later, when I became even more of a dancing fool for "the Negro Welshman," a sexy, sharp-looking Freedom Rider more than half my age, I thought a hell of a lot about Bayard and his gut-bucket, "in the life" laugh.

* * *

Once upon a time in "Dixie," a young "mulatto" man stationed himself outside a Virginia courthouse, dead set on challenging the state's miscegenation law, with a courageous (or foolhardy, depending on your point of view) sign proclaiming, "I am the product of interracial love." Despite the KKK's dismal prattle about "a mongrel race to come," this handsome protester, with an aquiline nose and a striking, sensual mouth, was surely the best possible advertisement for any future joining of the races. After some watchful colored folks bailed this curly-topped, blue-eyed beauty out of jail, he begged to meet me in DC during Bayard's march: "Jarrell Rory Gulliford, at your service, Mr. Metcalfe. My mom and pop heard you in Spain and when you shared some spirituals with the Welsh miners during their strike." Oh yes, how could I fail to recall the emerald valleys of South Wales, dotted with deep collieries, and the mean, stick-in-the-mud bosses who cared more about their "pit ponies" than their endangered workers? The starving, cast-off miners had stoically put one foot after the other, all the way from Swansea to London, in desperation and dogged protest, and, in Piccadilly Square, I sang for the down-on-their-luck men and made damn sure they got fed.

I did recall Rory's mother, of course; how could I forget her? She was the only Negro nurse I ever came across in Spain. In fact, we posed together for a picture, one that became quite an item in the "black and tan" press, with the caption "Negroes Doing Their Bit In Spain." She laughed and said, "My husband is going to be jealous as hell when he gets a load of me with Dark Gable!" Rory's intrepid mom was plunked down in a makeshift wheelchair; if I remember correctly, she was recuperating from some kind of bombing incident and was hightailing it home to Harlem, due to her injury.

"My nursing days are kaput for awhile."

"What will you do, dear heroine?"

"Visit some old friends, talk about the fight in Spain. Maybe take up a collection for folks here."

So that incredible Negro nurse was his mom! To say I was stirred by his inherited idealism and unbeatable looks would be an understatement: the moment our feasting eyes locked, I knew I wouldn't be a satisfied man until I had this appealing young protestor in my arms. I thought I was done with this sort of lovesick, puppy-dog foolishness, that I'd put it to rest with Maceo. I wasn't exactly "DT Sweetie" anymore but even with a few more pounds and a silver curl or two at my temples, I was still a man to be reckoned with in the bedroom department. Dark Gable's behind-closed-doors diet at the time was mostly a slim, doting actress and maybe (rarely) an inviting young Baptist tenor or a worshipful, in-shape stagehand.

I let it slip to the comely young Master Gulliford that I could use some help with my bookings and correspondence, back at my fancy Harlem address, and if he could use a little change, I'd be happy to have him around. "Wow! I'm honored. Given that I've been a certified jailbird of late, I'd be plain lucky to have such a cool job." It didn't take too long for the pretense of employing him as my boy Friday to fall by the proverbial wayside. I swear on my Aunt Della's fancy, chiseled gravestone, children, that Dark Gable didn't deploy his usual winning moves or surefire scripts; there was no slick Don Juan or Casanova savvy seduction. Rory gently held my large hand at first, "drylongso," as Gullah folks love to say: simple as that. We were side by side, working at my long teakwood table on proofreading an interview related to "Negro Stars in Support of Civil Rights," when he calmly reached for my hand. It felt absolutely no-fuss, pretty damn electric, and yes, necessary. "Well, Mr. Goldilocks, do you know what you're getting into?"

I felt, at times, when mouth-watering Rory was curled up in my bed and counting sheep, like a spellbound botanist before an especially fine species of butterfly. It tickled me that he started calling me LL (for living legend) almost right off the bat, and on those first nights together, when our wholesale passion was at its height, when the showy uptown elms and sycamores turned red and gold, LL, full of lust-struck wonder, would kiss the small keloid near Rory's left hip, a souvenir from a Freedom Ride, and bless the beautiful body that my golden-limned lover had bravely put in the path of bigoted cross-burners and crowbar-carrying hoodlums. Rory, who had once been scalded with Sanka, doused with ketchup, mustard, and malted milk by lunch counter hecklers, confided to me, over a fine supper he prepared, that the student Freedom Riders from Fisk (Maceo's alma mater) had, every one of them, under Diane Nash's steely leadership, signed their last wills and testaments before getting on their crazy, noble bus from Birmingham to Jackson. Spiky Bull Connor had commandeered their Trailways bus and ejected them at the border, in some Klan-bedeviled backwoods, and, so help me, the fast-thinking kids still managed to sneak back to Birmingham (aka "Bull Connor's City") to resume their Freedom Ride. Can you imagine? Frankly, I never failed to be touched by Goldilocks's down-South tales of courage and coping: how, in the Parchman penitentiary, Rory and his Freedom Rider friends hummed in their cells, did routine "cockroach counting," and brainstormed a makeshift Monopoly set out of a jailhouse sheet and some stiff slices of stale bread.

I also enjoyed hearing a thing or two about his parents. "Mom thought Pop was being so brave, so radical in marrying a Negro nurse. Then he clued her in to the fact that there was a whole history of wayfaring sailors in Cardiff marrying West Indian women and hauling them back to Wales. 'Proof,' he told her, 'it's in the blood.'"

* * *

As if gallant lunch counter protests in Nashville and risky-as-hell Freedom Rides weren't enough, Rory signed on to be part of the busy field staff for Freedom Summer, a courageous voting drive meant to be the new tip of the spear of the Movement. In the land of spiky filibusters and grandfather clauses, of phony-baloney literacy tests, Rory's job entailed long days spent knocking on Delta doors to coax scared-to-death Negroes to register to vote in careworn towns with almost lyrical names, like Ruleville, Indianola, and Tchula.

"Baby," I warned him, after he got his marching papers and headed to Mississippi, away from my dubious employ and king-sized bed, "you're going to get your sweet ass shot off and that would definitely be a waste of negritude, or, dare I say it, 'mulatohood'!"

"I have to go, LL!"

The Freedom Summer recruits, most of them dewy white college kids (with only a dim awareness they were essentially Caucasian "shock troops" or, to put it more bluntly, lily-white cannon fodder), were on hand for mass meetings in sanctified churches, their gospel pews always in danger of being torched or bombed by riled-up bigots; remember, southern Negroes didn't dub Birmingham "Bombingham" and one section of town "Dynamite Hill" for nothing! The fledgling crusaders also put together altruistic Freedom Schools, which aimed to teach deprived youngsters and even old (but never hopeless) sharecroppers a little Negro history. That became Rory's second task and his favorite part: inspiring Mississippi kids, accustomed to "whites only" libraries, watching their wondering faces light up like a full-blast April moon or a living room lamp when they learned the Negro anthem, "Lift Every Voice and Sing," or put on their very own production of *The Cat in the Hat*; yes, that delighter of children, gleeful Dr. Seuss, had arrived in sparring, sweltering Mississippi just in time for spirited Freedom Summer.

* * *

Well, it was clear as a ragged rooster's crow those rednecks meant grisly business when the corpses of three Freedom Summer workers turned up in a remote backwoods dam: the chilling disappearance and murder of

James Chaney, Andrew Goodman, and Mickey Schwerner on the first sultry day of summer had cast a fierce pall over the whole Don Quixote-ish project. Staff members warned the students, ingenuous lambs who had entered an accursed lion's den: "If you stay, we can't guarantee that you will get out of this summer alive." The young idealists were demoralized by the callous offing of their brave friends, so Rory begged me, pretty please with sugar on top, to come to Mississippi to sing and boost the group's morale. Pete Seeger had been on the red-eyed scene already, strumming on the same woeful day the assassinated trio was dug up, so the FS crew opted to have a Negro singer of some note to likewise shine a spotlight on their slain friends and the shameful day-to-day realities of the Magnolia State—like poll taxes, drive-by shootings, Molotov cocktails, and, Lord in heaven, lily-white cemeteries: Mickey Schwerner's fearless folks had wanted him six feet under beside his murdered coworker, Jim Chaney, a Meridian native, but that was, to no one's surprise, illegal in Klan-controlled Mississippi. Was I scared? Hell, yes. Was it relentless lust or true bravery that caused me to show up at the FS battlefront? You tell *me!*

The volunteers were housed with samaritan Negro families of small means; because of this arrangement, I had precious little one-on-one time with Rory, but it sure did my beating heart good to see him again, to witness, on my two canvassing excursions alongside him, Goldilocks's even-natured way with Mississippi folks: no-nonsense cotton pickers, corn pullers, and brickyard haulers; surprised Delta housewives, some in curlers and shyly offering sun tea to "the strangers at the gate"; snuff-chewing but still polite, even respectful seniors in overalls; and, of course, a few obviously-taken-with-Rory FS volunteers, both male and female. Once, two flabbergasted old ladies on a creaky porch swing put their hands over their mouths when they recognized me, even under my Foster Grants, from a current television variety show, maybe, or a few of my old "race films"; the bolder, gap-toothed one, by the name of Nerola, insisted on an autograph and a hug ("Gimme some sugar, Dark Gable!") and the other, Miss Essie Mae, who offered us canvassers a delicious glass of mint lemonade, was satisfied with just a sweet aw-shucks handshake.

The Delta, with its impressive vistas and hot, shimmering fields, really does cast a powerful spell. How could any wide-awake Negro mislay the beauty of the world far below the Mason-Dixon Line? After the Great Migration, too many years in fast-track city places, like Harlem, DC, Hollywood, and Greenwich Village, I suppose, kept memories of the Delta's shameless beauty locked in an attic trunk, covered with sticky cobwebs. Oh, the catfish and hush puppy South, with its cooling riverbanks and redbud trees, its hooded riders and hopelessness, yeah, the

South, man, like a fickle girl, a dazzling ingénue, could really bolster or break your damn heart.

* * *

One stifling night, sitting on a back porch step, my busy crusader in dungarees (with his "One Man, One Vote" button) confessed: "I know you think I'm always Young Mr. Bravery or something, but it's a real struggle sometimes getting my lungs to cooperate when actual danger's part of the mix. As a Cincinnati kid, I had pretty bad asthma; before those lunch counter sit-ins in Nashville, it would flare up at the mere thought of the sure-as-shit wrath about to come my way. I'd have to steady myself and sometimes reach for my old pal, the inhaler. After class the other day, I had a mostly minor attack, and of all things, started babbling to myself in French: *J'ai peur*, 'I'm scared,' I uttered out loud, wiping off the blackboard, as if I was back in my Saint Louis Square days in Montreal. I plunked down in one of the kid's desks to steady my breathing, and my hand left a big sweaty imprint on the wood."

Lord, I regret, with all my heart, we weren't any place I could have hugged Goldilocks, held my baby close for a spell to make the heebie-jeebies disappear; damn it to hell, I wish I'd put chilly propriety aside. Of course, Rory's worried admission of fear and sudden asthma has played in my head over and over, like a broken record—since a tearful male Mississippi Project volunteer came to my door to announce that two sharecroppers found the south side of Rory's school in terrible shreds, blasted open to the sky and stars, the stifling Mississippi night, and beyond the splintered desks, they spotted Rory, fairly covered in debris, sprawled across his little Freedom School's front steps.

* * *

My love, my one and only Goldilocks, lay stunned in the hollow of a coma for three nail-biting days, and on the hellish third day, no, no, my boy Rory didn't roll the stone away; my mute, curly-haired Apollo didn't rise like triumphant Christ from his rocky tomb: he left us.

* * *

After Rory's unbearable passing, as a discreet member of "Doctor King's Queens," I broadcast to the hilt, to Hattiesburg and beyond, my public support of CORE, the Mississippi Summer Project's voter registration campaign, and Carpenters for Christmas, volunteers working to rebuild a burnt-out Baptist church in Ripley. I was strong-willed, more determined than I'd ever been, as if I were sheltering Goldilocks (who was now part of Bayard's roll call, which included the little dynamited Baptist girls of Birmingham) blazing within me like a beacon—as if I were two Duncans, one, an activist songbird, the other, a new-minted soldier, burning with the hope of an unbowed generation that flatly refused "the separate but equal" South. My baritone came back in full force: oh yes, at times, in my soaring church solos, there seemed to be a ministering angel prodding me, or maybe the lionlike Virgil that encouraged Martin from trial to demanding trial.

So, as fate would have it, I lived to see Bethena-Vernadine Mathis Gulliford for a second time: she showed up in the Magnolia State to claim her golden boy's body. The Spanish Civil War heroine declared firmly, definitively, to CORE: "We'll bury him in the Delta, not in Cincinnati. *Here* is where he worked and hoped and fought. Right here!"

The wake was chockablock with Freedom Summer folks, including several Freedom School kids, some in dime-store glasses and pigtails, fast-learning pupils Rory taught to belt out "This Little Light of Mine." Settled in a relatively quiet porch corner, immune from the curling smoke of Chesterfields, Pall Malls, and Camels, Bethena shared some riveting tales of life with her husband, Aron, who'd died of leukemia when Rory was in college: "With whites, it was easier to pretend I was the 'dashing Welshman's' cook or maid. Do I look like anyone's sorry-ass maid?" With her silvery French braids and still custard-smooth skin, she looked like a Negro empress to me. "To colored folks, I might as well have been some house hussy willing to sleep with the massa!"

"I get the picture!"

"You know, it's wonderful to see you, Mr. Metcalfe, after all this time. Who could have imagined we'd end up together again?" She downed a finger of scotch, wiped an errant tear, and reminisced, "When you met me, Mister Movie Star, to jog your memory banks, they'd just dug me out of the rubble, thanks to a Fascist bomb. And now the same mess befalls my sweet son but he doesn't . . . I guess I've got my own cheerleading self to blame for teaching the boy he could outbox any boogeyman. Maybe nobody, not even a genius like Maceo Mitchell, can really take in three hundred years of hate. Beneath those curls, my kid was really tough; yes, he was: don't forget, he came from miner's stock on both sides."

"Bethena, I can't find the words . . ."

"You don't have to talk, Dark Gable, I know what he was to you. Oh Lord have mercy, how can anyone not fall in love with you?" ∎

OF WALKING IN
Aaron Coleman

I have taken the risk and liberty
of empathizing with the ill and braggadocious
brothas walking around Saint Louis

shout-singing their favorite pop hip hop songs
in order to perform a riddle and posture
of freedom. I caught myself singing, too,

getting louder and louder as I walked
across another cavernous pandemic night. Past
questions of hope and hopelessness. I trudged. I made

up the song I sang as I went, trickling down
patterns and headlight shine, but I
know I felt the big black weightlessness

in the practice of letting go
of public fear and private shame
in public space. Untaken, but noticed.

DRAFT NIGHT: NAUTICAL BROTHAS ASSOCIATION

Aaron Coleman

For Zion, Ja, RJ, Matisse, and the rest of us

I see the tall, young black men crying on national tv,
bowing their heads weeping, even sobbing.
Their voices gasp and spill, stutter and fly
as they reach for the crutch of word and steady sound.

Broad shoulders jitter and sputter as their muscles
make movements I have never seen before
and only felt happening inside myself
while weeping wildly in a car on the side of the road
with a woman I love. Or alone. In a dark, wet field, tired,
surrounded by the company of night.
(In an empty gym once, too, and in a foreign quiet
living room...but where am I now?—I distract myself.) Here,

buoyed by the night, bathed blue and American in soft electric light:
I watch these men on live tv with wonder.
What blackness is becoming is releasing

some stitch of pain, some wall of fear
to find our way to unknown pains and fears, yes, but
I saw so many young giants in the culture crying, letting go
of tears of joy and something else
floating away, out in the open, in front of teenaged strangers
donning jerseys stitched with their new cities and names,
in front of black and white women, young and old,
in front of uneasy white men in suits and money, in front
of bright screens, microphones, and the silent eyes of cameras.
I always knew there was something blue inside of freedom.

My guess is we won't sink, even though there's no rest as we
crest with the water. There's a river flooding the city inside us,
there's a surge bloody as history, silty as time, leaking past
the sandbags, crossing the makeshift shores that keep the kin

I love. I watch and feel this American spectacle the way I imagine
a cruise ship custodian watches and feels the ocean at night
as he mops and shines the deck, biding his time.

"I COULD ALWAYS JUST HEAR SOMEBODY RUNNING"
Aaron Coleman

*~Fred Moten (in conversation with Saidiya Hartman on
"The Black Outdoors")*

Reeling here out past the woods where
somebody's running—listen, gone river the edge
where feet leaped slick

and swum faith so across it was
a choice a swimming in
rude ripped scent-lifted safe

locked tracked place
hold nevered breathed
in mudfish catfish gill-lit

fish maw heavy-heavy in air—rich stench so
moody sexing the water—light
might moon the current to

take you, touched terror,
safely across itself
a savoir for a second only

in a second second deadly—
becoming leeway
becoming a way from

what you hear, here, howling
animals—not hounds, not us—in sites
of no and could and always

splayed black gravity
floating across remembering
pine needles and hard feet

          tree sap leak help me help
you reach past
          the sum of life split with its

death—together land gasps
          separates and bloodies
the night thrush sensorium the in

          being seethe, the wayward out
that fails the end, here
               hold on to me

SUNDAY
Aaron Coleman

Texarkana, 1939

We heard you before we saw you
come pealing across our sky
from the same side as the sunlight
then right over our heads—were you waving
down at us? Who could see you smiling?

A moan above a buzz—
plus me and Sis and the girls
with our fingers cupped over our eyes
chasing after you

damnnear all morning before
you wheeled your way down
to come say hi to us—

least that's half what it sounded like, some tongue
or accent I didn't know. Spanish? All the way from
Spain? No? From where now? Oh—

Well you were grand and smiling.
For some reason, less frightening
than other men, I guess. You in your high boots

asking for nothing. Maybe showing off a bit
but hey I'd show off too, if I had a flying
machine I could drive across the sky.

Seemed the whole world was asway, swept
in wide gold colors. And that afternoon blue.

The field was your open palm, the day was
my resting hand. For once. And there we were

with you. Got me
caught up in the kind distance of your face, I do
know that language. But mostly I forget the rest—

Where were you going? Boy, if I could just take off and go
anywhere—and do it by myself?

I'd be a whole 'nother thang up there in the air, alive
looking down and way out
past Texarkana, past Red Lick, the Depot—Domino!

All this blown land, this blown light—
Sure, I'd come back sometime.

YOUNG AMERICANS
Louis Chude-Sokei

Excerpted from *Floating in a Most Peculiar Way: A Memoir* (Houghton Mifflin Harcourt, 2021), by Louis Chude-Sokei.

My new job tutoring students for the college's affirmative action program was much better than scrubbing pots and serving food in a graduate dorm, which was how I'd contributed to my tuition payments up until then. It was also better than working for Great-Uncle Irving in his carpentry shop. Our relationship became more difficult for us both to tolerate the deeper I got into college. He may not have had a high school or college education, but he was smart enough to be certain that the ideas he heard me talking about were an absolute waste of time—and money, because I'm sure he occasionally helped my mother supplement my tuition. Most of the students I tutored were African American so the job not only delivered escape from Great-Uncle but also a way to render my political stance so clear that it wouldn't seem as if I were hiding from either of the two African student organizations, which I was.

The new job proved controversial at home. Great-Uncle Irving and other members of my family considered affirmative action a sign of intellectual laziness and a dependence on charity. We didn't need such things. Others would assume me unworthy of my place at the university and assume we were scroungers.

Beyond this political push and pull, the affirmative action program shaped my political consciousness in a more intimate way: it was where I met the first person who would break my heart. She was African American, which was immensely significant. So was the fact that she was studying African history. I assumed her field of study was why she'd been open to dating me. She was the most beautiful woman I'd ever seen, so I was happy to exchange whatever Africanness I could still conjure for the relentlessly imagined pleasures that consumed me when I thought of her.

My mother was working very late or taking a night class as she often did. I'd cleared the living room and the bedroom so I wouldn't have to explain why the house had so much stuff everywhere. I'd installed cheap scented candles from a liquor store. But by the time we turned off the 10 freeway onto Crenshaw and the neighborhood took on its distinct shape and feel, my young lady's arms were crossed. I assumed she was nervous; many people who exited the freeway here got nervous. To make her feel comfortable, I pointed out places that mattered to me, where family members or friends lived or where you could get your hair braided for cheap or hear music on the weekends. I indicated a row of houses where black fraternities lived and showed her the Jamaican restaurant that bore my mother's maiden name.

After a moody, withdrawn silence she said, "I didn't realize you lived in the ghetto."

It took time to register what she was saying.

"I mean, this is the *ghetto*. You grew up in the *ghetto!*"

Maybe this was a simple mistake, I thought. One had to live here to understand the differences in streets, topography, and culture. The ghetto was, of course, over there, on the other side of Crenshaw Boulevard. It was south of Century or on the other side of Inglewood Park Cemetery. From the top of Slauson where we lived, you could see it spread out flat and wide with long swaying palm trees that reminded us all of the Caribbean and me of Cousin Cecil, who could shimmy up them in a flash. It was definitely up near Normandie and Vermont, and if you got so far as Hoover, then even God couldn't help you.

No, we didn't live in the ghetto. We were near it, moved through it, and had learned to respect it as one learns to respect an angry sea. We lived just close enough to breathe with its ebb and flow, hear its roar, and feel its spume.

After passing Great-Uncle Irving's church, which I showed her in hopes of getting us back on track, she said, "You're not really African at all. At least not really."

At first it seemed a compliment to my assimilation. I was eager to find something positive in her words. We were here for a reason, after all, and what I was—or what she thought I was—was clearly crucial to its fulfillment.

When we were alone in my mother's house and the candles were lit, I made my first move, drawing her shea butter smell into my lungs. She recoiled. She said she felt that she'd been duped. She'd accepted my affection for non-black things like the science fiction books I read and the music I listened to but that was because she assumed I didn't know the codes of black America. That I so adored David Bowie had required much of her, but she figured I couldn't have known better since I was a foreigner. But for me to have grown up in what she—and admittedly most people in Los Angeles—called the ghetto meant that I should have known the rules. My way of speaking or presenting myself had to have been pretension. I'd hidden or perhaps rejected my true *ghetto* identity.

This difficult knot came when I was far from receptive to complex ideas, given my hopes for the evening and her smell deep in my lungs and my fingers aching for touch. But I knew I'd failed. Needless to say, we didn't have sex that evening—or ever.

Her rejection would have much to do with my now-changed relationship to the city I'd grown up in and something to do with my increased focus on more racially charged topics as I soon passed from undergraduate to graduate studies at the same school. That need to intellectually overcompensate for a failed racial identity or a general cultural alienation would be shared by many of the graduate students I began to know. So many of them were either immigrants themselves or rejects from cultures and communities that had bruised and still haunted them. A new community began to shape itself, one where our radicalisms were largely products of individual betrayals and personal failures. It became a home of sorts but then eventually, for many of us, careers.

* * *

I remember a T-shirt I'd see at reggae concerts, spoken-word events, hip-hop shows, or African culture festivals in the park near Great-Uncle Irving's house. It read MARCUS (as in Garvey), MALCOLM (as in X), MARTIN (as in Luther King), and ended with ME. They were sold all along Crenshaw Boulevard along with other clothes emblazoned with the colors, slogans, and images of black radical politics. The message on the T-shirt suited the obsession with racial leadership that seemed necessary for social or professional advancement on campus. For example, these T-shirts had also become popular on campus among members of the newly renamed Afrikan Student Association and other black activist groups. Students wore these clothes, often with leather medallions embossed with images of Africa, and there were now drum circles in the quad and homemade incense burning everywhere. It was like when my mother and I had first arrived in Jamaica. Africa—or at least a version of it—was everywhere.

Students I knew who'd been prejudiced against African students and central to the usurping of the name African Student Association were suddenly transformed into oracles of the race, complete with dreadlocks and African names. But I now understood. These acts and performances were necessary given the pervasive doubt cast over our very presence on campus. We were assumed to owe our places there to affirmative action. The more our qualifications were questioned, the more radical we black students became. Racism did not discriminate between and among us, so I decided that it was more important a problem than whatever internal wounds we caused one another, even heartbreak. Whatever traces of resentment I felt towards my fellow students I could chalk up to my cynicism and frustrated desire. And graduate school was like having your heart broken every week.

I cleared my shelves of science fiction and threw out Bowie and Prince and all the music they had led me to. I bought a few of those T-shirts from Crenshaw Boulevard, collected bales of incense from Muslim brothers on the corner, and took to traveling through the streets of the city attempting to put myself back together. With help from marijuana from the reggae shop next to the restaurant that bore my mother's maiden name and cheap alcohol from corner liquor stores, Los Angeles became the canvas for my reinvention, along with my classes, meetings with activist groups focused on everything from protesting racism to organizing rent parties and poetry readings, and the occasional drum circle. There was much to understand but even more to prove.

Still, no amount of Afrocentric or gangsta rap could hide the fact that in the weeks and months following the breakup I heard Bowie's "Young Americans" in my head whenever I thought about my young lady. And I thought about her often. That song had been a hit the year my mother and I arrived in LA. Its lyrics referred to leaving Washington and the notion of the ghetto, but for obvious reasons the chorus made me wince most of all: "She wants the young American, *all night!*"

When longing turned to anger, I recalled that my young lady didn't even live in the neighborhood. Being African American gave her the authority to determine who was in or out of the racial community. Despite what she'd called the neighborhood, almost nobody who lived there or nearby used the word "ghetto" to describe it. Hip-hop, at least for our generation, was to blame for a new geographic elasticity around the word, which had become fashionable among many of the black students on campus. The location of "ghetto" expanded until it became larger than any map could hold yet so small that only they, the arbiters, could tell where its borders were.

I should have told my young lady that my family knew and understood poverty very, very well. In their eyes, what they were surrounded by in that part of Los Angeles was not that. In their countries, "ghetto" meant something else. It didn't mean hot and cold running water, a television in every or any room, fast food on every corner, free education, and regular electricity. As immigrants, they were also held hostage by an optimism fueled by those they'd left behind. Folks back home wanted only good news about America. Tales of racial suffering or economic disparity were seen as cases of those with wings to fly complaining about the thin air above.

I didn't tell her these things because they were too difficult to think or to say at the time. The anger that gave rise to such thoughts now quickly turned back to longing, and I had started using the word "ghetto" like everybody else to emphasize the racism that I now agreed shaped and maintained the community.

My family was incensed to hear me refer to our neighborhood that way; they had long since tired of my tendency to explain everything by way of racism. For them "ghetto" described a way of life, or rather the acceptance of that way of life. It was a synonym for choice, therefore it could be judged. There was nothing racial about it. Speaking perhaps for them all, Great-Uncle Irving once said to me over the dining table, "Boy, this racism is better than your daddy's genocide so shut up and keep breathing."

He stopped speaking to me for at least two years after that, which I welcomed. What I didn't welcome was Aunt Pansy's greeting me with the sadness of a funeral, especially when I began twisting my hair into dreadlocks. This was the price to pay for becoming black, I thought. But because what I was becoming was actually American, I began to blame my parents and family for everything, especially for not understanding who or what I had become. They were immigrants after all, still fighting battles they had already lost back in their old countries.

I may have alienated my family, but I thrived on campus and in the broader neighborhood around Crenshaw and South Central, becoming a significant figure after participating in more protests and events than I could count. I published a black student literary journal with funding from the English department and local black businesses. People looked to me knowing I had a gift for identifying racism in any situation or context and was always ready to speak out in classes and in the neighborhoods. The universe was indeed black and white. I'd discovered the formula and was achieving my middle name, Voice of the People.

I joined the ASA (the *black* one), even if it meant that the now-name-less African student group looked at me with suspicion. That didn't trouble me, since they all thought of me as Jamaican now, with my twisted-up hair and the accent they could never quite place. When the ASA gave me an award for my campus and community activism, it was my young lady who presented it to me. And when she hugged me on stage and her shea butter scent went immediately into my lungs, the clarity I'd found began to dissipate into what seemed like smoke rising from a near horizon.

I carried the award home and stared at it for hours, ignored it for days, and then stared at it again for an entire weekend. It looked like glass but wasn't, and my name and achievements were stuck to it with plastic film. Eventually, I accepted that I deserved the award. Not for my achievements but for the depth and scale of my failures.

I welcomed the riots when they came. I wanted the entire country, or the parts of it that I'd struggled so much to fit into, to burn. As the violence spread, I made my way back to my mother's house from campus, staring down grim white faces in the opposing traffic. I spent the nights of smoke and fire and sirens drunk on cheap brandy and even cheaper marijuana. I walked the length of Crenshaw and sat in the park. The last time I saw my young lady was there, at an African pride festival, her pregnant belly festooned with cowrie shells, her hair wrapped in West African fabric, her feet stamping to rhythms churned out by Rastafarian drummers. On the streets during the riots, everyone was listening to rap on boom boxes and in cars, shouting out the lyrics and screaming, "Fuck the police!"

In my headphones was David Bowie's *Diamond Dogs*.

"This ain't rock and roll, this is genocide."

I wished I had the courage to burn something without losing anything. And in the darkest hours, I wished I had nothing to lose.

After the riots, the petty grievances of campus life became harder to justify with inflated talk of "the struggle" or "the people." I was exhausted, hollowed out, reduced to ash. I wanted more than anything to be an immigrant again, or at least go back to the beginning of the story that had brought me to this country, hopeful and naïve. I wanted to be African again. ∎

WANTED, OR
"IN SEARCH OF A COOK"
celeste doaks

~When Mid 19th century civil rights icon Mary Ellen
Pleasant arrived in San Francisco, her services were
auctioned off as a cook. She agreed because it was
customary for colored women to serve as domestics, but
she had stipulations on her hiring.

Much like sautéing sea scallops, she approached
the culinary world gingerly. Knowing a cook's job
was a man's game during the Gold Rush, she stepped delicately

onto the wharf. Bids flew in abundance between splashing
waves. A shout for $200, then for $350. But she held out,
held breath as close as kerchief nestled in bosom.

She'd eye a hot pan this same way, listening for oil's first
sizzle, before placing mollusks. Sensing when the browning
began, she refused *all* cleaning. Her hands would touch

no broom, nor wash a single dish. And suddenly, quicker than
a spatula's flip, she accepted $500. Now the rescued bivalve
could rest, and continue cooking at its own pace, plate side.

MY BABY'S A GHOST
celeste doaks

I know my baby's a ghost
who whispers secrets, during
my labored slumber. She shifts,
tells me *your stomach*
is my holding cell. I'm eager
to escape.

People don't know
my baby's a ghost who reads
tea leaves in amnion
and prods me to speak
her predictions out loud.

For the first spell
I start to sweat, then dizzy
and faint. I wake up
murmuring. "Mix *bek*
into your morning tea,
let it steep, then drink
for focus."

How does she know
I'd been having trouble
writing and what is *bek*?
When the spell slowly lifts
I wonder, is this the language
of apparitions?

THE ANNOUNCEMENT
celeste doaks

Over the steaming peas and carrots, I try slipping it in.
I tell my parents we're driving West, between discussions
about the raging virus and best places to buy layered masks.
Another spell nears and I'm struggling to stay present,
as Mama's eyes pool with confusion. *Such a long, unnecessary trip,*
she says. I don't confess that we've been ordered straight to Kansas,
the sunflower state. Filled with so much yellow, one might expect
to find Oshun there. *What if you go into labor?* She asks. I laugh,
grab a piece of bread, the butter slick as my lie. *Of course,*
I won't mother. If so, we'll be in Lebanon by then and Devin
used to palm a basketball pretty well, so I'm sure he can pull
a baby out from between my legs. Just then dad enters with snapper,
fire red and sizzling, as my lids start to drop. A warning, an appetizer
to her possession.

EUCALYPTUS TREES
celeste doaks

"Mammy Pleasant's eucalyptus trees are still the pride of Octavia street, but there's not an agency in San Francisco that wants the job of keeping them alive." *San Francisco Chronicle,* Jan 25, 1974

The Eucalyptus trees and a plaque have recently been named "Mary Ellen Pleasant Memorial Park." It is currently the smallest park in San Francisco.

Like Pleasant they stand,
their spindly frames defiant
against a grey blue sky.
On Octavia street, no one
tends to their decaying limbs.
Now they're an eyesore,
unless you want their oil
for insect repellant or
in your new perfume spritzer.
Or maybe you'd raise an eyebrow
if you knew they've been used
to combat Malaria.
You also never stop to think
how they detoxify the air,
convert CO_2 to O_2,
how each of *your* breaths
depends on *their* respiration.
How disrespected they
must feel, lining your prim
sidewalk, as the Suits
and Square-Toes pass
on their responsibilities
until one day, in a final fit,
the oil in all those branches combusts
into roaring orange flames.

SAY OUR NAMES:
AMERICAN ELEGIES, 2015
Rachel Eliza Griffiths

MIRACLE RIVER
Rachel Eliza Griffiths

A woman had been squatting in the woods just above the river that was named after a war. Everyone who remembered the war would have said it was more like a defunct battle, a quarrel of wills over rights to water. The books in which the battle had been mentioned, in one or two unremarkable sentences, had died too when the small local library burned down nearby. The remains of the war and the books were carried off in trucks by annoyed men who were insulted by the sheer amount of ash the library had left in its burning.

For the ghosts of the quarrel, ghostly enemies and ghostly heroes, there was a story that always changed. What was most consistent was the fact that the water was ungovernable and unnamable in its need and memory. In town a single word—*miracle*—was repeated about what had happened there on the bridge between the whites and others. For both memories, *miracle* was a cunning word. A word such as this, which could be cited by both the believer and the skeptic, was promptly recycled into something empty and picturesque. Meanwhile, the river, which they derided and abused, pulled back its rage and worked to fill its emptiness.

Instead of something elemental, it offered incidental proof of human life. Over years it became a raucous jetsam where sticks, sneakers, plastic bottles, diapers, condoms, tampons, and bleary fish floated together in symphonic gargling. And where, in the summer, children dived and drowned.

With the quarrel between whites and others put to rest in memory, Miracle River had been mostly left to the children. When asked by those children what had happened there, as if they could *feel* the story in the water and it itched them, the grown-ups feigned wonder. They spoke of it the way the world will marvel at a girl who has gone missing or a family that packed up overnight and left without a trace.

When they were growing up, the grown-ups said, that river was something else. They lied about its innocence and their own. Instead, they praised its pastoral qualities, citing nostalgic days when it was young water. Water that was going somewhere and with a purpose. They lied about Miracle River until they liked their lie more than the brackish stench that forced them give it a name that was the opposite of what they really wanted to call it (Horse Piss, God's Spit, Pus Bucket).

As passengers in fast cars sped across the cement overpass where the name of the river was featured in white lettering on a demented, rectangular green panel, they marveled at its charm and surprise. They said its name aloud as they drove across its white-brown face. Promptly and cordially, they then forgot it.

The woman knew they forgot Miracle River because it was, in truth, an unremarkable river. No one had extra time for marvelous distractions, however plain, when there were mouths to feed or bills that required postmarking. A proper miracle was getting out of the post office without spilling blood over the last book of stamps, without leaving internal organs on the scales.

But she imagined what they might say if they knew about the city beneath the underpass, the wooded empire where she lived, where she was not alone, where she often followed the tracks of wild beasts, two- and four-legged. Years ago, unsure of what exactly had been chasing her all her life, she'd run away, certain that the world liked her better being lost rather than dead.

What might anyone say about this city where each night her human heart thudded against the rustlings of owls and rats, where the crispness of inconsequential mornings tucked itself beneath her skin and made her bones ache. The woman stumbled along muddy banks alone in her thoughts. She felt rather pleasant when, weather permitting, she could also sit out on a flat, high boulder in direct sunlight and wait for her torn clothes to dry.

In sunlight and moonlight, she found herself singing. When the woman got tired of talking to The Questions, which had taken turns ridiculing and saving her since she was a very young girl, she opened her mouth and spat standards, show tunes, and spirituals. Lately, The Questions looked at her as though they expected that any day now her body would be found in the water, snagged on the cool tip of a breaking branch. This woman sang over The Questions and their ridicule of her, of how she had turned out. They taunted her anyway. "You're a bum. You're the Nothing you promised yourself you would become. You're one of those crazy bones the dogs won't touch."

The woman knew that The Questions were smarter than her, better looking, wiser. Their decorated shoulders squared. They did not slouch. Their eyes were time colored, their mouths always moving and using her voice. They were neither female nor male but contained the traits of a third gender that the world could not name. Their arms were muscular, softening only when they'd worn her out from their ranting and frothing. They gave her answers that often scared her, even when the answers were soft and loving.

The Questions were on to her, knew that it required more strength than the woman had to keep her mind quiet. The Questions knew how to channel her electricity and how to poach her plain common sense. They leaned on her, shocking her fingertips and teeth with their demands until her hair stuck out from her head in ashen naps.

Sometimes the woman saw herself in the river water, but there could be a Question standing behind her, armed in regalia, a red coat with neon-yellow epaulets, so that she could sense its presence, could sense the delight it would take in holding her head under the streams of raging current. Whipping around to confront a Question, she only understood that she had to think more quickly in order to capture one. Otherwise she herself could be captured. Standoffs and truces were no longer viable. Still, the woman would then resume trying to see her features in the water and became frustrated when her face failed to assemble itself.

"Yes," the Questions assured her, "you are Happening. Asking us what happened to you means you are invested in a story. A fair but easy question. We are invested in something far greater. Would you like to begin with your version, the version of a lunatic, the catechism of a madwoman?

"Very, very well, you'll have the first turn. You tell us Why. Then we'll tell you the truth."

Lately, there were no Questions. That troubled the woman. No visitations, no sightings of tall figures hidden behind neutral trunks of birch. No blurred pale faces lurked in the brush, in the thick rippling of brown and white water.

She missed The Questions that made her laugh until her sides ached. A Question would wipe away the tears that ran down her cheeks and encourage her to let her entire body fill with light. Another Question might sing her to bed as she curled herself inside a mansion of cardboard boxes, nylon string, and vinyl tarp. Sometimes a Question would arrive as she sat alone, looking up at the bridge that she had crossed years ago when she'd left home. "It's unlikely you'll go back over that bridge ever again," the Question might say. "So why don't you dance with me?"

"Right now?" she would reply. "In the middle of everything?"

But the Question would already be pulling her up by her hands to her feet. The dancing Question, who wore nothing but sequined overalls and a smile so incandescent she found herself smiling as her head filled with James Brown, Mayfield, Gaye, or Gaynor's "I Will Survive." The Question, who spun and snapped its finger saying, "Aw yeah, girl, aw get down, baby," wouldn't let her forget the words "Oh, as long as I know how to love I know I'll stay alive" as they twirled in shafts of sunlight that cut tunnels through thick, doomed trees.

Sometimes a Question appeared like a child, peeking out shyly from a rotten log. This Question wore patent-leather Mary Janes and pink ribbons in its hair. "Can you hold me? I can't find my mother," it would say, coming towards her with tearful eyes. She never said no to the child as she gathered the Question up into her arms and rocked back and forth for hours, for days, until the presence of the child was inconsequential.

The Questions occupied the air between her thoughts. The Questions, which a doctor might diagnose as a schizophrenic condition, to her were vibrations that could take the forms of the world, of the flesh, and she was forced to translate, to listen, to judge the fever in her own body as a feat rather than a fear.

When she was five or six years old, or perhaps younger, she remembered them being near her, though nobody else could see them. The woman had enjoyed having this secret and could remember the first time a face appeared at her bedroom window and asked to come inside. She'd known, as her mother had taught her, the difference between Strangers and Nice People. The face at the window was Nice. She helped, pulling its arm, as the Question climbed inside of her room.

"I'm Fern," she'd said in her friendliest voice. "Who are you and why don't you have a room of your own?"

"I'm How," said the Question. "I'm lonely in my room so I thought I'd come to yours and we could be friends. This is a very pretty room and it's very nice of you to let me stay with you."

"How long will you stay?"

"I'll never leave you," said How. "Doesn't that sound good?"

She had nodded, comforted. The next day when she tried to describe How to her mother, she had been surprised at the Question as it pressed a finger to its lips, reminding her of their invisible, secret pact.

As the years went on, she was introduced to How's family—Who, When, Why, Because, Where—and other relatives. She liked some of the family and hated others but realized it didn't matter. That was how families worked. None of them were going anywhere, none of them would ever leave.

Once they convinced her to run away, they helped her get herself settled under the underpass. They taught the woman how to hide in plain sight, how to find feasts in garbage, how to stay clean despite the filth of other peoples' ideas of her. They imbued her with their ideas, their paranoia, and helped her escape her unrelenting pangs of despair. Even when they were troublesome and attacked her, she forgave them. The Questions had been there for her when nothing and nobody else could. They gave the woman visions that sent her to other planets, other worlds. When she returned from her travels, they were waiting and smiling, hopeful that one day she would find a home where they could be stars, supernovas, moonlight together forever.

Until that discovery happened, a mitochondrial burning surged through her skin. Maybe she was dead, the woman once thought. Or was it more proof, molecular testimony, that nothing was dead, nothing dissolved, nothing finally after all, not even bones or words?

* * *

She couldn't tell The Questions, even though they already knew, about the swimming pools that appeared behind her eyes wherever she went. Blue ovals and squares, azure rectangles with diving boards that appeared in the corner of her vision like black specks, jumping away from her grasp when she tried to concentrate on them.

When she realized that the swimming pools would never go away, she decided that she actually liked their company. Nobody suspected that she was capable of thinking about something so simple, so blue, so bright. And fun! Swimming holes, as she had heard people from the country call them, were intended, primarily, for fun!

Maybe, she liked to tell herself, each time a hole appeared inside her eyes, or in her dreams, it was about the return of her young cousin, Didi, who had drowned years ago.

Maybe Didi was trying to send her a message.

The woman had often wondered whether her cousin was mad that something so shallow and so public had pulled her teenaged body down to the floor of its sunlit mouth and swallowed her life.

The drowning had happened years ago.

Didi, who was easygoing and pretty, who had been teaching her how to do cornrows right. Didi had insisted that she learn how to part properly. You got to part it like *this*, her cousin might say, sighing, but with patience as she took the rat-tail comb from her to use on the half-bald blond Barbie head her mother once used while taking some cosmetology classes. Didi, who didn't like scrambled eggs unless she could smother them in ketchup, who always slept with one of her hands under her cheek, who didn't like the taste of banana, who wanted to be a scientist when she grew up.

After Didi drowned, Fern barely spoke at all. Her mind clung to familiar words but often she could barely remember why she was holding them on her tongue in the first place. Her long silences made her mother and her friends uncomfortable. Didi's mother, Tina, understood and would only wrap an arm around her niece, squeezing her soundlessly.

But none of that mattered.

No one possessed any citizenship where Fern lived now. There was no way for her to be tracked in the impossible wildfires of the country where she had settled. The wooded empire. No one would see the smoke, the ashes in her mouth, her heart. She'd let them all off the hook. They wouldn't have to feel guilty for not trying to find her, not trying to explain the way she had snapped. The sensation of branches breaking beneath her swollen feet, which stuck out of her ripped sneakers as she made her way through the woods, muttering loudly that she was glad she had nothing extra, no food, no company, no final nerve to offer The Questions, who stole whatever she couldn't nail down. Even memories.

"It began before your mother died," a Question insisted. "Was it Didi?"

Fern wanted to say that it was more complicated.

Not a singular event. More like an erosion of her hairline, her edges thinning until one day she herself could see shy, pale scalp pulsing at her temples.

Yes, her mother had died around the time Fern graduated from high school. Sometimes Fern couldn't remember the date unless she thought about graduation, since her mother had died before that.

She hadn't been there when Fern walked across the stage holding a single long-stemmed red rose. Fern's mother hadn't been there to hear the mothers of her friends insisting that Fern's mother, an angel who was surely clapping her wings, was looking down from heaven and throwing roses of her own.

Uncle Daye had been her only blood relative present. Waving his bony Jesus arms, his cheeks sunken from nightmares and good times, he'd stood up on the metal chair in the overcrowded auditorium and shouted her name. He was six foot six. She had tried not to turn her head even though she could see the blades of his long arms blurring at the edge of her vision.

Fern Daye! Go on now, Fern! My niece, my girl, Fern! Hey, hey, go on, girl!

Uncle Daye, shaking and yelling as though he were a Vietnam soldier again, back in a rice paddy with leeches on his throat. Day-Daye, as her mother had called him, had obviously decided that Principal Keen didn't know shit, didn't know that there was no fucking way he was going to hold his applause while his only living niece walked, carefully, one foot first and the next foot following, tentatively, along the trip wire of youth in modest white patent-leather heels from Payless towards her Future.

All Fern knew then was that she could not fall when she reached out to accept her Future, the parched diploma, which was encased in deep-blue leather. The Future reminded Fern of her heart, which she distrusted as much as she did her Future.

According to the world, The Future would be a husband, three children, and perhaps a moderate dedication to the same church that was also giving her a cash prize for her achievement in attendance. Without her mother or her Aunt Tina, who had died a year after Didi's drowning, Fern and Uncle Daye had learned to tolerate each other.

Between his disability checks and the fast food jobs Fern took when they needed money for house repairs and taxes, they didn't have to worry about being put out on the street. For years, their small house sagged beneath an arrogant tree that bloomed above her grief and tore through its seasons without regard for her or for Uncle Daye's growing inability to discern the difference between whiskey and water, peace and war.

Fern had moved into her mother's bedroom.

There, she stopped sleeping. Sometimes Fern's mother appeared at the foot of the bed, silent and dead, wearing her work clothes. The ghost would fold her arms and stare at her daughter without speaking.

If she forgot to turn off the television while in a fretful nap, Fern would surface from a forgotten dream to find her mother sitting at the foot of the bed, her back still, as she watched *Fresh Prince of Bel-Air*. Did this ghost, who resembled her mother, even have eyes? Could a ghost appreciate Will Smith's dimples? Could ghosts laugh the corny, helpless way the living did? Because Fern didn't think ghosts could cry. A ghost that cried didn't make much sense to her.

She would wait then to see if her mother moved. The moment Fern blinked her eyes, she was alone again in the room, only aware of Uncle Daye's loud farting on the other side of the wall.

His legs had gone bad so he no longer stayed in the basement the way he once had when her mother was alive. He used Fern's old room.

In spite of his war legs, he had a steady stream of women who came to visit him. Introducing every one of them to her as his "friend," he would maneuver them away or around her sadness.

First, there was quiet in the kitchen as she imagined her uncle trying to explain what was "wrong" with his niece. Next, he fooled with the radio or one of his scratchy bootleg CDs from the tower that he kept stacked on the counter next to the CD player. All of the music was for fucking, she thought. Teddy Pendergrass, Luther Vandross, Al Green, Marvin Gaye, Donny Hathaway.

Fern wanted to ask him why didn't he have any CDs about women singing that way because she knew that women sang about it too, maybe even better. She'd grown up on the music so it lived in her. The loving part, at least.

With Uncle Daye there was a predictable story once he found his game was working. Across the music there was drinking, hollering, boasting, and the remembering of Back-in-the-Day, That-Nigger-Who-Used-To, and I-Wish-a-Motherfucker-Would. Then, maybe, food.

Uncle Daye would offer other things to his friend in a low voice.

Finally, he would stand outside Fern's bedroom door to see if she was awake. Because of his asthma, she could hear him breathing hard.

She imagined him there, swaying with a raggedy erection, holding some woman by the wrist before guiding her, stumbling and chuckling, into his niece's wallpapered room. Then the mattress springing a fuck-song. Never longer than three minutes and twenty-nine seconds, which was why it didn't bother her. She'd read about heart attacks, earthquakes, and natural events that had lasted longer. Thunderstorms.

In nightmares, Fern screamed, briefly, at the top of her lungs. Over time she wondered whether her screams were not so different than the way Uncle Daye's friends screamed beneath his thin loving in her old, girl-ish room with all her stuffed animals watching their intoxicated shadows.

Fern found a stingy peace in the idea that both pleasure and terror were short-lived, intense, and unsustainable. Waking at night in her moth-er's bed, soaked in sweat, Fern was often uncertain whether she herself was submerged in water.

When the water in her mother's heart broke, birthing her death, Uncle Daye was sitting innocently in the front yard braiding his hair while listening to the news. Black Baby was close, flirting and waiting to give him her dizzy, pint-sized whiskey smile.

After her mother's death, Uncle Day sometimes appeared at her high school, swaying and stinking from Black Baby's good loving, insist-ing that he had to walk her home. He had to keep her safe. Fern remembered how her uncle's mouth had moved as he recited his slurred vows. He wasn't going to let nobody wipe their feet on her Future. She remembered walking and being embarrassed until she wasn't. She often walked around, her mouth moving and torrents of words falling and splashing on her swift feet. Fern often felt Didi's ghost fingertips pressing her shoulders. Strange yet soothing, the way that touch happens under-water with no air.

That was, perhaps, when an unfamiliar Question announced its name.

"I am Why," the Question had announced.

On the morning of her mother's funeral, Fern remembered sitting in the church. She kept asking the Question to repeat itself because it wasn't speaking up. Why wasn't loud like the others. She couldn't make out Why's whispering.

Don't you have a name? There is nothing without a name, not even death. I think it says that in the Bible. My mother read the Bible all the time and wrote our names in it so don't act stupid like you didn't never have a name. I can't breathe under all this water. What is the name of the sky? Is it the ocean? Didi said I can wear cornrows to the funeral but Miss Haywood is coming over soon to give me some bangs. You like bangs? I have a big forehead so it's okay. Why do you keep asking me to explain? How do I know what I want? I don't know why anyone wants to know. Who is asking? Who is asking? Why will it ever matter?

"I don't know you," she said aloud, repeating herself loudly so that death could hear her. How could something so sad be so hard of hearing, Fern thought, raising her voice until she was aware that people were pointing at her and shaking their heads, whispering *shock*.

She and Uncle Daye stood in the half-empty church singing "Amazing Grace" while the Why stung and stung, singing its name through the tulle of her head until she fainted and the clammy sweat from her skin turned her wispy bangs into a puffed, storm cloud that covered her shut eyes.

* * *

Uprooted, neither fruit nor flower, without seed, root, season, or home, Fern roamed in the privacy of her wilderness. Inside of the woman whose flesh sagged and ballooned around its bones, she paced. She answered The Questions when they were kind to her, when they were soft like her mother's voice used to be before they lost Tina and Didi.

No, no, it wasn't selfish of her to withdraw. She was mad in a new way, Fern insisted to The Questions. It wasn't selfish at all. How could her mother have known her heart would burst?

"I'm *not* fooling myself. I stopped doing that years ago. When all my friends left town, riding off in search of their Futures, I walked to the stable and shot my shining white horse between its eyes. I'd shoot it again. Only it's died. It's really dead. The knight is waiting in a field. He must be wearing rusty armor. He must be bony like God. All I dream of is diving. Going under the water where Didi is giggling and sticking her tongue out at me. Happy for me because I'm not afraid anymore of getting my face wet."

* * *

In fact, Fern was squatting not very far from where they grew up.

It was just that no one looked for her. Who had time to search for a black girl who was believed to be in her right mind but who had run away from her responsibilities? Didn't this girl assume she would be punished for her escaping? With no relatives to suggest she should be in the hospital, or take mind pills, or fly to Jesus, there was nobody and nothing to be blamed.

Uncle Daye had despised the police so Fern had known that he would never call them to file a report when she went missing.

Fern enjoyed imagining the people in the cars that raced across the bridge above her head. The people looking down at the water who might or might not notice the army she was assembling. The Questions required her authority and her governing. She would not allow the world to disturb their work.

But, like The Questions, she could sometimes hear the voices in the cars that slowed.

"What was that? Some kind of animal down there? No, it was only a shadow on an old tree. It looks like a soldier. I thought it was a body floating in the light. Slow down before it runs off. I want to see something. I don't want to see what it is. How much trash is in this river? Was it possibly a woman—that thing? Did it *look* like one? Was that an actual woman down there on the bank, on the shining rocks, in the breeze?"

* * *

Miracle River would outlive her and the past that lived in it.

There was a rumor that during an evening in 1900, a man was lynched from the big branch of a tree that leaned its hallowed arms over the river. The rumor included a white man who drowned while trying to make certain the knot was tied good around the black throat that had, allegedly, dared to whistle at his daughter.

The branch broke.

The nearly lynched man pretended to be dead, and because he was so good at pretending his death, he floated his body like a raft of driftwood down the currents until he was out of sight and free, unaware that the men who had tried to kill him were using sticks to fish his facedown executioner out of the river's furious ripples. The quarrel about which man deserved justice or death, or its variations of pretense, would not sink to the bottom of their eyes.

When Fern dipped her feet, her hands, her face, when she relieved herself, bathed herself, rinsed her hair and used the travel soaps she collected from scavenging, when she braided and unbraided what was left of her hair and song, when she heard Didi's inviting whisper, when she cried and laughed, the water gave her something as elemental as blood, as freedom.

If she was very still, Fern could kneel on the rocks, leaning over so that her face appeared. If she looked past the first face that floated unhappily on the surface, the face that now resembled her mother's but was more aged, if she could focus, concentrating on the darker notes the river sparkled, she saw the face of a child there.

Herself and yes, her child.

* * *

She and Pluby had made a baby together just before or after they graduated. She could only recall the general sense of when it happened because she remembered that her mother had already died.

Pluby always told her that he was going to marry her.

Fern had laughed and said she didn't like marriage. She recalled how she'd once said it easily to him, as though she had simply stated she had an allergy or lacked an appetite for ice cream. It looked sweet but she didn't have a sweet tooth.

But she had always enjoyed his teasing, his promising.

When he figured out how to fuck her without Uncle Daye catching him, he visited. Uncle Daye's Black Baby was Pluby's boozy collaborator. *Shit, Black Baby could be trusted to look out for a nigga*, Pluby joked. Fern and Pluby had fumbled, humped, sucked, and fingered until they were both exhausted by the friction of their virtue. Of *her* virtue.

"Yo, I know I'm your first nigga," he said on the day that he finally got her to pull her panties down to her knees.

With Uncle Daye semiconscious from his fiery trysts with Black Baby, she and Pluby became bold. Almost nasty. Black Baby might as well have been Friar Lawrence.

It stopped as quickly as it began because Nadina found out.

"You won't have the life you want with E Pluribus. You gonna fuck with a nigga named *E Pluribus*? You want to do that with your life, you go right ahead. You won't even have the life you *need*. The only need that Pluribus motherfucker understands is his own," said her friend, softly, trying not to look disappointed. Trying not to judge her but very clearly judging her. "He make Losing It special for you?"

"We went to McDonald's afterwards," Fern said shyly to her friend. When the words hit the air, her desire for E Pluribus shattered.

"You're more beautiful than that, Fern."

"It's not the Big Thing y'all all think it is."

"Girl, but I'm talking about the *bigger* thing," said Nadina. "Love. You know—love. Get you a love like how your mama loved you. This nigga bought you a Big Mac and a two-dollar apple pie and you gave him first-rights pussy? Oh, Fern, I wish I could say something profound instead of saying it the way I am. I'm not good with words, with reading. I draw and shit, paint and shit. You know I'm more of an artist than an author. But you? I know you're intelligent. All-around-the-way smart, Fern. You stay on the honor roll. Shit, honor roll been your best boo, your best friend. You read all those classics and you mean to tell me you were able to let him get on top of you, inside of you, classical as you are?"

Fern shrugged, pulled away when Nadina tried to touch her.

"I just don't think it's the End All Be All. It's more like the Middle Of All. Maybe not even that. Nadina, I don't have religion the way the rest of you do. Plus, y'all church girls the first ones to open your legs. Nothing's wrong with Pluby. His dick is cute. You're jealous. You want a dick too."

"Sure," said Nadina. "I wish you could hear how dumb you sound. I don't think I've ever heard you sound so fucking silly."

"Listen," Fern said. "I really don't want the whole crew to know. I wouldn't even be talking to you about this if you hadn't just walked up into my house without ringing the bell."

"The screen wasn't locked. I only ring the bell when the screen's locked."

"No home training at all."

"Anyone could have walked in on you two," said Nadina, "and seen Pluby's ass in the air."

"Next time you want to borrow my books for those basic tests you always fail," Fern said, rolling her eyes so that she wouldn't begin crying, "take your cheap black ass to the library."

* * *

Then Uncle Daye is getting on the bus with her.

The bright morning light washes cracked plastic seats. He isn't speaking. Black Baby is tucked inside the waistband of his pants. The sloshing, liquid sound of her, whenever he shifts, is ugly. When Uncle Daye sits down, three people near them get up, rolling their eyes, and sit elsewhere.

Fern is used to his scent, the whiskey, the Egyptian oils he wears, the smell of war that won't ever be rinsed from his eyes and hands, the military shave of his jaw. He has cleaned himself up yet people are still terrified, she observes. In a way she can't explain, Fern likes that everyone is afraid of them and will leave them alone.

She is reassured by the heat coming off his body, the bitter smell of his life. He is wearing a light-blue button-up shirt and work pants that don't have holes in them. His hair is flattened by the generous assistance of Royal Crown. The pomade restricts his Indian hair, forcing it into jet grooves. She can smell the cloudy oil melting around his hairline. He is also wearing cologne, which feels a bit inappropriate, given the situation. She should know the name of Uncle Daye's cologne because she bought it for him at Christmas. It reminds her of Drakkar Noir but something richer, a scent reserved for grown-ass men. Drakkar was for boys.

She doesn't want to think about Pluby. The way his voice had changed when she told him she hadn't had her cycle for two months. She remembered how she had whispered *cycle* instead of *period*. So that, she hoped, he would understand that the absence of blood was a serious matter.

She remembered pushing the small popsicle-shaped proof over to him while he buckled the Malcolm X belt on his Cross Colours. She no longer thought of him getting hard inside of those baggy, candy-red jeans.

Her finger had trembled as she pointed to the pink line, so faint he had laughed in her face at first, saying quickly that he wasn't the father. Hell no he wasn't. Couldn't be the father no matter what evidence she had against him. How could she, how *dare* she, being the Non-Tenderoni-Un-Around-The-Way-Girl that she was, ruin his dreams, set him up Public Enemy style, trap him in a Me-Against-The-World joint. Incarcerate his life with Responsibility when he had Big Plans, Big Dreams. A Future.

She had gone to Nadina and showed her, panicky, the positive verdict.

Fern remembered how her friend had only hugged her and said she was, using his full name as she always did, going to visit E Pluribus.

Sunday evening, Pluby came over to her house and rang the bell, refusing to come inside when she invited him. He would not look at her face. The black eye he had was shiny, funky fresh. He gave her a wad of money, courtesy of his mother, and hissed, "Sike!" when Fern asked whether he was still going to marry her.

Uncle Daye discovered the test in the garbage. She was honest with him about what was going to happen next. Apparently, Uncle Daye had done this before himself because he spoke gently to her as though she were his sister instead of his niece.

"Baby girl, I'll go with you," he said, to her confusion. "I'm your brother, and I don't want you going to no butcher."

* * *

When it got too cold or stormed, when Fern was able to find a warmer place to sleep, she left Miracle River.

Using the woods as a place where she could store her things, one of her prized possessions was a rumpled brown bag inside which was a small plastic bag of her classics. She never left these in the woods, though she was willing to leave other things that were more important to her survival.

At the shelter, she allowed herself to enjoy lukewarm meals, hot showers and rough soap, and the bewildering sensation of sleeping in a room with other women. Why were they called shelters? Fern thought of women as shelters, the way her mother, Didi, her Aunt Tina, and her girlhood friends like Nadina had been her shelters. Yes, shelters were mostly inside things to her. Like the classics. In her classics, Fern recognized herself, even as she escaped herself.

At night she listened to shelter women who fucked each other, women who moaned alone while they listened to the fucking, women who ordered the fucking women to stop, women who snored through all of the fucking, and women, there was usually at least one, who would wake them all just before daybreak with lung-ripping screams. She barely recognized herself among these lost women except that she knew she was one of them.

* * *

In the woman's dreams, the branch always snaps before the man, who resembles Uncle Daye, falls into the river, the rough golden rope floating behind him as though he has fallen from the sky, fallen from heaven, fallen straight through the bottom of hell only to arrive at something beautiful and blacker.

The woman, once Fern, imagines Uncle Daye's death.

It is morning. Black Baby is, finally, a widow. An empty bottle in hard light sits on the windowsill where her mother's jade plant still grows and waits for her touch and voice.

Her uncle is hanging from a rope tied to the light fixture in their old kitchen. He plays dead beneath florescent stars.

* * *

The news anchor will describe a mysterious woman and the story, so sad and incredible, will bob and resist the river until, finally and ecstatically, it sinks to the bottom of the world.

Listeners will pause and try, unsuccessfully, to see the smiling teenaged girl whose blurry face appears on their screens. In seconds the adults who know Miracle River will allow themselves to remember how ugly it is, how greedy, how it let a black man live and a white man drown. They will say the word *shame* but will be talking about something else altogether, something that is long ago and has nothing to do with the black woman, estranged from her own mind, who memorized her classics and refused shelter whenever she could.

When the nicely dressed woman segues into the weather forecast, the viewers will be relieved. Blameless and overworked, they can listen to the weather, concentrating on how the rain and wind will affect their weekends.

Perhaps a few of the old folks, who like to recount how the river, the rope, and the tree conspired to free an innocent man, will speak about Fern. They will talk about her uncle, who was found hanging in that kitchen. They will marvel at how clean it was and how the police took their time cutting the veteran, who had earned a Purple Heart, down from the blade of that ceiling fan. Wet lipped, they will speak directly to their memories about the grief of Fern's mother and what all happened to Tina and Didi.

Was her name Didi, they will go on, chewing their dinner while they try to remember whether Fern's mother died before or after her daughter's graduation. They will say Fern was a good-looking girl who could have ridden away, like the rest of her friends, into any future she wanted because, after all, she had actually been a smart girl.

Police pulled her, smart as she was, out of Miracle River, they will say.

There were some of those great classics found close to the heap where she lived in the woods. Lived like an animal, they will say, shaking their heads because they know what animals are.

That child had herself a natural name.

Was it Fern? She loved those classics of hers since she was a child. Remember how she'd climb up into that pretty tree and sit there like a bird. Sit up there all day with her beak in a word. Nobody going to remember that child after us and anyway who in the hell want to think about a world that will take you out of here for no particularly good reason in the first place?

The woman just wouldn't leave that crazy river to itself. She couldn't help herself because that's what water can do. That's why you have to think about what they tell you is clean and what isn't. Ain't no clean rivers I ever seen, not no more, they will say. I wouldn't use that water. Wouldn't let that river lick my big toe. Even if they paid me.

I can't afford to, they will say, clearing their throats and thinking about all of the times the rope didn't break, the river willing. ■

BEYOND & AFTER
MY ANCESTORS,
MISSISSIPPI, 2014
Rachel Eliza Griffiths

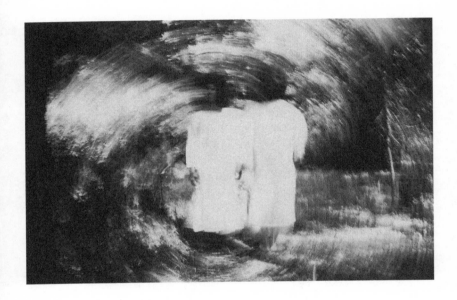

CLIMACTERIC
Rita Dove

I look around and suddenly all my friends have flown:
gone shopping, on a bender, off playing cards
while stink bugs ravish their boutique vineyards,
cooing over grandkids in lieu of hugging their own

frazzled issue—who knows? They're anywhere but
here, darkening my stoop on this sun-filled, vacant day. Not that
I'd welcome their airy distraction—not as long as the pages
keep thickening as I stir, lick a finger to test the edges

(illicit snacking, calorie-free)—but I'll confess this
once: If loving every minute spent jostling syllables
while out in the world others slog through their messes
implies such shuttered industry is selfish or irresponsible,

then I'm the one who's fled. Ta-ta! I'm not ashamed;
each word caught right is a pawned memory, humbly reclaimed.

SHAKESPEARE DOESN'T CARE
Rita Dove

where Sylvia put her head. His Ophelia
suffered far worse, shamed by slurs, drenched
merely to advance the plot. "Buck up, Sylvia!"
he'd say. "Who needs a gloomy prince
spouting iambs while minions drag the river?
Sharpen your lead and carve us
a fresh pound of Daddy's flesh
before the rabble in the pit

starts launching tomatoes!"
Shakespeare's taking no prisoners:
he's purloined the latest gossip
to plump up his next comedy,
pens a sonnet while building
a playlist for the apocalypse.
When you gripe at reviews,
he snickers: How would you like

to be called an "upstart crow"
just because you dared to write a play
instead of more "sugared sonnets"?
How's them apples next to your shriveled
sour grapes? As for the world
going to hell (alas! alack! whatever),

ditch the dramatics: He's already done
a number on that hand basket,
what with pox and the plague
bubbling up here and there,
now and then—afflictions
one could not cough away nor soothe
with piecemeal science. So chew it up
or spit it out, he might say,

although more likely he'd just shrug.
What does he care

if we all die tomorrow?
He lives in his words. You wrestle,
enraptured, with yours.
What time does with them
next, or ever after,
is someone else's rodeo.

A HAPPY BLACK MAN?
Peter J. Harris

When your history includes apocalypse, it behooves a militant falsetto like me to become *The Apocalypsonian,* courting risks that help convert ugliness into beauty, reimagining my contributions to the current cultural conversation, and communing always with the twin philosophies of African American cultural rejuvenation: *keep on keeping on* and *let's get it on!*

After forty-two years of cultural work, starting with a 1978 rant in the *Black Scholar* against police harassment of the MOVE family, I'm no longer called to rant. I'm now driven by a life-affirming question: *When does the season of celebration start?* I'm not in denial. I am simply embracing the implacable ethic of all seekers: *fiddle as you fight*—if I may riff on Gwendolyn Brooks's more linear "First fight. Then fiddle."

Robin D. G. Kelley, in his book *Freedom Dreams: The Black Radical Imagination,* writes: "Trying to envision 'somewhere in advance of nowhere,' as poet Jayne Cortez puts it, is an extremely difficult task, yet it is a matter of great urgency. Without new visions we don't know what to build, only what to knock down" (xii).

Enter my See You . . . Faces of the Black Man of Happiness campaign (@seeyou247), which excavates and spotlights historical photos of men and boys—from the 1800s to mid-twentieth century—*emanating a sense of joy.* These Legacy photos assert and illustrate our humanity, honor illuminated moments, and pay homage to men who now are all ancestors. Each photo offers viewers invigorating opportunities to savor vitality and to see their own image reflected in a wellspring of historical faces. I want campaign viewers to study each face, to search each face, to smile back at each face, to embrace the humanity emanating from history.

I want campaign viewers to literally see another public face of black men.

And during this inflamed season of COVID-19 surging into our lives on top of the ongoing torture of MAGA incompetence and mendacity, I also view these photos as counterpoint and counterspell to the brutal videos and photographs of police killings that have saturated newspapers and social media around the world—including, most stunningly, Mr. George Floyd being suffocated to death for eight minutes and forty-six seconds by a Minneapolis police officer, which galvanized international outrage. Just as it takes only a lethal sequence of time for our breath to be snuffed—actually and *then again* in viral videos!—these See You photos exquisitely celebrate the everyday joys of life and the lives that these photos preserve.

As a journalist, I'm thrilled that smartphones have become an indispensable tool—a golden megaphone!—capturing rampant extralegal brutality. And I'm actually grateful for the web-savvy folks whose posts illuminate the hypocrisy of "protect and serve" by circulating videos of white men and women literally spitting curses into the faces of white police officers showing *biblical* patience. Other memes show cops' tender treatment of mass murderer Dylann Roof (among other white boys). These videos and photos viscerally animate how the random biology of "white" skin is considered valuable and worthy and has often been allowed to become a protective fetish.

But with the See You campaign, I am refusing to make a fetish out of my own death.

* * *

See You is a community engagement program of the Black Man of Happiness Project, which I founded in 2010 as a creative, intellectual, and artistic exploration of African American life and history from a refreshing, life-affirming new angle. See You's title was inspired by the refrain in my poem "Praisesong for the Anonymous Brothers," first published in the 1996 anthology Soulfires: *Young Black Men on Love and Violence*, edited by Rohan Preston and David Wideman. (Just so you know I did NOT borrow from the movie *Avatar!*)

My research began in the 1993. I was licking wounds after a second divorce and I asked myself when I'd ever be happy. My instincts as a cultural worker kicked in, and I asked myself, *What is a Happy Black Man!?* Needing a hug, I began my sporadic—and frankly ineffective—hunt for a critical mass of Legacy photos of joyful black men. My investigations had me searching databases at universities, libraries, and government agencies, as well as asking friends for referrals to scholars. Along my research timeline, I was referred to a professional at the National Archives, who couldn't quite conceive what I was asking.

"You know," he said in a phone conversation, "black history hasn't been very happy."

In October 2017, I got lucky. I found myself at the Altadena Main Library, requesting help from Melissa Aldama, adult services reference clerk II. Excited by my query, Ms. Aldama assigned Helen Cate, library clerk I, to conduct research on my behalf. Ms. Cate began her research by sitting with me and absorbing the specs I outlined: historical photos in

which black men could be read as exhibiting joy, or happiness, or content-
ment, or dignity. I did *not* want photos of entertainers or athletes. I wanted
images of Everyday People. After our meeting, Ms. Cate initiated her
research by writing to librarians; almost casually, she wrote that she was
searching for assistance identifying photos of black men "emanating a
sense of joy." Honestly, this elegant turn of phrase distilled what was
actually motivating me and became a poetic, yet rigorous, framing device!

In addition to Ms. Aldama and Ms. Cate, I was also helped by Yago Cura,
bilingual outreach librarian at the West LA Regional Branch of the Los Angeles
Public Library (LAPL). A few months before I met Ms. Aldama and Ms. Cate, Mr.
Cura had unearthed a few photos from the LAPL photo database LA Neighborhoods.
Those photos are not part of the See You campaign, but they remain a part of the
larger pool of Legacy images.

On June 19, 2019, I began the See You social media campaign with
weekly posts on Instagram, @seeyou247. The campaign was funded
in part by a seed grant from the Pollination Project (TPP). For eleven
consecutive weeks, I posted Legacy photos to Instagram in digital frames
designed by Julie Ray Creative. Campaign posts culminated with a glowing collage of all the images. Juneteenth 2020 was launch date for phase
two of the campaign, also funded in part by TPP. For seventeen consecutive weeks, I posted framed Legacy photos excavated in 2020.

For our See You campaign collaboration, Ms. Cate has searched
collections at the Library of Congress; the National Archives; universities, including HBCUs; black fraternities; and the Schomburg Center for
Research in Black Culture, among several others. Our search is ongoing.
So far, we've found some hundred images, from which I curated the campaign photos. Going forward, I will grapple with the dynamics, contradictions, paradoxes, and metaphysics infused into African American history
and culture, as I seek to publish a fine-art coffee-table book anchored by
the Legacy photos and featuring creative writing and essays by myself
and other artists and scholars. *I feel grateful and illuminated that I found talented*
teammates, trained researchers, who could help me culminate more than twenty years
of imagination, gestation, concentration, and exploration, and that I trusted to keep
me on this journey.

* * *

See You visually shifts society's view from death to life, from the past to
the present, from who we were to who we can and should be, *based on*
the most noble of our country's founding values. See You's magnificent Legacy
images allow us to trace the historical DNA of Black Male Joy and pursue what scholar Sarah Lewis calls "representational justice." Lewis is

associate professor of history of art and architecture and African American studies at Harvard University. "The endeavor to affirm the dignity of human life cannot be waged without pictures, without representational justice," wrote Lewis in her guest editor's note for the summer 2016 special issue of *Aperture* magazine. "American citizenship has long been a project of vision and justice."

The See You campaign, point blank, pure and simple, does not flinch from the healing we need to seek and cultivate *even as we reel from public-space violence*—police killings, racially disparate sentences in America's courts, and their viral reflection on social media. These magnificent images teach us again, prove to us again, that at their best, my "big brothers" always, always, always retained their inner life and stoked their inner light. I value this intimate resistance! I value this *individuality across time*! I value the sacred work of helping to restore these men and boys to a humane place beyond stereotype. I can barely capture how thrilling it is to actually unearth these images of joyful and dignified forerunners, these powerful touchstones from the past who compel and inspire me to value every breath I take in the present! These See You images are part of a growing collection of visual reminders that my instincts were right, that if I continue to trust my intuition, I'll be rewarded with hundreds more photos. No doubt, we have, oh yes we have, waded through hundreds of images of pain, and tragedy, and difficulty, and death, and ugliness. Yet, by not turning away, we have been drawn inexorably to the magnificence emanating from history.

This campaign honors peak experiences through the faces of anonymous black men and boys. I want the campaign to inspire people to cultivate their own peak experiences and contribute to peak experiences in their personal and social relationships. I want the See You Campaign to boldly contribute to a recharged emotional ecology and social atmosphere that are infused with beautiful art reflecting ongoing, dignified, and intimate resistance of black males to their dehumanization. The campaign provides evidence that emanating a sense of joy is a healthy part of what I call whole living, even in the midst of contemporary social challenges and as witness to a documented history of pain. I'm confident that the campaign photos reveal the incredible strength and dignity and humanity necessary to become and remain a Black Man of Happiness.

More personally, I KNOW that the See You campaign, as part of the literary, theatrical, video, and community engagement work of the Black Man of Happiness Project, helped me survive a dynamic season of fracture and challenge and frustration in my own life. That season culminated in 2014, when I lost to foreclosure my cozy, crooked house, my Inspiration House, perched in LA's Mount Washington/Highland Park neighborhood, where I'd lived for some fifteen years. During this season, stymied by an inability to find work paying a living wage, I learned in the most visceral and productive ways that imagination is my savior, creativity is my fuel, and curiosity is my richest currency. Through the storm, I floundered in fear of homelessness. I beat myself up. I curled into the fetal position, when I could sleep at all. I considered moving from LA back to my family in DC. Ultimately, I wasn't ready to leave. I learned to *embrace the profound discombobulation of the season.* And slowly, I earned peace by participating fully in my transformative rite of passage. I stood, knees oftentimes buckling, before an emotional and spiritual threshold tagged brightly with elemental questions that pulsed like cosmic graffiti.

Are you really a writer? A poet? A storyteller? You an artist or an administrator? You think cultural work is easy? These questions, and many intimidating others, danced and dared—to a blaring, funky, psychedelic soundtrack in my mind. I swore I could hear James Brown demanding: *You ready to get up and do your thing?!* In my new season of renewal, I invite you to come dance with me! And in the spirit of reciprocity, I'm delighted to dance with others, too, who have created several humanizing initiatives focusing on Black Joy. Projects include:

> Black Men Smile, a platform designed by the artist and scholar Carlton Mackey to "ask Black Men what makes them smile . . . and work to create sustainable environments where we can do it more often."

> *Black Joy and Resistance*, a photo book by Adreinne Waheed.

> *Sleeping Beauty*, a series by the photographer Kunjo featuring "intimate portraits" of black men while they sleep.

> Brother Breathe, Ashley Wilkerson's "trauma-informed, creative workshop," often held at the Tree South LA, specifically designed for black boys and men seeking peace, which was inspired by her brother, John John, who was murdered at the age of twenty-eight.

> Black Joy Archive, a project created by graphic designer Zoë Pulley in 2020 as "an outlet for black individuals to heal" and push back against "the notion that black lives can solely be viewed in a negative vacuum of struggle."

I also note that California Humanities, an independent nonprofit and partner of the NEH, awarded a Quick Grant in winter 2019 to Chapter

510 Ink in Oakland for a poetry workshop called Black Joy: Poetry with Young Black Men. The workshop culminated with an anthology published by Nomadic Press, edited by Daniel B. Summerhill, an assistant professor at California State University, Monterey Bay.

And in February 2020, the third annual Black Joy Parade was held in Oakland.

* * *

Why is it imperative that *historical* photos anchor my contemporary happiness work? As the scholar at the National Archives rightly noted, pain has branded the primary contours of African American history.

"The study of happiness never was a luxury to be postponed until more serene, peaceful times," writes Sissela Bok in her book *Exploring Happiness: From Aristotle to Brain Science*. "Yet it is precisely in times of high danger and turmoil that concerns about happiness are voiced most strikingly and seen as most indispensable. From earliest times, views of human happiness have been set forth against the background of suffering, poverty, disease, and the inevitability of death" (5).

The background for my happiness work begins in the era of the American avatar of enlightenment, Thomas Jefferson. Often I like to juxtapose his soaring language in the US Declaration of Independence in 1776 with the coarse and commercial text of his 1769 runaway slave ad in the *Virginia Gazette*: "Mulatto slave called *Sandy*, about 35 years of age, his stature is rather low, inclining to corpulence, and his complexion light." During Jefferson's lifetime, he legally "owned" more than six hundred human beings, including his wife's half sister, who became the mother of his children, whom he also owned . . . *And that's why I always stop right there for a moment to breathe* . . . If Thomas Jefferson could claim happiness as an "unalienable right," then for sure black folks coerced to America to make somebody else happy—and then die . . . For sure black folks have even more of an *unalienable claim* on that "unalienable right."

Still I "fiddle" for reasons far more expansive than my historical beef with Jefferson and his posse. Immersing myself in the See You campaign's Legacy photos, tracing the DNA of my happiness, motivates me way beyond my decades of analyzing and fighting whitelessness. Way beyond my desire to defend myself, to speak out against injustice, or to respond to crises. Put most simply, I am *electrified* by this research. *I get chills gazing at the photos in the See You campaign.* I've embraced this work as one of my callings, as part of my literary voice as a poet. This work consolidates so much of my intellectual and cultural and political evolution, which began as a student at Howard University from 1973 to 1977. Given our American journey, a happy black man is the *last laugh* of American history. Given our American journey, he's the very embodiment of the most pristine ideals of free thought and free speech, if he claims his inner *conceptual space.*

The Black Man of Happiness. Hear it. Feel it. Disturbing? Foreign? Intriguing? I want to find out what makes black men happy, by looking back, for sure, and also by asking them, by listening to them, by respecting their unique explorations of happiness, by encouraging eloquence about the labyrinth of our inner lives. I want to facilitate the creation of beauty out of our honest and creative testimony. To enrich society by documenting the inspirational qualities of unique individuals. I want to explore the transformational potential of black men ferociously and publicly living their joy. I hope to contribute to an era of (self) love, peace, harmony, and imagination; to foster individuality over conformity; to orchestrate black male *VoiceMusic* out of virtuoso solos; to identify the difference between being happy and *happy-go-lucky.*

To me, *happy-go-lucky* means, at best, the *veneer* we flash, a fleeting form of entertainment, a jolt of pleasure. At worst, *happy-go-lucky* means an update on minstrel *do dah day.* And *when I'm happy?* I'm in stride, synergies ringing like the fluorescent notes coaxed from a vibraphone. I rep an inner fortitude and fandango that catalyzes other folks, even when bank account's running on fumes, no lover's in the mix, and you need yoga classes to stretch what little income's trickling through the pipeline. The late cultural critic Albert Murray, interviewed in the anthology *Speak My Name,* edited by Don Belton, calls it "that dynamic equilibrium, which is always precarious, but which makes for what we call happiness" (45–46). I hope to ride waves of storytelling, memories, dreams, and visions, then splash down into a kaleidoscopic vocabulary that has become our collective reservoir—an *Oral History of Happiness.*

Front Porch: Stokely Carmichael (L) with Jack Crawford (R) during SNCC voter registration campaign in Lowndes County, Alabama. Douglas R. Gilbert, photographer, *Look* Magazine Photograph Collection, Library of Congress, Prints and Photographs Division (reproduction number e.g., LC-L9-60-8812).

*Helen Cate, research librarian. Design by Julie Ray Creative. Funded in part by the Pollination Project, #SeedTheChange.

This photo, which I call *Front Porch*, was taken by Douglas R. Gilbert for *Look* magazine some fifty-five years ago in Lowndes County, Alabama. Joy and happiness animate Stokely Carmichael and his host, Jack Crawford, during the Student Non-Violent Coordinating Committee's voting rights campaign. Joy and happiness hold hands. Like indispensable catalysts and enzymes, joy and happiness enable life-and-death communications during the life-and-death circumstances shrouding human rights work!

In this photo, transformational history pulses within *dynamic stillness* on a rural front porch. An urban youngen, enflamed with his mission to serve, connects with a big brother, an actual 'Bama, brave enough to host a firebrand. There are no guns, no weapons, on display, although violence was actually a living presence threatening their work to fulfill democracy for the majority in Lowndes County, "one of the most violent regions of Alabama, [where] guns were as routine as leaflets announcing a mass meeting," according to Charles E. Cobb Jr. in his book *This Nonviolent Stuff'll Get You Killed: How Guns Made the Civil Rights Movement Possible* (233).

Front Porch simultaneously captures a breathtaking moment in the lives of real people and reflects their richest interior dimensions of humanity and wholeness. So, yes a social media campaign, the See You social media campaign, can contribute to a restorative field of energy, spark new insights, start a cascade of *aha* moments, and expand our thinking beyond the least common denominator. A social media campaign can flood the ecosphere with healthier, more expansive definitions of masculinity, deepen meditations on our manhood, and translate the spiritual codebook into sidewalk practices, country-road practices, for African American men, and for those who work for our safety, sanity, opportunity, and fulfillment.

"If there ain't no beauty, you gotta MAKE some beauty," was how big brother Maurice White exhorted me in a spoken coda to the Earth, Wind and Fire song "All About Love." As *Front Porch* and all See You Legacy photos show, you also gotta FIND some beauty, you gotta EXCAVATE some beauty, you gotta REFRAME some beauty, you gotta PROJECT some beauty, and you gotta be a conduit for TOMORROW'S BEAUTY.

Three Men—Pyramid of Dignity & Joy: Two men with canes seated in foreground with another man standing behind them. Tintype (photographic print), late nineteenth century. Stephan Loewentheil Photograph Collection, #8043. Division of Rare and Manuscript Collections, Cornell University Library.

*Helen Cate, research librarian. Design by Julie Ray Creative. Funded in part by the Pollination Project, #SeedTheChange.

But these three men will not allow me to settle for even a whiff of sentimentality!
As much as I believe in the importance of See You's Legacy photos, as much as I trust what poet Ross Gay might call my "catalog of unabashed gratitude"—my aspirations, my visions, my hopes, and my ecstatic insights about the importance of these Legacy photos—I must make a serious admission, a painful concession, if I am to truly honor these (mostly) anonymous ancestors who *braved* the dynamics, contradictions, paradoxes, and metaphysics infused into African American history and culture.

No social media campaign will stop bullets fired by unaccountable cops, stand-your-ground vigilantes, gangbangers, or men gripped in the passion play of violence. No social media campaign can block society's virulent, historical flow of venom against black men.

Only we, as engaged citizens, can handle that business! Yet we need robust tools to help us remain resilient enough to neutralize that venom and persistent enough to help build a more perfect union. Ultimately, the See You campaign reflects my dedication to *wreaking happiness* . . . as another of my contributions to safety first, yes, and safety for all, yes, but yes yes yes to safety in the spirit of a Love Supreme, in communion with the most humane work of human ancestors on this land. For the rest of my time on earth, count me among the *fiddlers* dedicated to *The Apocalypsonian's* twenty-first-century mantra:

I See You, Man . . .
I See You Living . . .
I See You Live . . .
[A happy black man?
En garde avant-garde!] ■

3RD EYE ON ILL HIERARCHY: A LOVE SUPREME SEARCHES THROUGH SORROW

—(Arranged by) Peter J. Harris

Found poem: lines drawn from
advertisements by formerly enslaved African
Americans seeking reunion with their sold-off kin

… Information Wanted …
… I Desire Information …
… I Will Be Most Thankful …
                    any person or persons knowing anything of importance

of my parents   of my father   of my sister   of our five children   of
    my daughter

… sold to a man named …
… was purchased by …
… was left with a trader named …
                            (a trader then in human beings)

was last heard of:
13 years ago:
some twenty odd years ago:
at Halifax Court House in 1851:

                            (human trader in that place)
                    any person or persons knowing anything of importance
                                        concerning the missing parties:

… I was owned by …
… my mother was owned by …
… I was sold …
… separated when I was five years old …
… from Nashville …
… 15 miles below New Orleans …

I earnestly request:

pastors will please read to their congregations from their pulpits
ministers of Christian churches will do a favor by announcing
different pastors, especially presiding over Southern Churches,
    to read this notice

... I now go by the name of ...

the place is healthy and they can do well here
as the hand of time steals over me now so rapidly
I wish to see my dear ones once more
their mother still lives
any information will be thankfully received
gladly received by their sorrowing mother

PAINTING BY NUMBERS: HYMN TO THE MOTHER (CHARLES LLOYD)

Peter J. Harris

> Paint by number *(or* painting by numbers*) describes kits having a board on which light blue lines indicate areas to paint, each area having a number and a corresponding numbered paint to use … developed and marketed in 1950 by Max S. Klein, owner of the Palmer Paint Company of Detroit, Michigan and Dan Robbins, a commercial artist. In 1951 Palmer Paint introduced the Craft Master brand, which sold over 12 million kits. This public response induced other companies to produce their own versions of paint by number. The Craft Master paint-kit box tops proclaimed, "Every man a Rembrandt!" Following the death of Max Klein in 1993, his daughter, Jacquelyn Schiffman donated the Palmer Paint Co. archives to the Smithsonian Museum of American History.*

ballerinas in a *pas de deux* pirouette off wall of our living room
graceful sentinels reminding us of Ma's warning
never slam front door of number 304 where Moms has labored
to curate serenity for a family of 5 & a museum within our 2BR
apartment
books multiplying to become an intimate Black History Month
walk-through
LPs hinting at my future's eclectic cultural rambles
Andre Watts at the Hollywood Bowl   John Denver Take Me Home
Country Roads
Rachmaninoff, I learn, is not a stew   Leontyne Pryce stuns my ear into
evolution
was that Paul Robeson climbing Jacob's Ladder?
Moms' subtle brush strokes multiplied miniature blue numbers into a
haunting whole

~

playing grand piano by ear backstage at Hollywood Bowl
I've taken my place after managing logistics of artistic excellence

& outliving my mother   my working-class saint   we are fused
balance lush between us   I'm poised on cover photo of my own iconic LP

~

Mother & son manufacture beauty
wish Ma could see through my eyes
I now *volunteer* to pick up random trash in my hood
She don't have to remind me no more
you live here don't you?
don't need peer pressure nor permission to make beauty
perpetual prisoner of Her compounding Home Training

~

me and Ma on a bus headed to a gogo sponsored by an organization
studying U.S. national security issues. we get lost. She laments that
Daddy doesn't ask her about Her feelings. I tell Her let's record your
oral history. She pshaws. I say no seriously, let's do it. I don't want
to forget your voice. I start crying as we get off bus at last stop in
Georgetown and start walking to 21st Street, where the event supposed to happen. we can't figure out the route and decide to call for
directions. I pull out my cell phone which breaks in two. cell phone?
we're in a restaurant. using pay phone when I slide a paper plate down
a long table. plate slides past Moms and into the lap of a brother who
favors Brian Jackson. dude promptly goes off on me even though I'm
apologizing with sincerity. eventually he calls me a european-loving
so-and-so, and I guess it's because Moms is light, bright & damn
near white. suddenly it's clear that what was on the plate splashed
on another brother who was sitting next to Brian Jackson who's still
ranting. I throw towels at both men. I look at second brother and say:
are we good? are we good? and he says: what you mean? and I say
I've apologized. I've thrown you a towel. I've humbled myself. are we
good? are we good? and he nods yeah we good. and then I ask Brian
Jackson: are we good? and he says: Hell no! and I get pissed and raise
my voice. *how can we not be good? it was an accident up front. I have done every-*
thing a motherfucker can do to make good and you up in here insulting me in front
of my Mother. the other diners come into view. they are mostly white
folks dressed for D.C. office jobs. they're frozen in various poses of eating shocked at this intense tableau. I walk up close to Moms and put
my arm around her shoulders. we in complete alignment, you know,
and I say: *this is my Mother motherfucker and I love my Moms more than I love*

apologizing to you. you ain't *earned one more second of my time.* I wake up
with my arm around Moms and I'm crying. I play the kalimba to ease
into the morning...

~

turned 53 on April 26. four children in full stride (youngest close to
earning Master's). quit straight job as arts educator. savoring. tranc-
ing. becoming healthier mid-level elder—*surrendering*, you know, with
humility, curiosity, and hunger. resurfacing as a student among the
number. dropped my esthetic guard. psyched rolling up on the unpre-
dictable: the unscripted conversations: turns of phrase I've been too
impatient or overconfident to receive: the ecstatic concentration my
day-to-day distractions have corroded: searching the awesome night
sky: walking during lulls in all the talk and teaching: coaxing playfulness into my world

through all my Blues and dues, ultimately learned to peep cliché or *okie
doke,* the unethical, the easy or oppressive and *this chord change in my life
imprints me with depth of my formative ferment,* embodying and resting on
militancy, serving & creating community, collective work & responsibility, daring musicality, historical excavation, personal testimony & rev-
elation, erotica & love, social equality, community health & education,
women's rights & children's freedom. *Unlike then, I know that real currency
of humane living is changing for the better faster, recognizing when to play changes
instead of just listening to them*

~

Charles Lloyd's Hymn to the Mother   concentration in psalm   calling
through calling   invoking Her delicious reverence for life   illumi-
nating Her persistence   revealing hope She wore on oval face of an
abandoned child   echoing Her passions to live beyond prescriptions
of childhood diseases   shape-shifting Her contours beyond whims
& codes on bureaucratic forms   shaping invisible numbers sprawled
upon white cardboard   praising Her   harvesting Her   with musical
brushstrokes that shepherd my return to a modest 2BR crib across the
Anacostia River   an official orphan bookmarks another random chapter in the Sacred Book for Haunted Lovers   transcribes lessons from a
January mother with the summer name   an oracle named June taken
way way way too soon

SAUDADE: SWEET AND SOUR VAMP @ 54

Peter J. Harris

indigo rusting joints of a birthday
contemplation   a muscle car revving in neutral
cantankerous as Fred Sanford
this atmosphere of paralysis electrifying rhythm & overflow of time

exhale after cleansing cry is slow locomotion
of my Ancestors' invitation
Saudade   sweet and sour vamp   *decisions decisions*   consolidate & hoard
blessings or massage them into origami pointing in no other direction
than the exalted everyday?

impossible to predict when possession will implode into craving for my
adolescence Trenton Avenue serenades & harmonies

when my sidewalk skin rhymed with the wind

BOTH SISSIES
Le Van D. Hawkins

It's Friday evening over four decades ago. I'm at my church for our weekly junior usher board meeting, preparing for the upcoming junior Sunday services. On the third Sunday of every month, junior church members aged seven to eighteen took over the adults' duties—the junior choir in vivid purple robes sang modern gospel songs, and the junior ushers stood in the church foyer warmly greeting church members and visitors as we passed out offering envelopes, handheld cardboard fans printed with the face of Dr. King, and church programs that listed that Sunday's order of service.

The junior ushers were easy to spot in our usher uniforms—the boys in crisp white dress shirts, black clip-on ties, black pants, and black dress shoes; the girls wearing fancy white blouses with frilly bows, black skirts, and shiny black patent leather shoes. We'd steer the attendees into the sanctuary, where they were greeted by a junior usher standing in the center of the aisle. Right hands extended in welcome, left hands behind their backs, they executed a sequence of precise, well-choreographed moves that welcomed church members and visitors, then directed them to their seats. Later, during the services, we collected the membership offerings with the same sense of purpose, precision, and showmanship, then brought the gold-plated collection plates to the prayer table in front of the altar, left hands behind our backs, right hands holding the collection plates at our waists. As the minister began his offering prayer, every usher standing in the sanctuary—in the aisles, posted at the exits—would take their cue from the ushers standing before the prayer table as they emphatically dropped their hands to their sides in unison, raised and crossed their arms at their chests, then, finally, bowed their heads in prayer.

Extended hands, graceful turns on the soles of our freshly polished shoes, these stylish maneuvers originated at a Black Baptist church in Chicago less than a half hour's drive from my church in Robbins, a predominately Black Chicago south suburb. Representatives of various usher boards—officers, junior supervisors, or in many cases, the usher board's most graceful members—traveled across Chicagoland, where they were taught these procedures along with a series of hand signals that enabled the ushers to communicate while going about their duties.

The number of workshops grew rapidly. Soon, the trainers were supplying rudimentary training manuals for their trainees to distribute among the usher boards they represented. At our usher board meeting, we studied the manuals and repeatedly went over the moves described and illustrated until we had converted them into dazzling live perfection. Quickly, this dynamic new style of welcoming church members and visitors became so popular it was used in Black churches across the United States.

* * *

That Friday evening forty years ago at junior usher board rehearsal, I couldn't master a new sequence of moves our trainer/president/dictator-for-life seventeen-year-old Robert Monroe was teaching us. Our moves needed to be precise and synchronized. Every time we went through them, I was a few seconds off. *Every time.* I was fifteen years old and the only member of the junior usher board who couldn't keep up—out of everyone—including the seven-year-olds, the eight-year-old boy with polio, and Mr. Perry, our seventy-something supervisor. My feet began to shake; I could feel the sweat of humiliation draining down my face as my leg spasmed.

"WRONG, WRONG, WRONG," Robert yelled at me. "What kind of sissy are you?"

Robert took special delight in harassing me. He knew how uncomfortable I was interacting with him and he knew I hated being called a sissy. I was doing everything I could think of to squelch that description. My mannerisms were subtler than Robert's, something I thought made me more acceptable than him until one of my high school classmates sat across from me in our crowded cafeteria and loudly told everyone in the vicinity of our table that unlike Robert, I was a "sophisticated" sissy: one who couldn't be detected on first glance, but was a sissy just the same. My classmate explained, in front of me but as if I weren't there, if you watched me closely, the sensual way I rocked my ass against the gymnasium wall and waited for jock strap inspection—yes, it's exactly what it sounds like: points deducted if it was dirty; double points off if you weren't wearing one—if you watched the way my hand fluttered when I was annoyed and attempting to shoo someone away (according to my classmate, only sissies "shooed"), you'd *know* I was a male of the *sissy sally fairy* variety.

After all the work I'd done, I still behaved like a sissy???At the very least, I thought I had made the transition from sophisticated sissy (my classmate's description, not mine) to nice but kool dude (*kool* with a *k*, like Kool cigarettes). I gave my voice edge when I spoke, dropping f-bombs and making sure when I tossed out *motherfucker* it was "mutha" and "fucka," not "mothER fuckER."

"Oh you kool, now, hunh?" the best football player in the history of my high school asked me (in reflection, perhaps there was some sarcasm in his question) when he spotted me wearing one of my recent purchases from an urban store in "the city," which was what kool people called Chicago. My idea to wear the kind of clothes the kool kids wore instead of wearing tight high-water pants riding my ass was paying off! Soon, I would be just another dude, my past clothing choices forgotten.

That day in the cafeteria was a setback, yes, but I vowed not to give up. The next day in gym class, I stood up straight for jock strap inspection, so straight my spine began to ache. I had no choice but to roll it out on the wall, sighing in relief as forty teenage boys eyeballed me.

Yes, the *sissy sally fairy* variety.

Here's the big difference between Robert and me: I did everything I could to fit in; Robert did everything he could to stand out. A few weeks before this particular junior usher board meeting, Robert had gone to our sister school to pick up Michael Washington, our church organist. For the occasion, Robert wore a woman's black fur coat that stopped midway between his knees and ankles, large round women's sunglasses, and a bright-red turban and matching gloves.

No one would ever accuse Robert of being a sophisticated sissy.

Even if I'd owned that outfit, I would have known better than to wear it to a high school in the south suburbs of Chicago. The high-waters I'd worn before I turned kool were an accident—it had never occurred to me to wear something loose. I simply had to learn different behavior. A red turban and matching red gloves—that was no accident; Robert knew what he was doing. Then maybe he didn't. Maybe he did as everyone else did—instinctively gravitated to whatever attracted him, never realizing there were observers who would vehemently object to his choices.

Dozens of laughing students gathered around him that day, branding him, in case he had forgotten he was a male of the *sissy sally fairy* variety. A security guard had to break up the crowd. Though there was no social media then, word quickly got around about Robert's outfit and how he'd been taunted. Today, the incident would have gone viral, a video of Robert's outfit and the harassment he endured all over Instagram and Facebook, some posters mocking him, others angry at his homophobic tormentors.

When I first heard the news, I wondered how Michael had reacted when he'd seen Robert. Had he seen him and thought, What the hell? Had he worried people would see them walking together and think he was gay? Had anyone harassed them? Had he stood up for Robert? Or had he gotten so accustomed to Robert's ensembles, he'd simply seen what Robert was wearing as another one of his outrageous outfits?

I couldn't be seen with Robert except while performing usher duties at church. My mother demanded my brother and I stay away from "that Monroe boy who can't make up his mind whether he's a boy or girl!" Secondly, I felt I had done much too much work transforming myself to negate it by associating with Robert. If we were together, he would inevitably draw everyone's attention, then they would broaden their lens and close in on me. And as my classmate said in the cafeteria—IN FRONT OF EVERYBODY—ALL would be revealed.

* * *

"WRONG, WRONG, WRONG!" Robert yelled as I tripped over my feet.

While he barked at me, I had flashbacks of being humiliated at the local YMCA when it took me all summer to progress from "Guppies" to "Beginners" in swim class, something the six boys in my neighborhood did the first day we attended. I saw the exasperated and repulsed face of my older cousin when, after weeks of his instruction, I still couldn't ride the new bike I'd received for Christmas while my brother, thirteen months younger, hopped on it, pedaled, and sped off.

"Amateur!" Robert yelled.

"I'm not an amateur, Madame President. Your moves suck."

Everyone in the sanctuary, including Mr. Perry, gasped. No one, including Mr. Perry, dared defy Robert.

Suddenly, a black flash is moving towards my face. I duck as a Bible missiles over my head. The word of God rocketing over me at a thousand miles an hour. I was one Bible verse away from being decapitated. The Holy Book has a lot of pages.

"You almost hit me!" I yell at Robert.

"If I wanted to hit you, I would have." He snaps his fingers in front of my face for emphasis when he says, "I *would* have," the finger snaps sounding through the sanctuary like gunshots.

"I had to duck to stop from being hurt."

"Nice reflexes."

"You hear him?" I angrily ask Mr. Perry.

"He said he wasn't trying to hit you, Le Van," Mr. Perry answers meekly.

I loved Mr. Perry but he was no match for Robert and wasn't good for anything but calling 911 the day Robert finally decapitated me. Robert was always throwing Bibles at me. I was the only one who defied him, the only one who desperately needed to maintain a distance between us. I thanked God for Robert's hate but that night, I'd had enough. Forget my tormentors who ridiculed me and robbed me of my lunch money, and the ones who made me do their homework—Robert was my number one nemesis. That year, we did everything but arch our backs and hiss at each other. It was one outrage after another, and when I thought it couldn't get any worse, he modeled at our church's biggest event, the annual Palm Sunday fashion show and tea, and ruined the show I'd waited all year to attend.

* * *

My enthusiasm for fashion began around the time I joined the junior usher board. That year, my brother and I accompanied my mother to the fashion show for the first time. All our babysitters were at the fashion show—even the men. My uncles—my mother's brothers—were available, but with their exuberant profanity and drinking, they weren't allowed to look after us, so my brother and I grudgingly attended another of the million church events we had to endure. Funerals, weddings, prayer meetings, church business meetings, Mother's board meetings—we did them all. I didn't expect to *love* the fashion show and tea. To become so excited, I had to stop myself from bouncing up and down in my seat.

Everything about the Palm Sunday fashion show was larger-than-life and glamorous—from the overflowing auditorium (my future high school gymnasium, where, years later, my classmates would notice how my ass rode the walls during jock strap inspection) to the mistress of ceremonies exhorting us to "applaud till the roof caves in!" to a gospel singer with a classical contralto like Marian Anderson (*Who hung the moon and the stars in the sky? Somebody bigger than you and I*).

After the fashion show, there was the tea—elegant tables covered with white tablecloths set around a cavernous room that one day would become my high school cafeteria, site of some of my greatest teenage humiliations. Each table was sponsored by a church organization. My mother was in charge of the usher board's table. She nervously watched the judges pace from one table to another with their ballots and pencils, awarding points for theme, originality, beauty, and refreshments. Guests were served finger sandwiches with no crust and pastries I loved but rarely ate such as macaroons and petit fours. (Macaroons looked like they were cloaked in colorful designer coats! The pretty petit fours I could eat two at a time!) There was also frappé made of pink sherbet, vanilla ice cream, 7UP, and a variety of fruit slices and juices. I had watched my mother make the concoction, mesmerized by the way it foamed in the giant sparkling glass punch bowl.

The usher board had as their centerpiece a cake shaped and decorated as a replica of a red straw high-crown hat with its large brim curving down. To my seven-year-old eyes, the hat reminded me of my grandmother's favorite Christmas bell ornament. It sat atop an ornate silver cake stand. A pink ribbon hugged the crown; a burst of pink flowers sprouting through the ribbon—the details so exact I had to fight the impulse to snatch a flower petal off the cake and eat it to determine if it was really cake and candy.

"Everything on the cake can be eaten," my mother informed fascinated guests as they gathered around the ushers' table.

She and the women ushers erupted in screams and hugs after our minister announced the ushers had won the giant winged-woman trophy that stood proudly all year in a locked glass box in the church foyer, the name of the organization that had won that year's Palm Sunday tea table contest engraved on a gold plaque above the winged-woman's head.

* * *

Most of all, I loved the models I saw that Palm Sunday as they posed and twirled in their resplendent outfits. I wasn't old enough to be aware of the subtleties of color; everything I saw was viewed through the prism of the simple colors in my first crayon box. Blue! Red! Green! Yellow! Pink! Even the colors I thought boring thrilled me. White! Black! Brown! Gray!

I couldn't stop spinning and twirling. My grandmother thought it was cute. "Show me how they modeled," she smiled, urging me on. I twirled and struck poses as she applauded. Applauded like she was trying to make the roof cave in!

I twirled in delight until I heard, "Sissy."

I turned to my cousin Freddy, a few months older than me. Repulsed, he shook his head and frowned. I rushed across the room and punched him in the face. It may not have been the manliest of punches, but it was effective. This sissy gave him something to frown about. We fought through the house like UFC warriors, my grandmother, hands raised in distress, whooping hysterically. A few of her ceramic knickknacks crashed to the floor. She whooped some more. When my mother arrived at my grandmother's house that night, my brother hurried to her and informed her I had been fighting, my cousin effeminately mocking my fashion turns, mincing through the house as he made his case for having called me such a vile name.

Later that night, my mother whipped me with a limb from our apple tree.

"You know why I'm whipping you, don't you?" she asked me.

"Yes, ma'am . . ."

* * *

By the age of fourteen, I knew the colors magenta and crimson and could explain the subtle differences between the two, but apple tree limbs and my ongoing efforts to be nice but kool forced me to limit my descriptions to "pink."

That year, the year of my fourteenth birthday, my aunt was appointed chair of the Palm Sunday fashion show. She told me she wanted me to be the fashion show handyman. I thought my head was going to explode. I attended all the rehearsals the week before the show, carried heavy items, gave my opinion on the decorations, and was at the disposal of all the models.

I was a crack addict working in a crack house.

I loved it all, but with studied indifference, only allowing myself to be thrilled on the inside, occasionally griping about the demeaning women's work my aunt had me doing. Alone in my bedroom, I locked my door and spun and struck poses like the models I had just watched rehearse.

That Palm Sunday morning and afternoon, I hurriedly assisted my aunt and her committee, then changed into my dress clothes. My work was done. Time for the show! I excitedly sat in the crowded high school gymnasium and delighted in the fashions. On the inside. Indigo! Rose! Fern! Dandelion! Ivory! Obsidian! Gingerbread! Pewter!

There were only two male models in the fashion show—Robert and Joseph Cobb. Joseph took a hypermasculine approach to modeling. As the mistress of ceremonies described his clothing, he performed vignettes as he pimp-walked down the runway. In one, he slowly retrieved a cigarette out of an antique silver cigarette case. He stopped, returned the case to his front pocket, lit his cigarette with a shiny silver lighter, then blew fancy rings of smoke as he continued his leisurely stroll. The women loved Joseph. In his presence, they seemed to forget they were attending a church event and swooned and screamed like they were seated in the front row at a male strip club.

"Next, we have Robert Monroe," the emcee excitedly told the audience. Robert hadn't allowed my aunt to see what he was going to do or wear. He'd worked on his routine privately with the emcee, who'd assured my aunt Robert was "going to be outta sight!"

Robert sashayed onto the stage wearing the largest sunglasses I had ever seen; they practically covered his whole face. "Robert is wearing Jackie O sunglasses, which are all the rage," gushed the emcee.

"For women," a man snorted behind my brother and me.

I turned to the president of my church's deacon board. His wife, amused at his discomfort, put her finger to her lips to shush him.

"Robert wears a gray tweed sports coat with yellow flecks, a yellow silk pocket square, a yellow silk dress shirt designed by him, yellow linen pants, and pale-yellow socks," the emcee continued. "Mellow yellow!" Robert pulled up his pant leg and seductively revealed his shoe. "And dark-gray Stacy Adams shoes!" He playfully kicked his foot at the deacon, then dramatically swished his ass down the stage. My brother turned his attention to the floor. The deacon frowned as Robert stopped at the edge of the riser, then slowly began to remove his coat.

"Go, Robert, go," the emcee urged. "Let it all hang out!"

Robert removed his coat, held it in one hand, then swiveled, his back to the audience.

Then he froze.

I froze.

The deacon froze.

My brother groaned.

Robert had cut a large heart in the middle of his shirt, his sweaty naked back peeking through.

"Ladies and gentlemen, THE KING OF HEARTS!!!!"

The crowd roared and broke out in laughter and rapturous applause. Suddenly, Robert threw his jacket to the floor and dramatically stormed down the runway, his butt cheeks thundering in his tight yellow linen pants. I thought I saw lightning bouncing off his ass. "Are we having fun yet?" The emcee laughed. "Go, Robert!" The deacon's wife hooted; the deacon groaned. My brother shook his head. I looked around the gym and the deacon locked his eyes on me. He wanted an audience. He rolled his eyes at the stage and shook his head disapprovingly at the spectacle. If only he knew how much I hated him. I joined him and rolled my eyes at the stage. And hated myself.

It took several minutes for the crowd to simmer down after Robert's sweaty back and thundering butt cheeks. "Your president," the deacon leaned in and said to me as Robert returned for a curtsy, then dramatically turned his back to us, once again revealing his heart. "Peekaboo, indeed," the emcee chuckled.

The deacon called an emergency deacon board meeting and later informed my aunt Robert could no longer model at church events. It saddened her. I don't know if she felt it was wrong denying a loyal church member what he loved or if she just knew a good thing when she saw it. People talked about her show for weeks.

My mother was silent.

* * *

When I ushered the next junior Sunday, I felt everyone's eyes on me, a member of Robert's "crew," their close-up lenses moving in. That

Sunday, my usher turns felt like the twirls I did alone in my bedroom. They were taboo. Something I was mysteriously drawn to but also, something that caused me shame. I awkwardly attempted to make my usher turns more masculine and fell out of step with my junior usher partners.

My male classmates' taunts rose in their frequency and their explicitness. "Did you get Robert in the booty and recite Bible verses?" "When the Bible says, 'Come onto me,' do you and Robert jerk off and cum?"

I used to volunteer to travel with the senior ushers on Sunday afternoons to various churches located in Chicago's Black neighborhoods. I loved exploring the city. What I'd once loved, I started avoiding, fearful someone would see me in the same car as Robert. I no longer went on excursions to Chicago.

I had had enough.

I decided to have my brother nominate me at the end of the year for president of the junior usher board. In my convoluted thinking, I would take Robert's beloved job. He would never take orders from me; he'd quit first. I had a great chance of winning. The other junior ushers were just as tired of Robert as I was—especially the boys, my brother included. They, too, were the butt of jokes. Being a sophisticated sissy, I was never as flamboyant as Robert and damnit, I was changing. I wore kool clothes and watched my every move to make sure I was acceptable. How could I fail with such dedication?

After my brother nominated me, Robert stood at the head of the sanctuary, his face panicked as he looked around the room, tallying votes in his head. I smirked at him.

Before we proceeded to vote, Mr. Perry asked to speak. "There's a lot of work involved with being president. Rehearsals. Communication from our district and state. District and state meetings. Conventions. It's not just show. Or play." As he spoke, I realized he was telling the ushers I didn't have the ability to be president; only Robert did. "Then there's the choreography issue." Mr. Perry paused and shyly looked away from me. Robert eyed me and smirked.

He who smirks last, smirks best.

Humiliated and angry, I withdrew from the race. Robert smirked at me the rest of the night.

A few Fridays later, he once again mocked me as I struggled with a move. "WRONG! WRONG! WRONG!" he yelled. Once again, I called him "Madame President," this time adding "and fired supermodel." He angrily grabbed a Bible off the prayer table, the flash of black zipping towards me. In those few seconds, I saw flashes of Robert's smirk while Mr. Perry spoke before we voted. Then I heard my classmate call me a "sophisticated sissy" in the cafeteria.

I wanted out.

I decided not to duck.

I winced as the Bible crashed against my nose and mouth. I grabbed my face, wailed, and fell dramatically to the floor, blood dripping from my lip. I didn't have to do much acting; that shit hurt. One of the little girls screamed and began to weep.

Robert stood frozen, hand to his mouth, as Mr. Perry rushed to me. "I wasn't trying to hit him!" Robert told Mr. Perry. Mr. Perry ignored him and directed one of the boys to hurry to the restroom and grab a handful of paper towels.

I told my brother to help me up, then said, "Come on, we're outta here." I defiantly walked through the church smirking, my brother at my side.

He who smirks last, smirks best.

* * *

When my brother and I arrived home, my mother was in the kitchen preparing dinner. She had been a junior usher when she was young and later served as president of the senior ushers when she was in her twenties. As soon as I was eligible to join the junior ushers, she'd signed us up. Though my brother had been a year younger than the minimum age allowed, my mother had persuaded Mr. Perry to take both of us as a package. We hadn't had a say in the matter. Nor had Mr. Perry. My mother would be displeased we had walked out and would force us to return. I had to use the one thing that would stop me from returning to the usher board so I could continue cultivating my image.

I had to use my mother's homophobia.

"That Robert Monroe," I said.

"I told you I don't want you around that Monroe boy."

"I'm not. I don't hang with him. He just hit me in the face with a Bible."

"What?"

"On purpose. Look at my lip. It's bleeding."

* * *

That was the end of my ushering. *And* Robert's Bible throwing—he was put on probation: if he threw another Bible, he would be permanently kicked off the usher board.

A few years later, I attended the University of Illinois at Urbana-Champaign. During a visit home at spring break, I ran into Roy Fordham, who'd been a junior usher along with Robert, my brother, and me. We talked about college and shared the latest news.

"Did you hear about Robert?" Roy asked. "He lives in the city now and calls himself 'Robbie Mae.'" Roy grunted derisively, the way a man who secretly sleeps with men makes fun of the men he's slept with, so no one suspects he's sleeping with them. It was too late for that performance. EVERYONE knew Roy had slept with Robert. Including my mother.

Months later, I visited my church during another break. During the services, I spotted one of our church members urgently tapping the shoulder of the woman in front of her. The woman turned to the row behind her and suddenly put her hand over her mouth in shock. People all over the church were tapping, elbowing, and turning. Tapping, elbowing, and turning. Then a hand to the mouth in surprise or outrage. Or was it both? I turned to see what everyone was looking at—Robert.

I didn't know enough to think, *There's Robbie Mae.* But there she was, dressed in an exquisite crimson dress. On her head was a magnificent church hat. (Picture the one the late, great Aretha Franklin wore when she sang "My Country, 'Tis of Thee" at Obama's first inauguration—the majesty, the circumference, the oversized bow, the sequins—but in pink with streaks of crimson.) My quick fashion eye took in her satin pumps, pink as the peonies in my mother's front yard. The murmurs rumbling through the congregation brought me back to the problem at hand. I wanted to flee. I had just started to accept myself. I'd read all of James Baldwin's novels, attended gay bars in Champaign, and enjoyed being in the presence of my new gay friends. That day at church, I felt shame and a familiar fear. Robbie's feelings didn't matter; she was a thing. And so was I. I wanted to shout: *She's not a thing! She's a human being!*

I frowned at the gawkers until I caught Robbie Mae's attention—I was frowning in her direction. She stared at me, her face indignantly asking, *What are you looking at? You still think you better than me? Haven't you learned anything?* For a moment, I expected her to scream at me and call me sissy in front of the whole church. *He ain't nothing but a sophisticated sissy!*

I quickly turned away and kept my head lowered through the rest of the church services, afraid at any moment, a Bible would rocket my way.

During the services, the deacons gathered in the pastor's office and decided Robert needed to be reminded he was of the *sissy sally fairy* variety. They vowed if he entered the women's restroom, they would do whatever was necessary to get him out. How far would they go? Stand at the women's restroom door and shove him away if he dared attempt to go in? Call the police? Shoot him?

I don't know what is with straight men feeling the need to protect their women from trans women using the restroom. Apparently, it's a thing . . . because this was decades ago.

* * *

Decades ago, when I saw Robbie Mae in all her glory, I wasn't familiar with the words *trans woman*. I also wasn't aware of *internalized homophobia* when I began altering myself to please people who hated me. I hadn't heard the phrase *toxic masculinity behaviors* when I began mimicking the kool dudes' stereotypically masculine way of behaving.

Occasionally, the fears of a gay teenager living in a small town assert themselves in my adult life and I find myself assessing my body language and the way I speak. Am I kool enough? The teenage me flinches when I arrive at a poetry or storytelling event to perform what my ex-boyfriend once called my "fag shit." I can feel the fearful heartbeat of my teenage self nodding understandingly at my ex's embarrassment and self-consciousness. The adult me has vowed to read my fag shit until I am no longer fearful of owning up to who I am. The teenage me puzzles over why Robbie Mae and I subjected ourselves to scrutiny—he certainly wouldn't have. Then I realize Robbie and the me who shared my personal life in my writing weren't the ones altering ourselves to please oppressors. Robbie never hid. She defiantly entered our church on her own terms, worshipped her God, and made us deal with her presence.

I have no idea where Robbie Mae lives or whether she is dead or alive, but the expression on her face that Sunday remains with me—*You still think you're better than me? We're members of the same family.*

She lived her life as Grand Diva Ruler because good or bad, that's who she was. She was brave. I was not.

I still have a long walk to get to freedom. ∎

OFF THE WALL
Tsehaye Geralyn Hébert

Armed with a self-righteous can of paint in one hand, the lady in the flat, sensible shoes made a beeline from the automotive store on the corner—the *Evanston* side. What one had just purchased legally on one side of the street could not be legally purchased across the street—on the *Chicago* side—yards away. Buying a can of spray paint was the least one of them. On one side of the street there were lawns, a garden and sweet shops. Stores full of a hundred or more choices of shoes, food and more.

But not on *that side*. *That side* was full of corner stores and fast food shops. Wig and weaving shops. Bars carried over from earlier, more lucrative times, sat next to jerk after jerk shop, a taco stand, and a shady hardware store rumored to sell mostly stolen goods.

With only four choices at the auto store, red, white, black and silver, Josie said, "White," without giving it a thought.

"White," she said, as crisp as the name implied. The sound of a sheet drying in the sun and wind whipped on a perfect day, now having its corners popped for good measure. Black and gray were too maudlin. Red too violent. The cans of spray paint held in her bosom like an amulet, she walked right up to the large marks covering one side of the wall of the fast-food joint.

The marks had been painted by *his* boys. The deceased's posse commemorated the life lost, lives lost. No matter what affiliation, what age, what side of town, caste or class, there is no reason, no concept, no ideology that can explain away or condone murder. Save for self-defense. And one better be careful with that. Given the circumstances, the time of day, the zip code, and other factors, like the color of your uniform, it could go either way.

As soon as she began to spray-paint, a person or two stopped. One passerby and then another shouted out to her.

"Go on 'head! That's right!"

"Somebody ought to do it."

"Need to stop all this foolishness."

"Damn shame!?"

"Whaaat???!!!"

"What the f—"

Rising and swelling as did the chorus of citizens assembling and diminishing behind her, each with a commentary, Josie sprayed and sprayed. Then silence. Dead...silence. Just like the kid who'd been shot the night before, a block away from Josie's home, at that intersection.

By the time Josie got to the second can, shaking it as furiously as she had the first, two more stopped to watch. From the corner of her eye, sliding it as far to the right as she could without turning around, she scanned left and right again, then up and down. She continued to spray and spray and spra... and sppppsss... The third can emptied, she became aware that there were now maybe a half dozen murmuring behind her. A low unsettling rumbling rising.

. . . *sick and tired. I am sick and tired of the killing. These are our children. Not other people's children. OUR children. That was somebody's child! Every day I hustle off to teach verbs and adverbs only to learn yet another one is gone. Another Bearden another Micheaux Jackie Robinson...How many times do we* . . . She shut up the voices inside and continued.

Someone stood close, closer than most, close enough to violate personal space. But she would not turn around. It was a man—men smell and move differently—you *don't* have to see them to know they're there. She sprayed over the signs and symbols—signals that only one group "owned" that block, when all of them put together couldn't buy enough cemetery plots to bury half the people murdered in gang violence. Or, let alone put that same energy to other uses?!

"Do you know what you're doing?"

The voice assured and in command. She slid her eye to notice the navy blue, from toe back up to midcalf and back again. She kept on spraying.

"Yes," she said, angrily, without looking up.

"Whoa . . ."

"Aww man? Heard what that broad said?!"

"My children stand here. They take the bus here. They walk down *this* street when we visit friends. This cannot happen here!"

The black turned gray and now smeared ghost text easing forward and dripping down from beneath the white spray.

"Ma'am, it's a memorial." The blue uniform stood quietly, upping the volume loud enough for those assembled to hear, and carefully enunciating each word.

"This is for all of us who have lost our precious children. Why do we have to have a memorial in the first place? That's what I want to paint away, not the memorial! OUR CHILDREN are dying!"

"I know, ma'am," quieter than before. "I'm gonna speak louder now, do not get alarmed. You painted over the memorial for the uh . . . a member of a . . . uh . . . street organization, and I agree with you. A dozen or more people standing behind you might think otherwise. So,

I'm gonna raise my voice and when you're finished with what sounds and looks like your last can, I'll disperse the crowd and watch as you leave to make sure you get out of here okay. Agreed?"

"Yes," she said loudly as if she were angry with the cop who spent most of his time sitting behind the desk at the outpost, across the street on the Evanston side.

When that last can gave out its final hiss, when nothing more could be done, Josie walked over to the trash can, dumped all the empty canisters in and walked away.

I just painted over an impromptu mural, the cop said we let it happen. They let off steam and Streets and San takes care of it in a day or two with a call to the alderman. Friends and colleagues of the deceased gathered behind her, not knowing what to make of the spectacle: a schoolteacher type, gray hair pulled back in a large bun, painting away their wall.

The woman with the sensible shoes had just left her job teaching at schools in the worst Chicago neighborhoods, tortoiseshell glasses slipping again and again to her nose. She could have lost her life. Instead, upon seeing the mural, the unlikely graffiti artist parked her car and doubled back to the auto shop to buy paint. Returning home, she now walked away from the wall, taking the opposite side of the street rather than walk right up to her house a half block away. She walked past her home and up to the next block, turned right, crossed the street, and doubled back toward home.

Her best students *opted* for motherhood instead of four-year colleges and the scholarships awaiting them. They were afraid to leave the homes and sordid assorted stories of human misery that would chain them to the very neighborhoods their parents fled to. Those same parents escaped the Mississippis and Alabamas and the Emmett Tills of their youth, only to end right back in blocks and systems of poverty that have never ended whether they worked on the West side at Brach or at Parchman Farm.

"College isn't for everyone," guidance counselors reminded her.

Other balked at incurring debt.

"My parents told me *never ever* have debt."

"Even good debt?" She found herself asking.

A brilliant student passed on a scholarship because he knew how to cut hair. A couple hundred a day cutting hair, and that one would never return to flipping burgers or dipping chicken into hot grease at any house but his own. A promising senior wrote an essay only under condition that Josie would destroy it upon reading. It told how the now-seventeen-year-old had lived on his own since he was fourteen, when he held down his own operation.

"I don't do no drugs, Ms. Josie, I just sell 'em. Both parents in jail.

I been on my own since 14. Made it all this time, make it through these last few months, I'm out of here. I'll never return to Chicago. I'ma start me a new life."

Her job done; Josie walked away. The once pristine memorial detailed with the deceased's insignia that had taken half the night to create was now a shockingly white-gray mass of dripping paint.

Returning home from school, her son walked very slowly down the opposite side of the street. He paused long enough to make sure his eyes did not lie. *Was that his sixty-something-year-old mother? Painting the snack shop wall? On the Chicago side of Howard Street?*

Two men walked past, "Look at that ol' dumbass," one man said.

"Bitch coulda got killed out here," the other one laughed.

"Yeah man . . . but, did you hear what homegirl said to the cop?!"

The treasured late-in-life child walked more slowly. Unsure what to do, or if any movement would help or endanger her, he stood in a store doorway and watched from a short distance to make sure she was okay.

As he headed back toward home, his mother crossed on the opposite side and headed north and up the block. She didn't see him, and he pretended *not* to see her. She walked with purpose and intent, flat, sensible shoes slapping the pavement. As she passed their home, he hurried inside.

Was his mother losing it? Should he call someone? His dad? He bounded up the stairs, fumbled for his key, unloaded his book bag, dropped his jacket in one move it seemed. By the time he reached for the phone, the key turned. The lock clicked open. In walked his mother.

The brightest smile, and a white thumbprint smeared slightly aside her nose, a whisper of paint brushed along her cheek. Josie pulled off her sensible shoes and put them on the shoe rack. The woman who, in less than twenty minutes, had wiped out a memorial it had taken half the night to put up now pulled on her sensible house shoes.

He had not voluntarily hugged his mother in the last year or so. As she moved toward him, arms open wide, he was transfixed. He swallowed the lump in his throat, the one that eased its way up from his stomach now headed back down again. By the time she reached him, he hugged her back, and held on.

"How was your day?"

"Same old, same old," she said. "Nothing special. What do you want for dinner, honey?" ■

BROTHER ERIC GARNER
David Henderson

On his way to the grocery store
Eric Garner had no loose cigarettes to sell
to those who lacked the funds
to invest in a 13 dollar pack of smokes.
But even though Garner, a big Black affable guy,
had just saved the idle posse of plainclothes cops
the trouble of breaking up a fight, those same cops
decided on the spot to arrest him anyway on some
obscure aspect of their mission to interdict the sale of
untaxed cigarettes to indigent tobacco addicts.
Guilt or no guilt Eric Garner
would fulfill the Staten Island cop quota
in or out of the moment.
Garner was known to those local cops and they were
known to Garner.

Here they go again.

His denials did not prevent his arrest

for a man going to the store for his wife and kids
A family man of love & peace —- overweight, diabetic,
with heart troubles and another due process on tap.
Garner balks then just as quickly agrees to cooperate
with being detained rather than blowing his top over an
inevitability.
But the shortest and thinness of the cops wearing a New
York Yankee cap creeps behind Garner, and has to leap to
gain an arm around his neck. his arm bent at elbow is
grasped by his other hand making a ligature below
Garner's chin.

A video beholds the illegal choke hold.

As with the other four cops Garner is taken down.
They are seeking to handcuff him behind his back as if he
had been caught in the commitment of some crime.

Garner says,
I can't breathe, I can't breathe, I can't breathe —
and then ten more times of distinct repetition,
having only those few breaths left before his death.

Had Garner, perhaps, turned and grabbed that little
leaping cop before he could attempt that illegal
chokehold, Garner might be alive today — had he
slammed down as many of those criminal cops as possible
and fought them like a father protecting his family.

CITIZEN SANDRA BLAND DOA BEFORE JUSTICE
David Henderson

> *Texas Transportation Code: Texas Traffic laws
> concerning motorist yielding to emergency vehicles.
> When you see an emergency vehicle with red lights
> flashing and a warning siren, you should immediately
> move as near as possible to the right curb or edge
> of the road to create a clear path of the emergency
> vehicle to pass on the left.*

A lovely 28 year old young woman of African American
descent driving alone on a desolate prairie road in the deep south,
Texas USA. The flashing lights of an emergency vehicle, a police
car, comes up fast behind her. She pulls over at once and discovers
the police vehicle with lights flashing is following her to the side of
the road.

And some traffic cop "official" with a Texas Ranger Stetson, badge
and gun comes out from the squad car and stands at her driver's
side window. There they are alone on some desolate old prairie
road deep in the old south. She is attractive, sassy and speaks of
her constitutional rights. But when she refused to put out her
cigarette while seated in her car this "official" will eventually
order her out of her car at the point of a gun and force her to
the ground her hands behind her back, and lock together her
hands with cuffs tight as can be. Pain that causes her to cry out
complaints are ignored,

Attractive, sassy and, cussing, she calls him out of his name
To her he is the "motherfucker," and to him, she is the potential
mother who shall die.

For her failure to signal, Citizen Sandra Bland—was arrested—

three days later she was DOA before justice

QUOTE: It is said she was found hanging from a cell partition

with a long plastic bag tied around her neck.

The fingers that shaped the ligature bind with knowledge of the noose
The fingers that shape the ligature bind with knowledge of the noose.

NIGHT SHIFT
Charles Johnson

You go to work at the hospital at 10:00 p.m., as you always do, but you're feeling like a lot of people who don't want to leave home during the pandemic. Doctors and nurses, health care providers, people in grocery stores, teachers, and security guards like you—you all are supposed to be "essential" workers. The people on the front lines every day (and night) because certain goods and services can't end without society collapsing entirely, although some days it seems to you at this dangerous hour in history, when Americans are killing and tearing each other apart, that this sea change has happened *already*.

As a young black man, you were of course always at risk from the moment you were born. But even *that* abnormal wasn't normal anymore. After months of the worst pandemic in a century, you've witnessed the devastating toll it's taking on the doctors and hospital staff all around you. It's like they're fighting a war with never enough supplies, or a battle they feel they lose every time someone on a ventilator dies, which is daily, or when one of their coworkers contemplates suicide, or collapses on the floor right in front of them from fatigue. On top of that, there is always the danger of being contaminated by this devilish, mutating, poorly understood, highly politicized plague themselves and bringing it back home to their spouses, children, or aging parents.

That isn't something you have to worry about. You're twenty-five, but you figure you don't have a family. Not really. Not since your mother died fifteen years ago, right here in this hospital after a surgery she was too weak to recover from. That left your older brother, Jamal, and you to somehow cross America's racial minefield of dangers on your own. And you don't talk. You don't want to think about him being "family." You've been practicing social distancing with him since the day he started carrying a gun, selling drugs, and running with a gang called the Cobras when you were still in your teens. You didn't like them. The Cobras used to beat you up before Jamal was jumped into that gang. Him being a Cobra, and so angry, cynical and fighting all the time, always opinionated and pissed off, broke your mother's heart, and you never knew your father. He just wasn't around. Your mother had tried her best to put you both on the right path. Blackness, she said, was not a curse or condemnation. But you had to be careful in a society structured by an infinite number of ways for its citizens to fail, make mistakes, blunders, or be defined as criminals, wrong in some way, or involved in something illegal. She always told you to strive to be more, to be better, to just be *human*, and to see obstacles as opportunities—to stand for *some*thing, she said, because if you don't stand for something, it's likely you'll fall for *any*thing.

So you always tried to do better. To avoid the land mines that Jamal stepped on. Like him, you didn't finish high school, but you earned your GED, and you quietly do your best on your job here at the hospital. You don't want to become a casualty or just another statistic. You were wired, you feel, differently from him, and feared if you tried to help your brother, he might drag you down with him. You haven't seen him in—what?—maybe ten years, and that's all right. You learned you could do just fine by yourself, if need be. You try to read as much and as widely as you can, and sometimes you take online courses, even though your budget on a security guard's salary gets too tight sometimes and every so often you get behind on your bills.

Before walking into the hospital, you loop your plain black cloth mask over your ears, then push through the doors leading to the emergency room waiting area, which is near the corridor that leads to the locker room for those who work security. As soon as you step inside you know something is wrong. One of the other security guards, Jim Sawyer, always stands inside the entrance at this hour, taking note of everyone who comes in or leaves. But not tonight. And then you hear a smear of loud voices in the waiting room. A dozen angry young people, bloodied, bandaged and moaning, scarred and scared, wounded and willful, some dressed entirely in black, are demanding medical attention. Behind them, you see the receptionist, Kimisha Thompson, who you like and maybe more than like, because she's always good-natured, kind, has a beautiful, bow-shaped smile that lights up her eyes behind her glasses, never burdens anyone with her personal baggage, and will listen as long as you want to keep talking. But tonight she seems overwhelmed when you squeeze through this rowdy, unruly crowd, none of them wearing masks or social distancing, and ask her what all this is about.

She's wearing a white mask sprinkled with red hearts. That makes you smile because it so fits her personality. It keeps slipping up her nose and every so often she has to tug it back down toward her chin with her thumb and forefinger. Through the cloth, you hear her say, "There was a protest downtown. Don't ask me about what they were protesting this time, I don't remember. But when it got dark, some people started looting. Some attacked the police. One cop was shot and they took him to Harborview. Lucas," her voice, tremulous, sounds exhausted, "we're really shorthanded tonight. The doctors are doing triage. Right now we don't have enough ventilators or beds. Five of the security guards, one of them was Jim, tested positive for COVID when they showed up for work, and they're being quarantined at home. Your supervisor has been trying to reach you all day, but he kept getting a message that service to your phone was disconnected."

You nod slowly. That's one of the bills you fell behind on. You can tell this is going to be a very long night. What you don't know yet is that it might be your last night.

"Okay," you say, "I'll come back to take Jim's place as soon as I can."

Kimisha holds up one hand covered by a blue vinyl glove. Above her mask, you can see her gentle eyes—dark-brown pupils like chocolate drops—and pencil-thin eyebrows, but not her high cheekbones. Her silvery voice floats disembodied in the air. "No, one of the doctors—Dr. Chen—said they need someone right now in the recovery room in the east wing. That's where security is needed. You need to go there *now*."

"Are you going to be okay here by yourself?"

Her eyes crinkle. "I'll do my best. You go find Dr. Chen."

You hurry into the empty locker room, thinking of all the duties that await you at a hospital that is shorthanded and under siege. You change into your gray short-sleeved shirt, dark pants with gray stripes on the side, and strap on your duty belt with its keys, flashlight, radio, and a slot to hold your smartphone, then you pull on your turquoise latex gloves. But your mind is still chewing on what Kimisha told you. If the security staff is down five people tonight, who is going to do a floor-by-floor check of all the buildings every two hours? Who will be checking windows and doors? Who will make sure the security systems are functioning properly?

You wonder: Can *any*thing good come out of this ongoing catastrophe?

Dr. Chen, wearing a blood-splattered surgical gown, is waiting impatiently outside the recovery room when you arrive. You approach him cautiously because he always carries himself as if he's posing for a photo. Tonight, though, you can tell he's sacked and empty, running on the fumes. You place his age at sixty. Maybe sixty-five. For as long as you've known him, he's always been a perfectionist in an imperfect world, a physician strict about the right nutrition for his patients and the staff at the hospital, and he never trusts himself even to talk when he's tired, like now. When feeling numb after seeing ten patients die in a day from the virus, he balances his depleted energy by slowing down, breathing deeply, being ever more precise and mindful of even the minutest details, doing things "Tai Chi–style," as he calls it, for his father taught him the twenty-two-move Yang-style form when he was a boy. His motions as he waits for you are as slow as those of a man submerged in water, each posture or position he takes as he shifts his weight outside the recovery room flowing like the unconscious grace of actors in a Chinese opera.

You wonder for the briefest of moments what it would have been like to grow up with a wealthy, well-educated doctor as your father, someone teaching you survival skills that would stay with you for a lifetime.

"I just removed a bullet from the shoulder of a man in that room," he says. "I need you to call the police and keep him here until they arrive."

Yes, you think, that *is* the hospital's rule when someone comes in after being shot. You've had to call the police before to inform them about a shooting victim. Dr. Chen turns away, moving toward his next patient, and you step into the recovery room as if into a dream. The lights are dimmed so you squint to sharpen your vision, the room gradually snapping to shape, your gaze finally falling on a figure in a bed with chrome knobs and a metal railing. You step closer as he tries to lift his head to look at you. Your heart is fluttery in your chest, your palms feel wet as if your life is doubling back on you like a Möbius strip, because of course you know who this is, who it has to be in a country coming apart at its seams.

This is the night that was bound to come.

You find yourself standing speechless over this wounded man. Wounded tonight. Wounded so badly earlier in your lives. He recognizes you. You wish you could say the same for him. Ten years have passed since you saw him, and he is a mystery to you, looking as if he's aged two decades. He's stumbled into many racial land mines. He's been blown to pieces often. And now he's hooked up to IV tubes, wearing a polyester patient gown, and still groggy from his presurgery injection of midazolam. An angry Saturday-night knife scar stretches from just below his left eye down his cheek to his chin. His skin is rough from the hard alcohol-and-drug-driven life he's been living with the Cobras. His voice is flinty, fractured every now and then by a chest-rattling cough.

"Can't stay here," he says, weakly. "He'p me leave."

You blink to refocus your eyes. It's been a long time since you've seen an OG. An original gangster. "You were shot . . . I don't understand what happened . . ."

"You never will," he says, rolling his eyes. "That was always your problem. You never get angry enough. When them protesters started bustin' into stores, me and a couple of my boys decided to liberate a little merchandise. You know, for reparations. White people owe us *every*thing. We *supposed* to be dead. You know that, right? Some pig saw us. He shot at me and I shot back. I told my boys to bring me here. I keep tabs on my square younger brother. Knew you worked security here. So he'p me outside, okay?"

"Jamal . . . you shot a cop?"

126 CHICAGO QUARTERLY REVIEW

"Yeah. He ain't the first. Probably won't be the last either. Cops, they just another gang."

"You still runnin' with the Cobras?"

"That's right. They're my family."

"I thought *we* were family."

He gives a shrug, the corners of his mouth pulled down. "We were, but diff'rent, like Momma always said. Aw 'ight? You gonna he'p me or not?"

"I can't let you go. I'll lose my job."

"Right. Your li'l job. And *I* could go to prison. I'm on parole, man. They're lookin' for me. They'll put me *under* the jail. And I can't do no more time. Just get me outside, let me hold that cell phone of yours, and I'll call the brothers to pick me up. After that, you'll never see me again."

You leave a silence, and lower your head, pinching the bridge of your nose. Here was a land mine your mother never told you that you would have to face. You imagine what might happen when the police catch up with him. Suicide by cop.

"Don't make me do this. It's not right. It's crazy. In your condition, you won't get far!"

"Let me worry about that, okay? My boys will pick me up. Li'l brother," he laughs, raising his eyebrows, "welcome to the real world. There ain't no right or wrong."

You don't reply to that. Unlike Kimisha, he was never one to listen. For a second, you want to ask him what sent him to prison but decide you really don't want to know. It doesn't matter. He's family. And you can't abandon family, no matter what happens. Despite your differences, and regardless of the risk to yourself, you know you cannot deny his request. For better or worse, good or ill, you are bonded by blood.

He tries to rise from the bed. He can't do it alone. Before you can think, you're unhooking him from the IV tubes, lowering the railing on his bed, and helping him to stand, moving slowly, calmly like Dr. Chen, focusing on each thing you do as if it will be the last thing you ever do. Awareness of death, you realize, makes every moment precious, a gift that must be managed carefully. Jamal holds on to you for support as you guide him to a wheelchair in a corner of the room, aware only of his pain and confusion, which somehow you accept, no matter how much you want him or this plague-racked world to be otherwise. From the recovery room, it's a short distance to one of the service elevators only used by the staff. That takes you down and spits you out at an exit at the back of the hospital. You hope your supervisor is too busy to be at the screens that monitor all the entrances leading outside.

Jamal struggles out of the wheelchair, clumsy and Chaplinesque. He bends over briefly from dizziness, there on the loading dock. You give him a look that says, *Go*. And he smiles, barefoot and wraithlike in his gown, before limping off into the darkness. As you watch him disappear, a sadness washes over you as you surrender to the certainty that your life will always be interwoven with your brother's, contaminated by his, just as one day you likely will be infected by a virus so difficult to control but, unlike him, you know you'll survive all this as you did the racial minefields of your childhood. And move on with your life.

You walk back into the hospital to check on Kimisha and call 911. ■

OUR PAST BOWED LIKE THE BRANCHES OF A MADRONE TREE
E. Hughes

I have taken with me what is left: your pajama pants
Pawpaw's sacramento flannel robe the worn leather belts creased
by your hands.
     I've scavenged
       the photo albums and filed them in an archive. Let them dry
like Nootka roses between pages,
        wanting them
          to leave me with stains of magenta.
  Imperfectly kept, pressed between my longing.   There is no name
for our grief—
            just its sound
the way its music leaves   the mouth
          demanding the body
             buckle.
In late summer,
      I sat sweating in your living room,
           flipped through albums of us,
    counted our dead. Our past selves bound
          within the confines of light
marked and shuttered against time,
      trying   to find ourselves within the promise of
           future. In the west,
       the sun lifts herself
   over the Sierra Nevada and closes on the ocean,
          shutting us in at the end
of her book. A bandit of light,
       a halo shown around the wound—
           the source of so much
  fluorescent pain. What else should we call this
          song of memory? The history
of ourselves fettered
     in some secret, uninhabitable place.

BECKWOURTH PASS
E. Hughes

—California, 2015

The oak, redwood, and laurel alike were dying or dead—
ochre and combustible as matches. My father was not

as thin as I had remembered him. His belly protruded
over the band of the seatbelt as I tried to remember

what the trees were like before they caught drought—
deeply green and heavy with leaves and life. Maybe?

How easily I had forgotten what my eyes had grown up
seeing—even if at a distance. Words were difficult to find

as he drove the car—I had saved all summer to buy—
sputtering at an incline. He had not wanted me

to drive almost 1,800 miles alone over an unforgiving
mountain, through a salt desert and midwestern prairie—

now greener than the Sierra Nevada's expanse of trees.
He had wanted me to find someone else to take his place

on the journey, to pack their bags in with the last
of the belongings I had gathered from my mother's house.

This stuff he said *is too heavy for this little car*
            to tow, to carry such a far distance.

My father has driven more than one woman he loves over
this mountain: First, my mother when they eloped—me,

only a shadow in my mother's womb and an unbearable
decision—*To break it or to let it live?*

My father's eyes were on the road when he asked
if I remembered the time he took us sledding.

*Pooh, remember—how slick the ice was? How steep
the slope?* He grinned. I did not respond as if to say—

I remember nothing. Yet, someone else's blood staining
packed ice entered my mind. The crack of skull on frozen

ground, and my father's hand leading me up the slopes
regardless. When we arrived in Reno, we stopped at a diner

and he ate more than I had ever seen him consume—
a sign of sobriety. Again, he said *Remember*

*when you were little? How we used to feed the ducks
small pieces of bread? We had fun. Didn't we always have fun?*

I responded *Yes,* in pity for my father, *I remember
the ducks.* When he asked this, he seemed stuck in time,

nauseated by the demands of the past. *I want this part to be over—
this painful journey* I thought to myself before he lifted his head

from his plate to ask: *I was a good father, right?*

MEET CUTE IN
SAN MATEO COUNTY
E. Hughes

My grandmother tells me there were clubs
    like a string of pearls draped along the dark
neck of a woman up and down the peninsula,
    music and lights at night warbling along
the coast of the bay.

I know what she wants to avoid. The past and its routine
    burden of memory. The year was 1960:
Myra had just turned eighteen, was fresh up from Texas—
    running from that three-room house, her Mama's
church—the heat of the minister preaching fire

and brimstone—and those opossum carcasses
    Daddy Buster would carry in to stew after working
the crop. I can imagine her—thin ankles, a fresh press
    in her hair, the drawn-out drones of B.B. King
calling her further and further from home

and into the watering hole where she would meet
    my grandfather— the twenty-eight-year-old slick
in a pinstriped suit, who would part the crowd, take her
    hand and say—
                Pretty woman, my name's Jimmy.

THE WAY WE WERE
E. Hughes

As her feet tap the brass pedals,
I recognize my mother—her mouth
once framed a gapped-tooth smile,
now eroded by periodontitis, where
implants stand now perfectly white drilled
into the old sockets of her jawbone. Her
fingers manage melody without score.
In music, she is no longer frightening—
the dark circles perched like phainopepla
beneath her eyes now something I see
in my own reflection. At the breast of
the piano, she sings—*Memories light
the corners of my mind* and I cross
the chasm between us, to stop her
playing this wounding

part of the song.

A FISHING STORY
John McCluskey, Jr.

Charleston is soon to be visited by a company of representative
Negroes, perhaps the most intelligent, the most cultured and the
wealthiest in the United States. . . . For the trip up the Elk river
over the C. C. & S. railroad Superintendent McDermitt has
placed a private car at the disposal of the gentlemen of the party
and they will no doubt enjoy the novelty of the outing very much.
— *Washington Colored American*, Sept. 14, 1901

Booker T. Washington was not an easy person to know. . . .
I found at the end of the first interview that I had done practi-
cally all the talking and that no clear and definite offer or expla-
nation of my proposed work at Tuskegee had been made. In fact,
Mr. Washington had said about as near nothing as was possible.
— W. E. B. Du Bois, *Dusk of Dawn*

The outer office, smelling faintly of rose, had been so quiet that
the professor now thought he should have walked in shoeless.
But that was only if he knew for certain that his best socks still
bore no holes worth displaying to the most powerful Negro in America.
From a padded bench within the inner office, he had waved off an offer
of tea before the door had closed almost soundlessly behind the secretary, a short woman with stunning white hair framing a deep-chocolate
face. She had not smiled during the introduction and had turned only
slightly to glance backward as she left the room. Du Bois surmised that
she was hired for this office only for this meeting, that she had probably
picked out the fresh roses in the porcelain vase on her desk.

The room for the meeting with Booker T. Washington had been
arranged by the railroad baron, William Baldwin, who had attempted
more than once that the two of them meet on a vague matter of transition. On this day they agreed to meet in Baldwin's second-floor office
in New York City. The professor was not surprised by the paintings
or photographs of behemoth locomotives along the walls. Nor by the
uninspired furniture. The chair had no padding and was the best of New
England hickory, no doubt. The desk was mahogany from the Caribbean.

Though not yet in his midthirties, Dr. Du Bois had long concluded that the Wallaces, Carnegies, and Rockefellers of this world could mix and match opulence with spartanism in the blink of an eye.

Directly behind the desk was a large window, which presented the limbs of an ancient oak tree before the forest of tall limestone buildings beyond. From the window in his own Atlanta office, the tree would be a spreading beech against a background of red brick buildings. From his host's Tuskegee office during an earlier visit, he recalled a maple in its October blaze against Georgian buildings of even darker red. *We see different worlds,* the professor concluded.

He was just beginning to identify the specific sources of noise among the wash and blare of the street below when he heard the door open behind him. He started to rise.

Booker T. Washington, the Wizard of Tuskegee some called him by then, had put on a little weight since the last time they'd met. Still he walked like a man much heavier than he actually was and looked now slightly weary about the eyes. He was Du Bois's elder by twelve years. Not shaking hands, they exchanged smiles as Washington moved around the half-standing professor.

"Welcome to New York, Dr. Du Bois," Washington said, both now fully standing.

"Still a place too loud for my tastes," Du Bois said, "but a pleasure to meet again." Washington nodded their sit-down.

"Yes, it is my pleasure, too, and I must agree about the noise. But it is the laziness that the big cities incite."

They had touched on this during the brief times they had met before in gatherings in Boston and New York. But the professor sensed an urgency, no, an unfocused pressure in these first minutes. Perhaps Washington had walked past the very same cluster of young Negroes he himself had passed earlier. They lounged on a corner between his hotel and the building where he now sat. Yes, to be sure, three or four could have comported themselves less loudly and he did ask himself why they were not on jobs this time of the morning. On the other hand, he reasoned, perhaps there were simply no jobs to welcome their skills. As he passed, he had nodded, touched the brim of his derby. One or two nodded in reply, smiling no doubt at his beard and cane.

"Perhaps the cities offer more than they can supply," Du Bois said.

Washington found a cigar in the canister atop the desk. He laid it before him near a bronze ashtray before he spoke. "Bring skills and the cities will provide work."

Du Bois smiled. They were off to a fine start. "Perhaps work will find them when white workers and their bosses don't fear them. Oh yes,

I have seen the same thing in Philadelphia and there, too, you can find laziness and unfortunate poverty, but that is only part of the story, as I tried to say in my book."

The Wizard said nothing, thinking.

The cities invite sloth and crime. Families break up easily. Girls sell themselves. Boys get drunk and gamble their lives away. Philadelphia or Filthydelphia? And who was it who told him about the neat professor sitting before him now strolling into the neighborhoods of ne'er-do-wells with his trim little beard and cane and gloves, tapping on doors and asking to interview folks on how they live their lives? He had not read The Philadelphia Negro, *but had listened to a lengthy summary from his trusted confidant, Scott.*

He covered the trace of a smile as Du Bois continued.

"That book was a difficult one to write. I had to interview hundreds of families in their houses. That is, when they let me in. Most did and many, mostly the mothers, gave me a window into their lives . . ."

Their infants bawling up a storm, too, with the smell of cabbage or onions all around. And the men, the fathers during those mornings and afternoons?

". . . of course, my time was limited as was the span of their attention. But I listened and watched and learned."

The professor thought to the time limit for this very conversation. Washington had offered an hour amid a very busy afternoon of fundraising. Though Baldwin had generously offered his office for the meeting, Du Bois was not completely sure of the purpose of the meeting. He had already turned down one offer to work at Tuskegee seven years before. They had been civil during two prior public encounters and at a meeting in Chicago and in Washington's absence he had given a vigorous display of support for Washington's business programs, not only in Alabama, but elsewhere as well. There had even been that July invitation to join Washington and friends on the West Virginia rivers, despite his book review of Washington's wildly popular life story.

"My belief, as you well know by now, is that the knowledge of social science is desperately needed by those men in power. Now the heavy shadow of their prejudices blinds them to the need for the proper policies that can help to elevate the Negro . . ."

There was a time and place that they could have met far from this loud and crowded city with perfectly healthy young Negro boys loitering on corners. But, for Du Bois's untimely illness , he could not join them in West Virginia. Du Bois had eagerly accepted his invitation a few months back. Did something change? He bore no grudge for Du Bois's recent review of the book tracing his life to date, none at all.

The professor knew that Washington had heard his championing the power of scholarship before and would be on guard for more. So what was to be expected this afternoon? Was Washington prepared to offer a job once more, but with specific terms this time? Still, his Nina would not hear of it. She never liked the south and after the death of young Burghart, she loathed it even more. And Tuskegee of all places? Yes, the school grounds were clean, nearly spotless, and the buildings designed by the Negro architect tasteful. Taylor was his name, yes, yes. From MIT or such from close to Harvard. Du Bois recalled all this from previous visits. But there was no culture to speak of. How many there had heard of Wagner or Bach or Strauss? And the library was less than serviceable for his needs. Would there be a respectable budget for its expansion?

"We missed you in West Virginia," Washington said abruptly.

The professor nodded. "I was looking forward to it, Mr. Washington. But I came down with the damndest cold."

From the street below, the bright laughter of walking women—two? three?—struck as a brief cascade of coins. A horse-drawn wagon rolled past on a slow clop-clop rhythm.

Washington remembered well the three weeks in West Virginia. A separate railroad car had been provided for the august body of men who had journeyed to West Virginia for the camp outing. And a fine homecoming it was for a favorite son who grew up just a half-day's ride away by horse. The Charleston crowd was proud, with bright blue-gold-red banners flying from tree limbs above the street leading to the car. Then at home in Malden, former schoolteachers smiled and waved. One woman pushed a chubby child to him and chimed that the boy would be a strong debater like he'd been in high school. In neither place had there been lines of men asking for favors. He had returned to West Virginia on several occasions, but this one in August was special.

That first evening, after a hearty dinner of duck and tasty venison, the campers talked of the advancement of the race in all things business and commerce. Some smoked the best cigars from Cuba. T. Thomas Fortune, unrobed as always and without shame guarding his mistress, the best whiskey available. Their Negro guide, Timmons—named by Watkins from Chicago "Lemon Timmons" because of his complexion. Watkins was a master at nicknaming. Sometimes Washington wondered what did Watkins call him behind his own back? Yes, yes, it was Timmons who was surrendered the floor and attention more than the blazing fire. He spoke of the war barely fifty years earlier and area families, white, divided with a son in blue and another in grey meeting on trails in the high hills. He told in his slow, laughing way of barefoot Negro boys even now, loose in the woods while hiding from school, finding lead bullets in the trunks of black oaks. He talked of walking beside his wounded grandfather, who talked of the war in spurts as he scattered feed to the chickens in the backyard, and the grandmother, the true storyteller, who did not need a clear night to sense the North Star. He himself, this "Lemon Timmons," would run a hotel for the wayward and weary someday. Washington had nodded in approval of his dreams and lightly slapped his arm. He concluded that Du Bois would have questioned the guide closely on Greek philosophy, rather than encourage with a touch.

Yet death would enter the conversation as the fire grew down. The voices grew low, the silences stretched as the evening wore down. Death stalked through the darkness at the edges of their cabin, tapped at the windows, shadowed the once-new moon above. They talked of lynchings, well over two thousand, mostly in the Deep South, and one in West Virginia just in the last six months. As far as Washington could imagine, their guide and cook was the only one of their company armed under those starlit skies of their camping trip with the rushing river waters lulling them toward brighter days.

On the early evenings of those very first days of the planned camping trip, Du Bois had had long thoughts of the camp meeting he had to miss. When coughing spells interrupted the essay he was writing, he could only imagine his place among the company of men. From his window in Atlanta, he would look onto Mitchell Street and wonder about the Elk and Gauley Rivers gloried under late August light. What would be the colors in the crowns of the trees, just weeks ahead? Would it be anything like the colors in western Massachusetts? Or early autumn in the hills of Tennessee after his search to ring up a school while still a Fisk College student? And what were the smells wafting from Gauley valley? Were they close to those of the small Housatonic River coursing through the Berkshires where he'd grown up or even the valley near Eisenach, a favorite town of his in Germany? Washington did not telegram him to come anyway after the coughs and sneezes had run their course. Was that a sign of dishonesty lurking behind the invitation from the beginning? He could only guess.

It was just at dawn, he remembered. The rushing water of the upper Elk River, far from the sawmills near Charleston, was colder than he expected for August. He studied the palm of his hand just below the surface of the water as the guide and cook standing closely nearby boasted that all in the party would catch fish. He smiled when the man added that the fish would be proud to leap to the river's bank at the feet of such an august company. After all had cast their lines into the river, Williams immediately caught the first fish, pulling it in and shouting loudly as if touched by the Lord. Then, landing it on the bank, his laugh echoed across the valley floor.

"Hush, you ain't in a Chicago church," Jefferson said, and they all laughed.

From Atlanta Du Bois had imagined them emerging at dawn from the Pullman car parked on a side spur. They would travel by wagon to the fishing lodge, where no doubt they would be met by a smiling, dutiful guide. They would change into their fishing clothes and ready for the boats that would take them to the river.

". . . I believe that a well-funded program of research into issues and areas affecting Negro life in America, in the north and south, in the city and the country, that such a program would have profound relief for policies affecting education, health, commerce, and the well-being of our people." The professor leaned back, crossed his legs, and slowly stroked his short, pointed beard. The Wizard drummed his fingers again slowly.

What if they did not read, these railroad and oil bosses? After all, they were busy men. They might listen to a speech, but would they take the time to read about Negroes in the South? And what if they never worked with their shirts rolled to their elbows, their barely used tweed suit coats hanging on a rack? Would the ones of that class work and dirty their fingernails to join workers in Alabama? In Georgia? Had they even tasted their own sweat? Even the one who loaned this office for him and the professor to study one another for an hour?

"I am not naïve, sir," the professor said. "Science will not stop a mob. We both know well the fate of Sam Hose, his knuckles hanging in the window of a meat market on Mitchell Street in Atlanta. It will not stop a mob any more perhaps than a dozen Negro carpenters building houses in Lowndes County. But good policy might guide the thinking of individuals before they become a part of a mob . . ."

Washington shifted in his chair, willing away a wince from the professor's words. He glanced over the professor's shoulder to admire as if for the first time that afternoon the sheen to the mahogany planks in a standing closet. He wondered where to find mahogany and how to get it to Alabama. But he thought, too, of how either of their efforts, their sweat in different offices, their sacrifices and compromises, could stop the mob.

From nearby, seemingly outside, came the low moan of a tugboat. There was a bell from an approaching fire engine below. Two men cursed loudly while the oak limb moved barely in an afternoon's bare whisper of a breeze. In the second-floor office there was a beat of silence in the room.

Washington had worried that he might be only the third or fourth in the party to land a fish. Until one hit and he felt the electricity of the strike to his shoulder. As he had hoped, the others applauded when they saw the silver flash of a fish's underbelly twisting as the Wizard reeled it in. They oohed and ahhed when he landed it, claiming it to be the largest trout caught so far when he held it high. The guide smiled as he unhooked it. But none would slap him on the back. Yet.

Would the good professor have changed his clothes completely, before climbing slowly into the fishing gear? Would he have fussed with the galluses? Or complained about the poor fit of his boots? Then, after the worm had been placed on his hook by the smiling guide, would he have been gifted with beginner's luck and caught the first fish, to the grinning shame of the rest of the party? He, who would have thought he was pulling in a giant eel and not a medium-sized trout? And would he have even touched it, his flapping treasure?

"I understand both our and others' struggle in the red hills and black soil of the South. We both understand that failings there are visited upon our Northern cities. There will be the crowding, the spread of diseases, the charlatan preachers, the rent gougers . . ."

Washington was nodding in increasing rhythm to this.

". . . all of these will try to slow us down, but there will be progress and deep meaning in the progress . . ."

Washington managed another weak smile, still nodding.

". . . and the education of our young must hasten that progress, even as we speed toward our middle age. They must be given the mantle of hope to push ahead."

Then he leaned back in his chair and recrossed his legs.

"I can only agree," Washington said, leaning forward and fixing the point of Du Bois's Vandyke beard in his gaze. "I can only agree that there is so much work to be done."

The professor studied the toes of his newly shined cordovans, his closely trimmed fingernails, the fresh carnation in the pale-green crystal vase that sat at one corner of the desk. His mind raced quickly back to the river he could only imagine as he finished a draft of an essay during one of those late August afternoons in Atlanta.

Surely at night they would have relaxed after a dinner in the small clubhouse. If he were there, he would have tried to coax a conversation toward national or international commerce. Most would surely comment on the six thousand Negro troops sent to the Philippines to help Americans crush a rebellion, brown men sent to help defeat other brown men. Literature or art might not serve as a rich topic of conversation in that crowd of businessmen. Even his foray into the Paris Exhibition and his effort to serve Negro dignity in photographs to a doubting world audience had been hampered by the efforts of a Washington confederate. Even in mid-August perhaps a low fire in the fireplace, its reflection upon snifters of brandy. T. Thomas Fortune would have preferred Scotch whiskey, of course, and Washington himself would not have imbibed. But Washington would have remained as reserved as he was now. Probably sitting clear from the customary card game and singing. Could he ever sing in a loud voice? Du Bois sensed an aloneness there. And would the cabin at the fishing camp have been large enough for him to find a corner to read or write in while the others made what they considered to be merry? And who in that group would recall aloud that there had been a lynching in that state just a few months back? Even in his autobiography, the Wizard hardly mentioned the mobs.

His God? A blacksmith who owned his shop, a careless, small smudge or two across the forehead of his proud and smiling face.

The good professor might have enjoyed the quiet mornings of the next days as they all did. Their guide welcomed all with a smile as he prepared breakfast. A few took morning strolls along the Gauley with its nice roaring nearby. Du Bois would not have been with the others. He would have struck out on his own and studied the trees and birds like the genius Washington Carver might do. That man could be found on many mornings studying flowers, sometimes his mouth moving in silence. He and Du Bois should meet. Du Bois would have to abide Carver's religion, though. He had more religion in him than Washington and Du Bois together.

Carver's studies of the gift from peanuts and his religion could remake the world. Washington's gift was to shelter him. And Du Bois? They both were solitary men, yet truly needing no shelter.

". . . My plan is to research one subject in depth each year, then to publish my findings at the end of each year. I am proposing to start such a series soon in Atlanta. I will do this for ten years."

Washington tilted his head. "And at the end of ten years?" he asked.

"I will simply start the cycle again. To chart and demonstrate progress of the race to the world." Du Bois smiled. "I'm not a betting man, as you might have gathered. But I have confidence in my skills at research and confident that the race can move forward even against the brutish actors in our South."

"Yes, yes, though we do have our good friends in the North." He raised both palms slightly, looked slowly right and left.

"They need to journey with us to Georgia and Alabama and sit in the village squares and listen to the folk talk and go into the Negro shacks, sit in the churches and listen to the hymns."

"True, but these are busy men."

"So are we, Mr. Washington. So are we."

About to respond, Washington was interrupted by a single knock on the door. The short woman with the nut-brown face and halo of white hair entered. She slid a paper along the desk for Washington to sign, whispered something to him, then tapped the face of her wristwatch with a finger.

She half-smiled as she passed the professor on her way out.

"So very true, Dr. Du Bois," Washington said.

He would see the short, neat man at the river near a grove of white oaks. He tried to imagine Du Bois among tenements in Philadelphia with his cane and gloves, talking about diets and rent. As out of place there as he would be on the banks of the Gauley, perhaps, baiting a hook to catch trout. Through the trees he would be looking at the sky perhaps as the sun rose over the Alleghenies to the east. A solitary man with a son dead at the age of three in Atlanta. A wife near mad with grief, he had been told, and her incurable anger toward the South. Wanting to stay north after their son's burial, they said.

Looking heavenward, he might have been that morning. His God? A neat man, strolling down a paved street, not a dirt path, with a book under his arm, silently mouthing something in some long-ago tongue no one remembered or even cared for today.

Death all around. President McKinley murdered, to be learned only when the camping trip had ended and they'd returned to Charleston. The mobs, the violence of mobs beckoned assassinations at every level. Who bundled this madness? And what lay ahead for the race?

No. No Tuskegee for Du Bois, his mind was made up, his walk told him that much. But could they wrestle out a peace? Du Bois's review of his book was not altogether a welcome one. He and Scott often laughed aloud at the joke about him, that he'd never met a white man he did not like. How foolish such a joke. His school still stood, its doors open for the poorest of the poor. He smiled, but never grinned. What did they know?

At the river, just a paltry Niagara in its roar, he might have espied the Wizard of Tuskegee. He, too, knew loss. Two wives gone before the age of fifty. Probably standing a little apart from the others, even now as he sought perhaps parts of a script for the dinner with the new president, that cunning Roosevelt, within two weeks. A solitary man under it all, no real backslapping around, despite the seeming devotion from Negroes and wealthy whites who supported his school. Whether Birmingham, Chicago, New York, Boston, long lines of those seeking favors. That morning Washington might have looked up as he himself would have from, say, fifty yards downriver. Each would have waved before turning from the river, rejoining for breakfast and the ride to the base camp for home.

This afternoon with the roar of New York outside the large window behind Washington at the desk, they stood, shook hands, smiled. Perhaps one day they would break bread together. Just the two of them. This was not the time or the day. A chapter, just a chapter. In their civil parting might lie the promise to meet again through the smoke of conflicts—wars, really, all around them—and to continue the work of generations past and to help arm generations ahead. ∎

THE TRIP
Clarence Major

Antoinette said
Tomorrow let's take the train
up into the mountains.
I know a little out-of-the-way restaurant in a village
where the diners are farmers.

The food is served on long tables she said,
and everybody sits together on benches, side by side,
and fill their plates from large pots and bowls

placed in a row before them.
They eat and talk together about their work and their lives.
I think you will enjoy the train ride especially

as we cross the old railway viaduct into the village.
As we approach, you will see the village
perched up on the rocky spur of the plateau.

If the weather holds, and it's as clear as today,
if from the train window you look down,
you will see the river and the valley.

When we enter and sit among them,
they will look at us curiously, but never mind that.
In time they will warm to our presence.

SLOW DANCE
Clarence Major

In church grandma did a slow dance.
Her eyes and her skin remembered
centuries of human bodies
on rotundas handled by the calloused
hands of rude sellers of human flesh.
Sugar cane-cutters and cotton-pickers:
work-songs found their flesh to save them
and they saved the songs too to carry on.
In statehouses and in courthouses
the unfree debated and delayed
for centuries. Mother's mother danced
in church to music centuries free
with old cries of liberty. Iron shackles
could not hold the music in check. Her feet
knew the dance before she was born;
and all the world knows it instinctively.

IRISH NELL
Clarence Major

In Colonial Chesapeake Lord Baltimore in 1681
said to his servant Nell don't you know
that if you marry a slave you will become a slave
and all your children and grandchildren
and great grandchildren from now on into eternity
will become slaves? Nell said I'd rather marry Charles
than to marry you Lord Baltimore
and I would rather sleep with Charles
than with you Lord Baltimore;
and in that same year with a priest presiding
Nell married Charles and she worked the Boarman fields
alongside Charles and slept with Charles
and they had children one after another
and the years passed, and they grew old together
and people called him Negro Charles and called her Irish Nell
and eventually they both died;
but many years later people said
there is nothing in Chesapeake law
saying a white woman marrying a slave becomes a slave,
so Irish Nell in folk minds became White Nell
and all her children and grandchildren
and great-grandchildren were set free from bondage
because everybody knew a white woman in Chesapeake
could never have been a slave.

AT THE MARKET
Clarence Major

They are haggling over the price of fruit.
The critics of puckish malice
will see how brazen this argument is.
The seller and the buyer both
are susceptible to shouting.
It's obligatory that I tell the truth:
The argument is bogus.
It should never have started.
It started over three pennies.
I once read a retrospective on pennies.
It was a milestone.
The argument began
from the assumption that the blurry beginnings
of money correlated
with the beginnings of civil conflict;
and I would bet you any amount
that *that* is the gospel truth.

"TRYING TO DISCOVER": AN INTERVIEW WITH AHMAD JAMAL
John McCluskey, Jr.

I accept the risk of a cliché to suggest how often music is a lifeline. Music and the specific memory of song can guide you through haze to clarity, through seeming resignation to inspiration. My thought here is to the refuge of an overheated apartment on Cheney Street in Boston's Dorchester section in the early 1960s. My Aunt Janie lived and welcomed me there during my first challenging semesters in college. On fall and winter Sundays, I would be offered collard greens, baked pork chops smothered in gravy, sweet potatoes—comfort food that eased the anxieties of classes. It was there that I first heard of Ahmad Jamal. Noting the name first, I remember asking my aunt where he was from.

"I'm not certain," she said, "but I think he could be from another country."

I would soon learn that he was from Pittsburgh, no more another country than southwestern Ohio, where I and my aunt had been reared. In that apartment, I listened to his 1958 album *Ahmad Jamal Live at the Pershing: But Not for Me* over and over again, especially his signature tune, "Poinciana."

Ahmad Jamal   Photo credit: Studio Harcourt

These many years later I still connect his tune, indeed the entire album of eight songs, with soul food (in every sense of the term) and renewal.

How long can you keep it new and joyful and risky? This is a question I raise when pondering a long and productive career such as Ahmad Jamal's (over six decades!). His compositions are full of surprises, yet steeped in musical traditions from all over the world. The tightness of each ensemble he has organized over the years has been a marvel. As just one example, "Saturday Morning," from a recent album by the same name, shifts through a number of tones tied within a simple yet haunting frame. The bass and drum are as one, yet each still unique in their approach with each shift. It is an evocative piece throughout. (My first impression was that of the first moments of an early morning's open-air market.) It is the apparent simplicity of theme that captured the early attention of both Mr. Jamal's detractors and his most ardent fans. Yet he is still capable of arpeggios, sudden stops, atonal asides. A subtle complexity emerges. (One is reminded of Duke Ellington's six-note invitation and ultimate frame to John Coltrane's solo in their duo treatment of "In A Sentimental Mood," a slight figure from Ellington that welcomes the lyrical "stress" of the 'Trane train. The instrumental jazz vault is packed with such interplay.)

Mr. Jamal's work in the trio format is perhaps best known among his audience. He has composed and performed with larger groups, however. A gift to us and himself perhaps was when he performed in Paris for his seventieth birthday with the formidable George Coleman on tenor saxophone (*Olympia 2000*). The closeness of the trio is apparent throughout, but the interplay between the piano and horn is especially dazzling in "Night Has a Thousand Eyes" and "My Foolish Heart."

One need only listen to a range of his music from any of the six decades of his work to be, hopefully, renewed time again by this master. As of this writing, Ahmad Jamal is ninety years young and keeping on.

The following interview was done by phone in November 2018. The very brief exchange at the beginning refers to a missed call.

McCluskey: Mr. Jamal, how you doin' this evening?

Jamal: [*laughing*] I got your call.

McCluskey: All right.

Jamal: My apologies again.

McCluskey: No problem: these things happen. And I always suspect these things happen on the music stand and you got to go on and improvise around them.

Jamal: Well, I don't *like* for them to happen, believe me.

McCluskey: Exactly. Well, the questions that I have are short, and

I want to start out with questions under the heading of setting or place. In several interviews, you've talked about the power of Pittsburgh and the power of certain cities and I was wondering: What was it about Pittsburgh, aside from being your home, that made it special? And the same thing with . . . I think you mentioned New Orleans, you mentioned Kansas City as places where the music was extremely . . . not just important, but it seemed to crystallize in certain places. And I'm curious about that as an instructor—a former instructor—with issues around what was called the Harlem Renaissance, which became the Chicago Renaissance, or which morphed into the Chicago Renaissance. So back in the twenties and thirties, "the City" stood out in terms of attracting American classical music and American classical musicians—or jazz musicians, as some would call it—and I'm wondering about your view of that.

Jamal: Well, you know that's why . . . we are in error where we cite the "greatest this," and the "greatest that," "the greatest city." There's no such thing when it comes to man or cities. The great cities are Pittsburgh and New Orleans. Not the greatest. New Orleans is a great city, but not the greatest because that adjective is used carelessly. There are great pianists but no greatest. There are great boxers, but no greatest. And the same thing with cities. And certainly if you could use an adjective carelessly, you shouldn't use it with respect to Pittsburgh. But Pittsburgh is not the greatest city; it's *one* of the great cities for music. It's unbelievable. I mean, I went to the school that Erroll Garner attended. To name a few others, Dodo Marmarosa, who was a great pianist, and Billy Strayhorn, whose family I sold papers to when I was a kid and he'd gone with Duke. Earl Hines, Billy Eckstine, Kenny Clarke—an expatriate who went to France and never came back. Art Blakey, Ray Brown, Earl Wild—the exponent of Liszt—and a little tap dancer called Gene Kelly. Ever hear of him?

McCluskey: Oh yes, uh-huh.

Jamal: So it goes on and on and on. There are as many greats who have not left. Johnny Costa is a classic example. They're playing his works behind Mister Rogers all over the internet now. He was the pianist for Mister Rogers and he left Pittsburgh very sparingly. So we go on and on . . . We have some of the greatest players ever that emanated from Pittsburgh, and that's where I got all of my inspiration—from my mother, of course, numero uno from my mother, number one, and from the town of Pittsburgh, my number two.

McCluskey: Was that because the musicians hung out together? Or because of certain teachers?

Jamal: No, every group of people—every city has something to contribute. Whether it's Paris or Perugia in Italy, where the big festival is. Or whether Chicago or New Orleans or Pittsburgh. And every ethnic group has given gifts. If you want opera, you have to go to Italy. There's some spin-offs of course . . . We've got great opera, of course, exponents. But if you want to find out the source of opera, you've got to go to Italy. Ballet? You got to go to Russia. But you have certain things from all over the world—China, Egypt just to name two contributing factors. And as I said before, that's a phrase that I coined many years ago: American classical music. And I don't care who gets the credit for it, but that's what music is. Because there are only two art forms [in America]. And here we go to contributing cities, contributing ethnic groups, contributing factors.

There are only two art forms that put a smattering of culture in the United States and they are American Indian art, which is still not promoted, still undiscovered, for the most part, and this thing we call "jazz" that I refer to as American classical music. We've got a great civilization and we're about to blow it. It's the youngsters. They're about to blow it. We have a great civilization. What is civilization? When man devises ways and means to move goods from one place to another, whether it's by horse and buggy or by satellite. That's civilization. But culture's a different thing. Culture is how to speak to people, how to treat people, how to respect this global village that we're living in. That's culture. And we're about to blow it because we've got a lot of things with very little culture. The only smattering of culture—and I'll repeat that 'cause I can't be too redundant—is American classical music and American Indian art. And you have to go to Europe to see Duke Ellington on the tube every day. You used to be able to see Duke Ellington every day on the tube in some shape or form.

McCluskey: "A Train"?

Jamal: Of course. "Satin Doll" was Billy Strayhorn's, but it was associated with Duke. You can sell these things just as easy, or even easier, than you can this junk that we hear behind commercials. And if you don't have the mute button, you're in trouble!

[*laughter*]

You got to go to Europe to hear Duke or Dizzy or our great American classicists. Sidney Bechet: another one who left this country and never came back. He's a national treasure in France. And it goes on, I could expound on that for hours. And this is what we lack. And when you lack culture, your civilization is not going to last, in my opinion.

McCluskey: Well, that makes a lot of sense . . .

Jamal: And we're blowing it. We're blowing it here. Look at the confusion. No culture.

McCluskey: Exactly. And we don't appreciate the homegrown culture that we *do* have. I think it was Ralph Ellison, the novelist, who said American culture originally came from American classical music [or jazz], baseball, and the Constitution. That was America's gift to the world.

[*laughter*]

Jamal: That's great. I'll have to look that up and remember it.

McCluskey: The other part is—particularly on "Saturday Morning"—is this: You described once how you came up on that particular song, but more generally that you do some of your composing at home. Is that something new or have you been doing that over the years in terms of finding a comfortable place to compose?

Jamal: Well, I do most of my composing at home, ninety percent of it. I just did "Marseille"—which is a tribute to a city I admire in France. I released that last year and I composed that at home. Most of my compositions I do at home, since I was ten years old. I was writing for my small ensemble when I inherited the four strings or the three strings. I was writing for bass guitar and piano. Y'know, that was not just put together. I've been writing for many years. But most of my writing, to answer your question simply, is [done] at home.

McCluskey: Are you driven by a certain memory? Or you saw something on the street that day? Or you overheard something at the market? How are these ideas for the melody triggered?

Jamal: Well that's a very interesting question, John. I'm trying to concentrate now more on my writing because I'm getting settled at home. I'm almost to the point where I don't take any engagements at all. I took four engagements last year: Ukraine and Chicago and Costa Mesa and San Francisco. That's all I did. And I only have Princeton scheduled for next year, and Saint Louis, and California again, San Francisco. So I have time now to concentrate more, hopefully, on my writing, because I want to expand my book, my publishing activities. So I am inspired by many things. Mostly life itself. And that's an inspiration that most of us draw from. Whether you're John McCluskey or Ernest Hemingway, I think we're inspired by the life we live. Whether you're some of the very famous poets and writers . . . myself, I'm inspired by life itself.

McCluskey: I see. That's certainly true: I mean, you never know where you're going to draw it from. I was walking down the street once in New York and saw a hat, just a battered hat on the sidewalk. I stopped to look at it. A fairly famous actor/director, whom I recognized, stopped near me and did the same thing. We just stood there for several seconds then looked at each other and smiled and went our merry way. I have little doubt that he put something on the drawing board, figuring in the hat and its owner. I'm still searching my imagination to create the owner of the hat. But the point is it's something very simple we can draw from to do our writing. What you're suggesting is the same thing can happen in music as well.

But let me raise a different question. While you're composing now, I guess, is there any notion or need to do a larger ensemble, a larger group? Monk did a band. Mingus did a band. I don't know whether Horace Silver did a band. A larger band, I guess is what I'm saying . . . or orchestra? Is there anything like that down the road for you, or is that even important to you?

Jamal: Well I've done many orchestral things in my life. I did a project—two projects—with the some of the most talented voices in New York. I did both of those while I was recording for Chess [Records]: *The Bright, the Blue and the Beautiful* and *Nature Boy*. And I did a number of things orchestral years ago. *Macanudo*, which is forgotten. A project I commissioned Richard Evans—the late Richard Evans—to do. One of my favorite composers! He came out of Chess, Checker, and Argo [Records] as well. So I've done orchestral things all my life. In fact, I grew up orchestrally. I don't think in terms of two-pieces, I only think in terms of a whole orchestra when I compose. I'm thinking orchestrally all the time. In the future, I may do something. I have a list of things, including a project I did with the Cleveland Orchestra years ago—Cleveland Pops—years ago. Joe Kennedy was the writer/conductor. Not saying I've done everything, but I've done a lot of orchestral things, most importantly with the human voice. I mean that's one of the most important instruments in the world, the human voice. We wouldn't be doing what we're doing now without it. I often admire people who sing and I often . . . not regret, but reflect on why I didn't sing. There are a lot of musicians that don't. Duke didn't sing, Dave Brubeck didn't sing, I don't know . . . Charlie Mingus yelled a little bit, but . . . I don't think he sang. There's a few from my hometown that do and George Benson is one. He's from Pittsburgh as well. Another classic example of Pittsburgh talent. So I've done things with the human voice, I've done things orchestrally in the past. Not saying there's nothing I haven't done before, because that's not so. But I've done orchestral things many times.

McCluskey: Well, that's good to know. So I'll have to go back and do my homework in terms of finding those. By the way, you had mentioned, on vinyl, an album called *American Classical Music*? Is that still available?

Jamal: Only on my web page. You can only get it on my web page . . .

McCluskey: Okay, I'll make sure I look for it.

Jamal: . . . unless there's a pirate out there. There's always some pirates out there. You know, you might get one of the pirated versions, but for the bona fide collectors, get it from my web page.

McCluskey: Okay I'll go to that. I saw your group . . . I think it was at the Blue Note in New York. Maybe eight years ago. I'm not sure the exact year. But like all of your recordings, it was a very tight group. And it's almost like magic for me to hear that kind of tightness and what I also hear as playfulness in the group. When you compose and you've got the notes down and so forth and you go before the group, how do you build that tightness before you get to the stand—before you get to the public?

Jamal: Well, first of all, you can write all the notes that you want, but if you don't have the personality that can execute what you have in mind, it's not going to happen. That's why "if it ain't broke, don't fix it." That's why Ray Nance stayed with Duke so many years. And Johnny Hodges, and Paul Gonzalez . . . I can go on and on and on. And a classic deal: Freddie Green with Count Basie. From inception, he was with Count Basie. Playing that guitar without any amp. So I'm saying . . . In order to get that cohesiveness and the interpretation you want, you have to have a certain personality to do that. You can put notes on it all you want, but if you don't have the guys that can execute your thoughts, it ain't going to happen.

McCluskey: Well, how do you . . . I guess it's like being a good scout for athletes. You spot talent. You, in your case, you *hear* talent. What is it? Is it something special that you hear in looking for or searching for, let's say, a bassist?

Jamal: Well that's a very interesting question, John, and it's been asked to me very many times. But with me, I've been fortunate enough to have some of the best in the world. Israel Crosby is a classic example. Israel was one of Benny Goodman's favorite bassists. I was Israel's pianist. I was in with his group before he joined mine. So I was fortunate enough to work with these people who became part of my ensemble in later years. Vernel Fournier being another one. A classic example of how it works is my being Israel's pianist first. We worked Jack's Back Door in Chicago for many years. Of course, I never forgot Israel, and he never forgot me. He eventually became my bassist. So there's many ways that people have gotten together, ensemble-wise and orchestra-wise. But the main thing is exposure. When you've been exposed to this business as long as I have—I was playing professionally at ten—you run into a lot of musicians. Talented musicians. And eventually, if you're able to become or inherit the position of orchestra leader or ensemble leader, then you draw upon that backlog. That's what I've done all these years.

McCluskey: And so you've had long experience in spotting that special talent, identifying it?

Jamal: That is correct.

McCluskey: Just shifting here a little bit, I'm always curious when this question is asked to writers or to musicians: What other art forms engage you? Does painting? Does literature, dance, or opera engage you in terms of inspiring ideas? Or is it just something you're excited to view or to experience?

Jamal: You always keep an open eye and open ear, in my opinion. When you close your eyes and close your ears to other avenues and other forms of artistic endeavor, you're charting a dangerous path. So I try to be open. And to quote Duke about music: there's only two types of music—good and bad. I can't stand this inference about European . . . About classical music. You were talking about European classical music as opposed to American classical music? There's good opera and there's bad opera. There's good American classical music and there's bad. There's good ballet there's bad ballet. And there are good orchestras and there are bad orchestras. Only two types of music: good and bad. And this inference, that, "Oh, I play classical music," speaking of European. Well, that irks me. I mean, that really provokes me. Do you play European classical music? One of the things about Pittsburgh is that we studied both. If you're from Pittsburgh, you study Bach, you study Beethoven, you study Art Tatum, you study Duke Ellington. We don't separate them. The only thing we don't study is bad stuff. That's the only thing, the only line of demarcation we have. And that goes with food, with books . . . I have some of the finest books in the world; I haven't read them all, but I have some of the finest books in the world. And maybe I'll read them before I leave this Earth, but the thing is you always keep . . . everything depends on the knowledge that one possesses, so seek knowledge if it be in China.

McCluskey: Well, is there any particular painting or sculpture or book?

Jamal: I'm a still life person. Because when you try to reproduce the human figure, there's always a human flaw. And as opposed to photographs, yeah there's nothing wrong—that's the real thing. When you start painting the human figure, I find that's inconsistent with the original. That's . . . only the Creator can put here the original. The duplicates, they're very good, but I'm a still life person.

McCluskey: So not still life in terms of the human figure at ease or isolation but still life in terms of trees and flowers . . . ?

Jamal: Nature. Mostly nature.

McCluskey: This brings me to another question, a question of training, and that is: Suppose we have a Jamal Academy, a Jamal School. And we're looking at students . . . say, students about sixteen, seventeen. They're high school students. And it's your school and you have unlimited funds. So funding is not even a question. But beyond that, what would you want these students to know? And I don't mean the whole curriculum that will take you through the whole day, or six hours. But are there certain things that you want them to emerge from that school or academy with? I'm curious. I don't know . . . it could be wide open: history, political science, literature, philosophy, other arts. Whatever. But it's your choice, and you want to sort of mark the next generation of students coming out.

Jamal: The operative word is "options." I tell that to all the youngsters, to prepare yourself with options. "What do you mean by that, Mr. Jamal?" You know, as many negatives that are in the institution of higher learning, there are more positives. We don't know how to say yes or no—I'm simplifying it, but those are the most important words on Earth. *Some* of the most important. Not the most important, but some of the most important decisions in your life rest on your abilities to say yes or no. And when you're seventeen and sixteen and fifteen, you haven't developed an accurate answer to all the things that you're going to be confronted with later on. So I tell youngsters: "Prepare yourself with options." What are options? If you have only one exit door and a fire breaks out, there's a great probability that you're going to get crushed to death. So, if you're going to lose your bearing and lose your focus because your area of performance breaks down—you can't perform, you can't get the right venue or the right setting or the right this or the right that—you don't despair and become an abyss of gloom. You learn to conduct for a while. If the area of conducting breaks down, you teach for a while. If that breaks down, you write, you compose for a while. So these options you can only acquire by going to school and expanding your knowledge. And that's what I pass on to youngsters. Burt Bacharach is a classic example. Marlene Dietrich, he was conducting for her, because he was a good conductor. And along comes Dionne Warwick and Scepter Records for Florence Greenberg. And sixty million dollars later . . . It's not the money, but that's just an example of options. He had the option to conduct until he got heard, and then came "Do You Know the Way to San Jose?" and, say, "Raindrops Keep Falling on My Head," and this and that. And it's unending. But had he not received the option to know how to conduct with Marlene Dietrich, he might have been in trouble. He might have gotten disgusted. He came to the place where one of my great bassists was working, Jamil Nasser, who passed away—the late Jamil Nasser, who worked with me for years. [Bacharach] came to the Composite Club while he was in New York conducting with Marlene Dietrich, and he said, "How do you like these songs?" Jamil told him, "Keep writing." And that's what he did. And look! But he had options. So I tell all my youngsters, "Instead of despairing and going into addictive behavior, choose your exit doors. Another exit door that you've acquired in school. Teach for a while. Or conduct for a while. Or write for a while." So that's what I leave with all of my youngsters.

McCluskey: So, it sounds like a broad-based education. It gives them . . . well, in your even better word, "options." If they learn history. If they learn this. If they learn that. They can learn to maybe teach themselves . . . in some ways. Or explore, themselves . . . Things that they may not have—or even their teachers—may have not even imagined.

Jamal: Yeah, when you have your mind set, "Oh, I just got to do one thing," that's fine when you get a platform for that. But sometimes there are no platforms available.

McCluskey: One other question this leads me to: I know you've admired the work of Randy Weston. Randy Weston admired your work. Mr. Weston spent a great deal of time in West Africa and the continent. I had the good fortune of seeing him perform at the National Museum of African American History and Culture in Washington, DC, before his passing. Are there areas in the Caribbean, areas in Africa, that have, you know, inspired you in terms of opening another door or, to use that notion of options, musical options?

Jamal: Well, speaking of Randy, I was in Morocco on vacation when Randy was living there. So here, I have a good connection with his family. I didn't spend a lot of time with Randy, but it's quality not quantity, as I said before. And his son, Azzedin—the late Azzedin Weston—was my percussionist for a while. But to answer your question: Music is not confined to one continent or one area. And I'm inspired by sounds from all over the world. I know it's happening, but to our particular American transformation, American classical music has been disseminated and emulated and much to the credit of this great culture, it has changed things all over the world. And vice versa. I haven't had any need not to be influenced by other sounds. But I think what we've done here is very far-reaching, to say the least.

McCluskey: It's powerful and I don't know if anybody's ever put their finger on something simple or clear to answer that. But as you say, hey, it's all over the world. It's hummed in streets in the villages in Italy. It's hummed in Tokyo. They're playing Stevie Wonder all over Germany and France. Miles Davis's and your work, too. In India. I mean, as you well know, there's a power in the music that no government can stop.

Jamal: Well you know it's very sad commentary when you can't see Louis Armstrong every day on the tube or Ella Fitzgerald as I said before . . . not to be redundant . . . There's a flaw here, a major flaw. And not only that, it's going to have a very negative effect on our children. When you only recognize the products of civilization and there's no room for the cultural side of life, you've got troubles with your kids. You've got troubles! Now what do you have now? Kids afraid to go to school! Because they get murdered and butchered in school by other kids. And some of that is lack of culture. You know, if you have not instilled in society, "Don't throw stuff on the streets, don't litter," you're going to have a problem with just litter alone. Let alone these shootings and these terrible tragedies that are happening to our kids. By our kids, also! And inspired by lack of culture.

McCluskey: Do you see that lack of culture over your lifetime getting worse? How was it . . . Was there the same lack of culture, let's say in the 1950s, '40s? From what you're saying, it seems to have gone in a different direction and going fast in that different direction.

Jamal: We've reached an apex, John. We've reached an apex. It was bad, but we've reached an apex now. And to me, it's going to be some startling results in a negative way that we've never witnessed before. I mean we talked about anywhere from climate change, we have extremes in the weather, to the what do you call it the video games . . . I've never seen such nonsense! Why can't there be a *Star Peace* instead of *Star Wars*?

McCluskey: Or why not teach more music? You give everybody an instrument . . .

[laughter]

Jamal: It was bad before, but it's reached an apex now. We had lynchings before. But we have lynchings now, only a different form. A different form of lynching. I mean, people! Eighty-five thousand kids dying from starvation in Yemen. Eighty-five thousand. And you have parts of Africa . . . Years ago, I was in Sudan . . . one of my places I wanted to go since I was eleven years old. So I was finally able to go there in 1959. The ex-minister of interior, Sheik Abdul-Rahman, was my host. I went to Egypt. Doctor Shawarbi, one of the leading scientists, was my host there. But I wouldn't go there now. I wouldn't go now. There's chaos everywhere, but I have to start at home, there's chaos here and it's reached in apex. So there's a difference, yes. We're just sophisticated. It's more sophisticated, and certainly more nuclear than it was before. And when it gets to nuclear, you're headed for one of the worst tragedies known to man.

McCluskey: I worked with my uncle who is a truck driver when I was little. He liked to sing the blues, and one of his favorite songs repeated the line, "The danger zone is everywhere," which Ray Charles made, I believe. I said to myself, "Well this is some kind of bleak record." I was only twelve years old. He could sing that same song today, couldn't he?

Jamal: You know it's really something . . . I mean, it's quite mind-boggling when you reflect on it. And we're building, building, building. [I see this] every time I go to New York . . . I was there in 1948 at the Apollo Theater. I mean, I forgot more things about New York than most people know in three lifetimes. And they're still building, building, building. I don't like to go to New York anymore. I was there in 1948, it was the city that everybody wanted to go to. But not anymore! Not me. I mean it's really something. If you want things, if it's in the world materially, you'll find it in New York. A culture? That's something else. In fact, it's an understatement saying it lacks culture. It's madness there.

McCluskey: And not enough places to hear good music

Jamal: What's that?

McCluskey: Not enough places to go and hear good music.

Jamal: You know something? And I marvel at what Wynton [Marsalis] has down there at Jazz at Lincoln Center. I mean, it's incredible! And what they've done on the opposite end: Randall Kline with San Francisco Jazz Collective. Now these are buildings. Buildings like these should be all over America. There are only two and they're both powerful. To tell you the power, they're both extremely successful, too. Jazz at Lincoln Center as well as San Francisco Jazz Collective. Look at their brochures! So it shows their power. The power of music; the power of culture.

McCluskey: Well, what's the second one? I'm not familiar . . .

Jamal: SFJAZZ. It's San Francisco Jazz. Those are the two great edifices. One night, I along with Clint Eastwood—I was an honoree one year, before they actually built it, and Clint Eastwood has been a fan of mine for years—and Willie Brown, the ex-mayor, the three of us at a benefit, we helped to raise a million dollars that night for San Francisco Jazz Collective and they built the wonderful building. In part, I take pride in that I had a little bit to do with that and pride in what Wynton and Jazz at Lincoln Center have done almost single-handedly at the other side of the country.

McCluskey: And people are hungry for the music. But here's another question, perhaps my last question this evening: I attend, for example, the Monterey Jazz Festival, but I'm sure the question can apply to Detroit or Newport or other places. The audiences are older. We have a great time. It's a good three days of great music. How do we—and it gets back to your question in terms of the youth and culture—how do we begin to expand the audiences? I know the musician and composer have enough to worry about composing and making music and performing. They're not necessarily the ones to go out and beat the bushes for a younger audience. But any ideas about how one keeps the audience growing?

Jamal: Now that's a good question. A very good question. And I don't know if it's possible. You have the social media that's more interested in one thing: making money.

McCluskey: Yeah and the social media is pretty solitary, too. It's too often one person with one machine. It's not a group of people together listening to group music.

Jamal: So I really don't know because the thing is, if you don't put the social media to proper use, the only other thing is improper use. The opposite of positive result is a negative result. And until I see platforms like they have in Europe, it's going to have a negative effect. But why do I have to go to Europe to see Kenny Clarke on television? Or to see Art Blakey? Or to see Duke Ellington? I mean here, you have Duke Ellington. Now how much more sophisticated can you be than "Sophisticated Lady"? And I don't hear it, I don't see him. I don't see Fats Waller. And he was an all-around presenter of the art form. I'm not going to call him an entertainer. I'm not going to call this great stride artist, who Art Tatum even said he could stride better than himself. Fats Waller—what a gift! The kids should see him. They should see Billie Holiday and Sarah Vaughan every day instead of . . . Come on! Some of the stuff they have—and that's another statement—is pornographic that they're showing on social media. Now how is that going to influence the young minds? I don't know what's going to turn it around. I don't know. Let me tell you: unless the people change, it's going to get worse before it's going to gets better.

McCluskey: Well, it sounds like we got a lot of work to do.

Jamal: That's all I can tell you . . .

McCluskey: You know that refrain. And I'll end on this: The refrain that's in the poem printed in the CD sleeve for *Saturday Morning*. It was originally in French. The phrase is: "Life is simple. Why complicate it?" When I read the English translation the first time, I thought, "That can't happen. We want the complication at the same time we want simplicity, but you can't have them both."

Jamal: . . . you know, like I said: we've got problems here.

McCluskey: Yeah, we do. But you know, we'll get through it. I think powerful music like yours will help us pull through it. And we just need . . .

Jamal: I pray that I will continue to deliver on the artist's job.

McCluskey: I'm sure you will. I think you answered this earlier, but are you willing to briefly share plans for any project you're in the middle of now or that you see ahead on the horizon?

Jamal: My project is trying to *discover*. That's what life is all about, is trying to discover each day. And I try to go to the piano and discover each day and perhaps some of these discoveries will come out in the manuscript. And maybe I'll do a record. I'm thinking about doing a record with the San Francisco Jazz Collective this year. They wanted me to come back after we opened the season this year, they want me to open 2019. They sent me an offer right away after I opened the 2018 season, "We want you back again." So, they offered me a four-day residency there . . . in the hall that I said we raised money for, Willie Brown and myself and Clint Eastwood that night. I think I'm going to do a recording there.

McCluskey: It's a beautiful area to do a recording.

Jamal: Yeah, I think I'm going to do a recording there . . . if the Creator allows me to stay here.

McCluskey: Well, all the best for that. I mean that's a wonderful thing to look forward to, and I'm sure the record will be fine and powerful and be a success.

* * *

True to his word, Mr. Jamal has cut back on touring. In addition to the dates at Princeton University and in San Francisco, he has done only a few others in the United States. There were several appearances in France during the year following this interview. In 2019, his CD *Ballades* was released to rave reviews. The recording consists of seven solo pieces and three with his double-bassist, James Cammack. *DownBeat* magazine honored it as one of the best albums of 2019. In his ninetieth year, Ahmad Jamal still composes at his home in western Massachusetts. ■

SLAVE NARRATIVES
E. Ethelbert Miller

I slip indoors after searching
for hours for the North Star.
Rumors have been spreading
about how a fabulous day
is a night with no moon.
The problem with plantations
is that the pizza driver never
comes. Just yesterday my copy
of Ebony was delivered to
the Big House. Massa had
a fit. Now I'll have to hide
my Coltrane and Miles
records under the big quilt.
I hear slavery is hard
on the eyes but a beautiful
woman can teach you to read
in the dark.

INVENTION
E. Ethelbert Miller

Across the street Thomas Edison listens to
Bessie Smith and decides the blues are too painful
for anyone crying alone in the dark.

HAIKU FOR MALCOLM
E. Ethelbert Miller

X marks the spot where
the ground opens for a man
a black shining prince

AFTERNOON
E. Ethelbert Miller

In the dream I'm always
sitting in your apartment
looking out the window
at my life. Sunset is your
beauty kneeling behind
me. Slippers like two hands
near your feet.

1865
E. Ethelbert Miller

After Lincoln's death old people lost their dreams.
There was only emptiness behind their eyes.
There were rumors that spread about Africa and the big river,
places where the land gave birth to food and shelter.
Tired feet left every morning and every day we counted
a loved one among the missing. It was Shonda I tightly held
each night, I buried my face in the center
of her back. I held her tighter than slavery. I was man
and chain. I searched for the softness of her blackness
under her scars and all the false promises of freedom.
I loved her like the North Star I could barely see.

CRAZY HORSE
E. Ethelbert Miller

(for Shonda)

You always loved his name.
You wished his name were yours.
Imagine standing before white
people with this name. White
people afraid of what you might
do. Imagine being Sonny Rollins
with an Iroquois haircut. His horn
filled with beautiful sounds. His
notes high flying like Bird
who once played "Cherokee"
so fast they couldn't name it.

WHAT DOES A BLACK MAN WISH FOR?

E. Ethelbert Miller

You think of Ellison's light bulbs
as you stare at the candles burning
on your birthday cake.

What is the difference
between chocolate cake
and American cherry pie?

When a Black man is hungry
he wishes for a job not food.
He wishes for his back to stop hurting.

He wishes for solitude
when he is seduced by loneliness.
When he is lonely he wishes for love.

When the people in the room sing
"Happy Birthday" you realize
how old you are.

You no longer need to count
on your fingers because you
will never confuse 1950 with 1776.

When your eyes first saw the light
you cried because you were being
separated from blackness.

You cried while watching your
mother's cry turn from pain to joy.
Her face candle bright.

You have always wished for your mother
to be well, to light the way with kindness
and sacrifice.

You wished for your father's black hands
to always be reaching and lifting
and for the future to never be dark.

What does a Black man wish for?

You wish for everything even the
things you cannot carry. You wish for
nothing so you will not be disappointed.

The light from the candles turn blue.
You hold a knife in your black hand
ready to cut the cake.

But first you cut your wishes
into small pieces before you blow.
Now you blow and blow.

FOUR HAIKU
E. Ethelbert Miller

how lonely my arms
trees walk away from the wind
i now hold nothing

your hair turns silver
like waves cresting at the beach
love endless like sand

hug the open sky
flowers bloom when they are loved
the birds are flying

leap into beyond
the seasons change with each breath
there is nothing here

that's why darkies were born
David Nicholson

> *Mr. Frankie,*
> *why do I have to live my life*
> *like I was you instead of me?*
> *What am I, a zombie?*
> Mantan Moreland

(easy travel to other worlds)

Yearn for that lost city where women wear hats and gloves and men doff fedoras at strangers' approach. A kinder, gentler place. Suffused with plangent yearning for the lost dream city decades astray, after-school black-and-white flickering illusions: Pigtailed girls and freckle-faced boys. Wholesome mothers framed in screen doors wipe their hands on gingham aprons and call their children from play.

Yaller woman in long coat, hands tucked in muff, hair pinned 'neath feathered hat, mustachioed brown man in celluloid collar, curly-headed boy in knee breeches holding a sled upright. Under corner gas lamp, the street names painted on glass rectangles 'neath globe. Wintertime and a part of the city—LeDroit Park, Georgetown, Capitol Hill—where past gives way grudgingly to present. On rare, special winter mornings, horse hooves sound a muted clip-clop just beyond hearing. Sleigh bells ring. Time stands still amid silence and snow-shrouded houses and, for an instant, redemption seems possible in that vanished world . . .

(reconstructions i)

Honesty compels me to confess my surprise, as well as pleasure others might find unseemly, when I learned how prominently I featured in the second book of boys' adventures. From the first pages, however, I felt only shock, followed by disappointment and shame. He set great store in his ability to depict the way men speak, but never in this life had I said "gwyne" for *going*, "en" for *and*, or "stugent" for *student*. And as for the narrative, truth was not merely stretched—it was broken on the rack and the pieces scattered.

I do nothing without first seeking the counsel of the dear wife of my youth, and so I read aloud from it, choosing passages true to the author's intent but that nonetheless illustrated the validity of my complaints.

I had scarcely begun when she interrupted to urge me to seek recompense in a court of law. Such had been my first inclination and, indeed, the Hon. A. J. Calhoun, Esq., agreed the slander was actionable. In the end, however, Lawyer Calhoun concluded there was only the certainty of great expense, and none at all of satisfaction.

Night after night, long after my good wife had retired, I read and read again, leaving marginalia like the trail of some wounded insect. In the end, I decided to tell my own story, leaving out and adding nothing.

I was born a free man, as was my father before me and his father before him. My five-times-great-grandfather, brought against his will, served twenty years indenture before claiming his freedom and quitting the South. At first a small freeholder, he became a merchant. He and those who followed him lived quietly, increasing their worth without calling attention to themselves. My grandfather achieved some success as a sailmaker and ship's provisioner in Philadelphia, profiting handsomely during the Revolutionary War. His son, my father, also called James, the first to receive a formal education, was called to pastor a church in Boston.

He believed equally in the utility of labor and the value of education. Thus I was schooled in the mornings by private tutors and apprenticed to a smith in the afternoons. I resented it then, but my father's wisdom and foresight would prove my salvation.

This regimen continued until I was eighteen. I enrolled, then, at Harvard, remaining at home, there being no dormitory provisions for men of sable complexion. I took no umbrage, but instead used each offense—and there were many—as a spur to finish the course of study in three years. Shortly before my graduation, my father informed me of his intent to send me to Scotland to study medicine.

I refused. I wanted to return to whence our ancestor had fled, perhaps to open a school or find some other way of serving our unfortunate brethren. My father strove to dissuade me. In the end, he gave his reluctant blessing and—having been so long free we possessed no manumission papers—obtained letters from prominent officials and bankers attesting to my free status and the credit available for me to draw on.

These might have proved sufficient, except for my own missteps. Bondsman and roustabout alike laughed as I disembarked at the Hannibal wharf. I wore my best suit, a fresh white shirt, and a new hat (gold watch and silver-headed cane were authorial embellishments), hoping to inspire some measure of respect. The clothes incited only derision. Still, I might have fared better but for my own arrogance.

A notice affixed to a tree near the wharf advertised the upcoming elections. I had thought to seek out a leading clergyman or two to ask their advice on what service I might most profitably pursue. Instead, it being my civic duty, I postponed those errands to attend the courthouse. Scratching his lice-ridden head, the registrar stared as if I were some species of exotic animal.

"Mercy," he said, in the pinched, whining accent peculiar to those parts. "Never had no call to register no nigger before."

"And are not asked now to do so," I replied, "for I am a free man of color."

The constable I had thought dozing pushed himself off the wall, cheek bulging with a wad of tobacco. (It is commonly called a cud there.)

"Mebbe," he said. "But anybody kin see you ain't a smart one." He chewed ruminatively. When I did not give him the pleasure of a response, he spat, coating the toes of my polished boots with noxious juices. "Smart nigger woulda stayed wherever he come from."

In short order, I was seized, chained, and thrown rudely into the frame hut that served as jail. In the morning Judge Thatcher ruled my letter no proof I was free, the law recognizing only manumission papers filed with the court and certified by the legislature. I protested, cajoled, threatened, even, in the end, offered bribes. It was no use. I was declared property and sold in short order. Once James, a free man, I was now Nigger Jim, diminished in name and status.

Oh, the sorrow of it, the ignominy, the sheer and utter humiliation! Yet give her her due—though an emaciated spinster inclined to peevishness, Miss Watson was tolerably kind. I had only to hew wood and carry water, tend chickens kept for eggs and Sunday supper, perform such errands as she and her sister, the Widow Douglas, saw fit.

Still, kindness is as salt in the wound of slavery. I soon came to understand escape impossible. The judge had seized my money, allegedly for fines and court costs, and the jailers had plundered my luggage and clothing, giving me a rough shirt and breeches. I suffered barefoot, limping and bleeding, who had never before gone unshod. Penniless, clad as the meanest of slaves, what chance of escape had I? To be captured would mean branding as a runaway before being sold farther South into a short life of nasty and brutish toil.

To tell of the means by which I found escape, I must write of matters repugnant, though only in the most general terms lest I offend my dear Priscilla. Mr. Douglas had departed this life some fifteen years before, but his widow was just thirty-three, scarcely an old woman.

I began to notice her eyeing me, looking away and blushing coyly as if still a maiden. I feared she had decided to profit and was determining a price so she might convince her sister to sell me. But if her look was assessing, it was dreamy and somehow predatory as well. In due time she advanced her proposition. In the evening, once her sister slept, Mrs. Douglas proposed I quit my pallet in the kitchen to provide her a different kind of service. Stealthily, of course, and, to my everlasting relief, not to include the spinster.

I shall say little more about these matters, except to ask God—and my dear Priscilla—to forgive me. I was a young man, subject to a young man's cravings and the widow, God rest her soul!, still comely and with pent-up needs of her own.

Our intimacy conspired to allow me greater freedom and, once my errands were completed during the day, the balance of the time was mine to spend as I saw fit. I commenced to visit the town smith, progressing from observation to questioning to fetching coal and raw iron and work-ing the bellows. A plan had come to me: I must purchase my freedom.

When the time was right, I made my offer. The smith accepted readily—my labor cost less than he would have been obliged to pay a white man.

I had next to convince Miss Watson. At first, she would hear none of it, arguing that she would gladly allow me small sums, so long as I did not spend them on drink, tobacco, or gambling. The Widow Douglas agreed. Perhaps she feared bellows and anvil would leave me too weak to fulfill her venereal requirements, but the two sisters soon came to see the worth of my proposal when I offered to turn over a third of my earnings each week. We settled, after some negotiation, on half.

Those first few weeks the smith confined me to the most menial labor—stoking the forge, pumping the bellows, steadying the horses he shod. In the evenings, when he took himself to the tavern, I swept up and set the tools in order.

On one of those nights, instead of hurrying to finish that I might return for prayers and to service the widow, I busied myself fashioning a candleholder. Though simple, it was well-made and pleasing to the eye.

I left it where he could find it. Jealous at first of my superior skills, the smith soon saw the sense of taking advantage of them. In a matter of moments we reached an agreement, no more fair to me, to be sure, than the bargain I'd struck with my mistress. All the same, it was sufficient to begin to envision the day I might purchase my freedom.

I shall not dwell here on how long it took. In time, however, I gained my goal. Miss Watson hemmed and hawed, thus I took myself to convince the widow. All night we discussed the matter. In the morning, weary from our brokering, she arose from the bed to convince her sister. That afternoon, I took possession of the documents certifying me a free man.

I sought to leave immediately, knowing that lingering meant any white man might claim me for his own use or sell me for profit. Foolishly, I took myself to the river and attempted to book passage on the next boat. The ticket seller laughed. I insisted on my right—was not my money as good as anyone else's? Was I not as well-dressed (I had managed to purchase some more somber articles of clothing) as any white man?

An hour before the steamboat arrived, a crowd had gathered on the docks to see me served my comeuppance. They were not disappointed. At the captain's direction I was removed, thrown head over heels down the gangplank to the dock. When I presented myself to the ticket seller, he pointed to the sign not so much written as crudely drawn, and woefully misspelled. There were no refunds.

It was then that I threw in my lot with the boy. His father was worthless, a trifling idler, and Judge Thatcher had sent the boy to live with the widow. He was seldom there, preferring a hogshead by the dock and to spend his days lazing on the river fishing and smoking a corncob pipe. But he had a raft, crudely fashioned but capable of floating. With a little work and a store of provisions, it would suit to be poled north towards freedom . . .

(scraps from the cutting room floor)

Dim yellow lights the only color in monochrome Bedford Falls evening. Winding gravel walkway wends through park, skirting bandstand at center. Houselights flicker beyond grove of trees. Church spire soars pristine above highest branches.

Air redolent with honeysuckle and verbena, magnolia and bougainvillea, its spring softness palpable enough to cup handfuls. Soft laughter and the low murmur of conversation from curved-back benches off the path. Plink-plunk of a ukulele, faraway chords of parlor guitar. Boy in football sweater, leather helmet dangling from one hand, walks with girl in long skirt and saddle shoes.

House curtains open, windows raised to the summer night, high-ceilinged parlors and living rooms ablaze with light. Families cluster round enormous radios, shoulder to shoulder though it's only an advertisement for Gold Dust Twins washing powder. The boy and girl strolling hand in hand miss nothing of the broadcast . . . Up and down the street, radios are tuned to the same program.

"And now," the announcer says, deep, resonant voice jovial with shared secrets, *"The Continuing Adventures of Sam and Henry."*

The orchestra fades, and Sam says in a hoarse white man's black man's voice, "Say, Henry, who wuz dat lady I—"

"You mean her what—"

"Naw, de other one, down to—"

"Dass a nice place, but not ez nice ez—"

"You mean de one whar—"

"Naw, not dat one, de other what—"

"Aw, yeah, I remembers now. You and me, we's—"

" 'Cuz yo' momma 'n' mine, cuz. So how come when us'n—"

"Now see, dere you goes agin, all argufyin' an'—"

"I sho'lly ain't—"

"Is—"

"Ain't—"

"Is—"

"How you come to be so informed 'bout my is and my ain'ts—"

"Jes' knows. Same as I knows you's a little headstrong sometimes."

"But I come by it honest," Henry says proudly. "Mah pappy wuz a little Headstrong and my mammy wuz a little Armstrong an' when de Headstrongs married de Armstrongs, well, suh, dat's how darkies wuz born."

A burst of laughter erupts from each living room; laughter echoes up and down the street. A banjo begins, plaintive and tinny, accompanied by violin and mournful cornet, and then the singer—Is it Sam? Or is it Henry?—begins:

Tasked to plant de melons,
'Rected to husk de corn,
Servin' in silence 'n' sorrow,
Dat's de reason darkies wuz born.

Screen doors slap closed up and down the street. Children flit by chasing fireflies, like shadows on a screen. Teenagers in white bucks settle on porch swings. Ragtime plays on an upright piano, syncopated notes like popcorn on an open fire. A game of charades ends in happy laughter as the players drift onto the porch for hand-cranked ice cream. Fathers draw on their pipes and cluck their tongues over the sports pages. Gray-haired mothers in sturdy, low-heeled shoes rock slowly, clicking at their knitting. The harmonizing of a barbershop quartet comes from far away, sweet as the roses that fill the night.

(reconstructions ii)

Pay strict 'tention now, because I'm gon' tell you the truth of how it was. I wasn't never that fat, that black neither. I was near twenty-seven, a grown woman already come into her own, slim as a willow. And strong . . . Many's the day I worked alongside the men in the fields from cain't see to cain't see, every day of the week except Sunday 'less'n it was harvest.

If I had the gifts, I'd put this all down on paper so my words wouldn't just float off and bust like soap bubbles in the sun. But I count on you rememberin'. They might steal my story, yourn too, do what they want with 'em. But all us'n can remember and learn them that come after the truth of how it was. Learn 'em. Learn the younguns.

Everything changed the day Big Sam directed me to drop my sack and go up to the Big House. Got there and had to bathe usin' some soft, sweet-smelling soap, and then Miz Ellen gimme some dresses, clean drawers, and a pair shoes so confining I use to took 'em off any time she wasn't lookin'.

Once Ise all cleaned up, Miz Ellen begin to show me around the house I'd take charge of later when it come time. Wasn't all that grand. Mr. Gerald called himself a gentleman, but he wasn't nothing but some old shanty Irish. Left Virginia and run down to Georgia 'fore he finished out his 'denture. Started with a log cabin, back when it was just him and a few hands. Built up and around it once he started making some crops. White columns and mill-cut boards, but you could still see where the logs was. Jes' like you could see he wasn't no gentleman, much as he put on airs.

One mornin', right soon after I come, Miz Ellen bid me pick up a breakfast tray wid coffee and a plate of grits and cornbread. "That girl's a trial," she whispered. "But please, see kin you find a way to get along with her." Truth is I was gon' have to, 'less'n I wanted to go back to strainy labor in the fields.

Past noon and that gal still lying in the bed, great mane of red hair—auburn she called it—spread over the pillows. Miz Ellen called, "Time to get up," like she was speakin' to a chile 'stead a grown woman. "Day's a wasting."

That ol' gal turn' over mumbling and Miz Ellen motioned for me to open them heavy green curtains. Sunlight flooded the room, and that red-headed rascal sat up, cussin' like a turpentine-tappin' cracker. Miz Ellen's face tighten' like she'd bit into a persimmon wasn't quite ripe. Told her not to carry on so—she hadn't stayed out so late, she wouldn't been so sleepy. And Ol' Red, she cussed a few more times before she sat up and held out her hand.

I made haste to pour coffee, set the tray on the bed, and commenced to tidying up the room. Heard so much about life in the Big House when the house folk come down in their Sunday-go-to-meeting clothes, how grand it was, how Miz Scarlett the mos' beautiful thing on God's sweet earth. And here she was in that great big bed, a little old thing with scrawny arms and green-apple titties and one them pink, pox-freckled complexions.

Miz Ellen left once she seen I knew my bidness. No sooner the door close than Miz Scarlett told me to look under the bed. Damn if that ol' gal didn't jump out and squat on the thunder mug right in front of me. Soon's she finished, she reach under the pillow, come out with a little brown bottle. She open' it and took a sip, then pour some in her coffee. Took a little swallow, sat back, and winked at me.

My instructions was to get her dressed and ready, but oh my Lord, what a time! Drew her bath, washed her hair, then come on back in the bedroom so she could figure out what dress she gon' wear. Couldn't none please her. Pull one out the chiffarobe and hold it up while she looked in the mirror, she snatch it out of my hands and throw it down. Pretty soon we had us a whole mess of clothes on the floor.

Reason she so particular, see, she expectin' a special visitor, a Mr. Butler from N'Orleans.

Finally, after I tooken out all them dresses and hadn't none of them suited her, I said, "Miz Scarlett, I still think that green one there's the one you require."

She turned and glared at me, eyes flashing.

"Who the hell asked you?" she screeched, and she drew back her hand.

Oh, she was a slappin' fool! Man, woman, child, black, white, it didn't matter. But I knew one thing—*I'd* be the fool 'fore I let her slap me. I grab hol' of her wrist before she could let loose.

"Now looka here," I said. "My mammy the only one ever raised her hand to me. And you ain't my mammy, 'less it's some history here I don't know 'bout."

She struggled like a fish on the line, callin' me black wench this and black bitch that, screamin' 'bout how she was gon' have me whupped till my back was raw.

Ain't gon' pretend I wasn't scared. White folks didn't need no reason to deal a whuppin', and I seen what a body look like after. And then, alla sudden the fight went outta her, and she dropped down cryin'. She wasn't nothin' but a itty bitty little chile, inside, where it count. All she needed was somebody to stand up to her.

I did what you do with chirren cryin' 'cause it's somethin' they want but cain't have—stoop down and put my arm around her. "Hush now, Miz Scarlett," I said. "Ain't no need to carry on so. Get up now. We find you somethin' nice to wear. I promise."

Whole time I was brushin' her hair and lacin' up her corset, she goin' on and on 'bout this Mr. Butler come for her all the way from New Orleans. All that talk got me curious. Finally got her into that green dress, I come downstairs to see could I help in the kitchen. I heard Mr. Polk call out, "Mr. Rhett Butler, of New Orleans." Something strained-like in his voice made me crack open the door to peep. Soon as I seen, I shut the door so the white folks in the parlor couldn't hear me cackle.

It was a whole lot of white folks there, but Mr. Rhett Butler of New Orleans wasn't one. His mammy had to been one a them octoroons or sixteenthoons or whatever you wanna call 'em and his daddy some white planter rich enough to claim her favors. Tarbrush didn't hit him but a lick. You could see it, though, you knew how to look.

Show how young and ignorant I was, when he come back in the kitchen, I ast Mr. Polk what we was gon' do.

"*Do?*" he said. "'Bout what? Ain't gon' tell nobody nothin'. Ol' Red done made her bed. She want him in it, that's her business . . ."

(scraps from the cutting room floor)

The phone's in the hall, an old-fashioned wooden box mounted high enough so Annie stands tip-toe to reach the ebonite mouthpiece. Earpiece tipped to her ear, she listens, mouth souring.

"Aw, hell," she says. "Tell me they didn't." And then, "Awright, Miz Bailey, lemme finish first what I got to get done for myself this mornin'."

Hanging up the phone, she comes to the table, pours herself a cup of coffee, sips. Tipping a little into the saucer, she blows on it before she sips again, this time from the saucer.

"Some little motherfucker ain't had no more sense than to open the floor over the swimming pool," she says aloud to the empty kitchen. "And 'course everybody had to jump in. Like they jump off a bridge just 'cause some fool said so."

Standing, she goes to the sink, stoops, and retrieves a bottle from the cupboard beneath. She pours a dollop into her coffee, closes the bottle, then opens it again and swigs directly before replacing it under the sink.

"Naw," Annie says, sitting down once more. And then, more emphatically, "Hell, naw! They grown. Let 'em clean up they own damn mess."

(reconstructions iii)

We'd been up most of the night. Talking. It was early now or very late—I couldn't tell any more. I was at the painted short-scale piano while Rick poured two glasses of champagne. He was in his white dinner jacket, a red carnation in the lapel. He shot me a quick glance from his lined, weary face. By the time he found the desk pried open and the letters of transit missing, we'd be gone, too. A moment, long enough for me to run the scale from one end of the piano to the other, before he poured a third glass, cigarette drooping from tight, cynical lips.

Elsa leaned against the piano, all shoulder-length brown hair and glowing milkmaid's complexion, elegant off-white suit clinging to her slim figure. Long skirt cut close as a pair of slacks.

She sang, just for the two of us—"It Had to Be You" in a breathy whisper, stretching the last word, "true," till I threw a scatter of chords to end it. Rick studied her with hooded, predatory eyes and scowled.

"Drink up," he said. "One more to finish before we hightail it to the airport."

Elsa took the third glass, handed it to me.

"Here, Sam," she said. "You're going to drink with us."

I raised mine, looking at both of them, and sipped.

She'd made it complicated. Used to be just the two of us—me and Rick. Started when I come out of the club with my horn after a gig, seen him braced against a wall, two goons working him over. I set down my horn and waded in. I'm a sucker for even odds—that was my first mistake. I should have just turned up my collar and headed for the subway at the corner.

They were plainclothes, Heinze and Strasser, dirty cops collecting for a loan shark named Ferrari. Afterwards, in the holding cell, he said, "Just you and me, kid. Could be the beginning of a beautiful friendship." I should have taken myself and my busted-up mouth to the far end of the bench, left him to the yeggs and scarred-face pimps eyeing his shoes.

I didn't. That was my second mistake.

We skipped bail, caught a freighter to Europe, fought in Spain with the Lincoln Brigade, ran guns in Ethiopia, smuggled diamonds in the Congo, undercut Chinese warlords with Burmese opium. He would have died of fever in Thailand if I hadn't poled a dugout twenty miles upriver to a temple.

"He is fortunate you brought him to us," the monk said, draping a wet cloth over Rick's clammy forehead. "And now, having saved his life, you are responsible for him forever."

"Damn," I said. "Wish somebody'da told me that the first time."

Because Rick was weak and a coward, a man who stuck his neck out for no one, believed in nothing except himself. He repaid me by stealing the opium profits. When I finally caught up with him in Paris, the money was gone, sunk into a jazz club. I kept the books, hired and fired. At night, I sang and played the piano. Rick played host.

Give him this, though—the man had style. Germans marching into Paris, everything shot to shit, thousands of Tommies stuck on the beach. Just as we walking up the gangplank in Marseille, gendarme ask to see his passport again. And Rick, he look at him, say, "You want the real one? Or the fake one?"

I tossed back the last of my champagne now, pushed back the piano bench, stood.

"Takin' a little break, boss."

Rick nodded carelessly.

I waited outside for Elsa, a stoutish, ordinary man of the type called colored, full faced and full featured, brushed-back kinky hair. Elegant enough in white dinner jacket and black bow tie, cigarette in one hand. When she came out, I flicked away the cigarette and raised both hands, gesture both warding off and surrender.

"Oh, Sam," she said. Broad-brimmed hat shadowed cheeks wet with tears. Accent that could have come from any of a dozen strife-torn duchies purged from the map. "Sam, Sam, Sam."

"Hush now," I said. "No need to carry on like that. It'll be all right."

She clung to me as if I'd saved her from drowning, pulled back blinking away tears. I took out a handkerchief. Women cry when they're happy and unhappy both. They know happiness never lasts.

"Maybe you can start again when we get there," she said. "Trumpet. Like you used to."

"Cops took that." It was hard not to sound bitter. "Took it forever."

"Another piece of bad luck, then. Like me."

"I'm a grown man. I knew what I was doing."

"Oh, Sam," she said. "You can lie better than that."

"God's truth." I touched her chin with two fingers, wanting to cover her lips with mine. "You the best thing that happened to me in a long time. And I love you. Better than I do myself."

She sniffled, weeping again.

"I don't want to wait," she whispered. "Especially since I know so little. I mean really—Where did you come from? What did you do?"

We'd said no questions. And there hadn't been the need. Not till the night before when she told me about Victor. He'd come. Found her as he'd always told her he would. The Germans had gotten him in Paris.

He'd had a rough time, but he'd gotten away. She'd told him about us, cried, and then cried some more.

"Maybe somewhere sometime," I said. "But not now." I took out the papers that would get her to freedom. "Victor's waiting at the airport."

"But, Sam— I thought you and I—"

And we were going to. Cut out Victor, use the letters of transit ourselves. But I couldn't. I'd trimmed corners, skated close to the edge, lied, cheated, stolen, all the time using Rick as an excuse. This was different. I couldn't stomach another betrayal.

"We talked about lots of things last night," I said. "But I've had time to think. The two of us, this place, this crazy world—You don't have any idea what we'd have to go through."

She began to weep again, quietly this time.

"Chin up, kiddo," I said. "We'll always have Paris. Nobody can take that away."

She nodded. And then she wiped her eyes with the handkerchief and tucked it in the sleeve of her jacket.

"Kiss me," she said. "For the last time. And think of me sometimes when you play."

I watched her step into the taxi, raised my hand in farewell. I waited in the rain long after the cab had disappeared round the corner. The way I'd waited in Paris when I thought I'd lost her forever . . .

(scraps from the cutting room floor)

Dark shadows on the silver screen, mute ebon faces in train and bus stations, roaming city streets. Chauffeurs and steerers of fresh-air taxis, porters, housemen and charwomen, sassy back-talking maids, spook-scared crap shooters. Low clowns and minstrels. Beulahs and Annies and Roscoes and Sams (so many Sams!) in a sweet imitation of life, too full of sass and spirit to remain in the shadows. Too foolish, too brave, to understand they disappear once the cover's closed and the last reel stowed, they look at you with surprise and answer with a question of their own: "What? And give up show business?" ■

TALLADEGA 1925
Delia C. Pitts

You ask me, the two important events of that fall were the birth of my baby sister, Helen Inez, and the Ku Klux Klan rally that drove by our house four weeks later. Plenty other things happened, but those were the biggest. I was seven years old in 1925. Maybe you think the Klan ought to come first, before the birth of one more little colored girl in Alabama. But if you want a different story, you have to ask somebody else. I'm seventy-eight years old and this one's mine. Let me hurry up and answer your questions so I can get to bed. I need to rest up for the funeral tomorrow. Here's what I remember of that autumn in 1925.

Doretta was bigger than me, but that didn't give her the right to take up more than half the bed. It was my bed, my room. I was obliged to share the covers with my sister because Daddy Bob had finally sent Doretta to bed when there was nothing more she could do to help with the birthing.

Helen, Doretta, and Juliette Lowery, c. 1931

Her long legs and sharp elbows dug into my back under the worn quilt; it had a few holes at the seams so it didn't completely ward off the chill of the October night. I sniffled and used the edge of the coverlet to wipe my nose. But I didn't voice my complaint. Not when the shouts, groans, and cries from down the hall continued to echo through the dark house. A new baby was coming and I knew our Mama was in a world of pain.

The aches had started that morning while Mama rolled out the dough for the biscuits. With those little touches to her back and hips, I knew something was wrong. I was small, but I knew grown-up business.

After she set out the hot platter of fresh-made fried chicken and the biscuits on the table in the downstairs kitchen, Mama wiped her hands on her apron front as she always did and hung it on the hook by the back door. It was late October, but still warm enough we kept the screen panel in the door. Daddy Bob would replace the screen with solid wood slats on the day after Thanksgiving, the same time Mama started the chopping, slicing, and peeling for her Christmas fruitcakes. That's the way it always went.

That morning, I looked out to the back yard, where Mama had planted late purple and yellow pansies in a wide border on either side of the brick path. The stems of the sunflowers stood naked where she had docked the blooms at the far end of the yard. A row of dry stalks remained from the corn she'd brought in last month. Pumpkins still hunkered under their green foliage beyond the fenced dirt yard, where the chickens pecked at feed Doretta had scattered before dawn.

I sat at the table, swinging my legs under the red oilcloth cover. Doretta pushed the platter to me before taking a wing, showing off her manners for Mama. I snuck two biscuits from the plate and jammed a third in my dress pocket. Doretta frowned and kicked my shin under the table. But to keep the peace for Mama's sake, she said nothing. And I didn't yelp. When Mama saw our plates were filled and the buttermilk poured in both glasses, she went upstairs to her bedroom to pin up her braid as she usually did. She even set her coat on the back of the parlor chair, like always.

Our house was bigger than most in the colored section of town. It stood at the crest of Battle Street, at the high point where the land dipped and the road curved toward the courthouse in the town square. Our wide porch swept along the front of the house and curved around one side like the prow of a boat. Fat white pillars, pale-blue paint on the ceiling slats, green floorboards. Most summer nights I'd sit on that porch after supper, swinging my legs over the edge, listening to the grown-ups rocking, talking, and sipping bourbon or sweet tea as the sun sank. When

I hugged a pillar on that porch, I thought this must be what it would feel like to sail on a grand pleasure ship, looking across the ocean of tumbling green slopes and cotton fields toward the dark eastern sky.

Opposite our house was a low wall that marked the boundary of the Talladega College campus. Red bricks stacked knee-high on a grown man, with white stone slabs topping the wall for its five-block run. Right across from our front walk was a narrow break in the wall, space enough for one person to enter the campus on a cement path.

I haven't been inside that house for twenty-five years. You ask how I remember so much. But I see it clear as day. Directly past the front door was the main parlor, with a long velvet-upholstered settee and three straight chairs gathered around a red Turkish carpet. We kept the best lamp and the radio in the parlor. Opposite the settee were sliding panel doors. I think this had been meant as a sitting room, but Mama had outfitted it as a workroom. She kept her foot-pedal Singer sewing machine there along with the ironing board and suitcases filled with out-of-season clothes. When our Aunt Val visited from Sylacauga, she slept on a sofa tucked into an alcove off the sewing room. Past the indoor bathroom was a dining room whose high windows looked out over the back yard and garden. We didn't often eat in the dining room, except on Sundays or when guests visited. Then Mama would bring her set of fine white china with the pink flowers from the glass-front cabinet at the far end of the dining room. Those china cups were so thin you could see light dance through them if you held one in the air. I dropped a cup once; Mama wanted to whip me for it, but Daddy Bob held me in his arms until she quit her ruckus.

Between the front parlor and the dining room, a narrow stair led to the upper floor. There were three bedrooms, the two small ones for me and Doretta, the double-wide room along the back of the house for Mama and Daddy Bob. Doors from their bedroom opened on a balcony so narrow it only fit a single spindly chair and little round table for Mama's teapot and cup.

I was seven in 1925, old enough to dress myself and put on my own coat and hat for the walk to school. My navy-blue coat was a hand-me-down from Doretta. She was fourteen that year, as tall as our mother. Her face had stretched to a pretty shape over high cheekbones like Mama had, but her skin was taffy colored, much darker than Mama's pale skin. Doretta's slanted brown eyes sparked like she knew secrets and special tricks. Every Saturday night, Mama used a hot comb to help Doretta straighten her black hair until its undercurve touched her neck. I begged and cried, but Mama wouldn't press my hair. She said my hair would stay in three plaits until I turned into a young lady and went to high school.

That year, Daddy Bob bought Doretta a new tweed coat with a velvet collar in recognition of her starting high school. I didn't get anything new. Ever. The only used clothes Doretta ever wore were a pair of men's canvas pants. Mama cut down Daddy Bob's old tan trousers so Doretta could have proper pants to wear when she went rabbit and squirrel hunting. Daddy Bob said Doretta handled a rifle as well as any man he knew, so she deserved to be outfitted in a nice-fitting pair of pants.

I remember how Mama frowned as she trimmed those canvas pants, mumbling about decent behavior for young ladies. But she smiled when she skinned the rabbits Doretta bagged each Saturday morning. Mama refused to touch the squirrels they shot. She said they were fine for target practice but weren't decent food for proper folks. Daddy Bob always winked at me, skinned the little creatures, and made us squirrel stew himself. He said he learned the recipe from his mother over in Dahlonega, Georgia. Mama said if he was going to bring anything from Georgia when he come to Alabama, he should have carried some Dahlonega gold dust in his pockets. Every Saturday, same squirrels, same joke, same stew.

Daddy Bob was the most handsome man in Talladega, colored or white. None of the men who came to visit our house on Sunday afternoons for a smoke after church matched up to him. Daddy Bob was darker than any, with fine, smooth black skin that stretched across his gleaming skull and over the cords of his neck to disappear under his white shirt collar. The deep lines that ran from his nose to the corners of his wide mouth gave him a fearsome look, but I could always make Daddy Bob laugh by turning a cartwheel. Doretta could charm him by just flipping her hair across her shoulder, so we knew he loved us as much as Mama did. Maybe more.

Mama said she called him Daddy Bob because his own mother did; Wiley seemed too stiff and formal for him, Mama said. Daddy Bob made Mama laugh. A lot. His voice boomed when he imitated Reverend Daniels from the Congregational church. It shrank to a mewling whine when he mimicked a complaint from George Hopkins, who ran the general store. Daddy Bob always smelled of fresh cedarwood, tobacco, rich black earth, and the starch Mama used on his collars.

This October morning, Mama asked Doretta to take me to school. I resented that change because those short walks were the only times I had Mama all to myself. Even if we never talked much in those fifteen minutes, I liked sharing the search for leaves or the pecans the neighbor boys had missed. With its wide streets and deep lawns, our town was beautiful in the fall. Heavy oak and walnut trees darkened the wide sidewalks on the edge of the college campus. The smell of burning leaves drifted from smoldering piles along the curb in front of each house. I never visited the white part of town; I don't know if it was as beautiful as ours. I don't figure how it could have been.

Mama always nodded at each lady who waved from a front door on our way to school, bobbing her head, but keeping her brisk pace. I thought the women wanted to talk; their eyes sparked with looks that blended shy and hopeful when we scurried by.

I wondered if those neighbor ladies thought Mary Lowery was always in a hurry because she was stuck on herself. Mama's light skin matched the finest store-bought wax candle, ivory with a whisper of yellow. Her red hair was long and straight. When she unknotted the braid for Saturday-night wash, her hair reached past the waist of her dress. Each week, she let me brush out her braid with a boar's hair brush. Mama was slender, like a girl in a newspaper advertisement; she didn't have the heavy hips and chest of the other colored women. With her high cheekbones, pointed chin, and thin lips, I learned early on Mama looked white.

But I knew she wasn't. Her daddy, Mr. Michael P. Curry, was, though. White as rice, our Aunt Val used to say. She told me and Doretta plenty of family stories. I remember she saved certain stories for when Mama was out running errands. According to Aunt Val, Mr. Curry was the richest man in Alabama. He travelled across the state in a private railcar, upholstered in red velvet special ordered from England. I never met Mr. Curry. I wonder if Mama did. She never talked about him. Or about her mother.

Aunt Val told us Mr. Curry was a red-headed Irishman, direct from across the sea. She said Mr. Curry had made babies all over the state. Colored babies, white babies, one in every town where the train reached and he could stop his special-order velvet-lined railroad car. Aunt Val said Mr. Curry brought Mama when she was a tiny baby and asked Val to raise her for him. He gave her envelopes of money to help with the household expenses whenever he rolled into town. So, Aunt Val had the raising of Mama. She was the only family Mama ever knew. I never learned why it was Val got to raise Mama. I did wonder if Val might be more than just an aunt, but that was a secret the two of them kept for themselves.

Those secrets, that uncertain history, maybe that's why Mama was so busy, always rushing, always determined to get somewhere. Or maybe it was because she worked at the college, in the dormitories for the young colored lady students. She cleaned, washed, sorted, and dusted. She never had time to fritter with gossip on front porches. She was always pressing to get somewhere. Make something, find someone, be somebody.

But this day in October, Mama stayed home. She told Doretta to walk me to school. Doretta was all business and made the trip twice as fast because she had to get to school herself.

Sitting still through Mrs. Wilson's first-grade class was such a chore I'd almost forgot about my mother's pains by the time the school day ended. Doretta met me outside the schoolhouse gate. She walked faster than ever on the way home and I lagged behind, finding four small smooth stones to toss at that awful Tuttle boy, who danced just out of the reach of my pitches.

When we arrived home, our father was standing on the front porch, his big hands pushed into his pants pockets. The wrinkle above his nose was deeper than usual, but his eyes were flashing with excitement the way they did on Thanksgiving morning. By the time I reached the bottom step, Daddy Bob was guiding Doretta across our porch with his arm around her shoulders. They whispered in the darkened parlor while I took off my coat and remembered to hang up my hat even without Mama telling me. The air in our parlor was stale that afternoon, as if no one had moved through the room all day.

Clasping the coat collar at her throat, Doretta flew out the front door, leaving it wide open to let in a blast of late afternoon's chilled air.

Daddy Bob knelt in front of me, his hand clamped on my shoulder. "Juliette Marie, your Mama is going to have that baby now."

"I know, Daddy." I wanted him to see I wasn't a baby anymore. I understood grown-up business. "I could tell by the way she was acting this morning."

He smiled and patted me on the head. "I sent Doretta to fetch Doctor Carter. I want you to go down to the kitchen and put the chicken left from breakfast on a plate. You carry it to the dining room. We'll eat it cold tonight."

He hugged me to his chest, then chucked me under the chin. "And we'll save some for Doctor Carter too. Aunt Val will get here by dark and I expect she'll bring something too. So, we'll have plenty to eat. Can you do that for me, Juliette? Like a big girl?"

I stretched to plant a kiss on his chin. "Yes, I can do it, Daddy. I won't drop nothing."

I remembered two other autumn days when a baby had come. And the dark wailing that spread through our house after each death. Pressing my face into his shirtfront, I whispered, "Is this baby coming for real this time, Daddy?"

"Yes, it really is coming, sweetie," He stroked my cheek, then bent to kiss the top of my head. "And this time our baby is going to stay." Daddy Bob's voice rumbled through me.

In his arms, I remembered another afternoon months earlier. On a dare from Doretta, I'd snuck into the big bedroom when Mama was away at the bank. Doretta opened the top drawer of Mama's oak dresser. She pointed at a narrow blue box made of heavy cardboard and told me Mama might keep a pearl necklace there. Or maybe peppermint candy. As Doretta watched, I pried open that hinged box. Inside, on a white velvet lining, were six little shocks of black hair. They looked like a strange alphabet written on parchment. I touched one cluster of coils, stroking a fingernail over those soft locks. This was baby hair; no grown colored person had such silky curls. Doretta gasped; she snatched the box from my hand and snapped it shut. She pinched my arm hard and made me swear I'd never tell about sneaking into the dresser. I promised and Doretta dragged me from the room.

But even as I swore to silence, I remembered secret sounds I'd heard whispered in the dark, words slipping like smoke under the door of Mama's bedroom so many nights. Hushed sounds from Bible verses: *Amos, Jonah, Aaron, David, Micah, Daniel.* Prayers and psalms, songs and stories. Mama kept the names of each boy she'd lost in the seven years between Doretta and me. And other boys lost in the seven years between me and this new baby. All Mama had of her babies were those Old Testament names and tiny curls in a souvenir box.

I brought the cold chicken to the dining room like Daddy Bob had asked, but no one ate much that night. The casserole of green beans Aunt Val brought, along with her famous pecan pie, sat forgotten on the big table. The sweet potatoes went to the icebox untouched. Doretta said leave the dishes till tomorrow. After supper, I lay in my bed and read my picture book to Annabelle, the stuffed bear. I fell asleep to the murmurs of Dr. Carter and Aunt Val, their voices mingling with the deeper notes of Daddy Bob and the groans of my mother.

When Doretta pulled back the quilt, a rush of cold air awakened me. I could hear Mama and Aunt Val humming and moaning, their voices distant and small like they were in a well. But the men's voices had faded away.

"Doretta! I don't hear Daddy, where's he gone to?"

"Hush, he's right downstairs." She wriggled under the covers, then squeezed my arm.

I tugged on the sleeve of her nightgown. "But Mama needs him."

"Hush, I say! Mama's going to be all right in a little while. Just you hush now."

Doretta laid her warm hand over my shoulder and rubbed little circles until I curled under the quilt again. I drifted to sleep with my sister's knees pressing into the small of my back.

A flash of light startled us from sleep. Our father's silhouette filled the doorway. All I could make of his face were his gleaming teeth. His eyes were squinted by smiles. He approached the bed in two strides as we sat up shoulder to shoulder. He bent over the quilt and held out a tightly wrapped bundle.

"Doretta, Juliette, wake up! Your baby sister's come!" His voice boomed in the darkness. "She's called Helen Inez. Isn't she a beauty? Don't she look the image of your ma? Oh, but I tell you, she's your mama all over with that bright skin and all that pretty hair."

Little beads of sweat dotted his hairline, grabbing the lamplight in a gold halo over his face. His nose was shiny too; I could see his heart beating fast in the notch of his white shirt collar. Daddy Bob smelled like sweat and earth and excitement, the way he did returning from a Saturday hunt with a fine brace of rabbits hanging over his shoulder. He rumbled and chattered at us for several minutes, but with the baby clasped to his chest we couldn't tell what Helen Inez looked like. We just knew she was beautiful.

When he left at last, we sighed and squirmed under the quilt again. Doretta's knobby knees jutted into my hip and back as we wriggled.

"Think Mama's all right?" I whispered. "I don't hear her. Why's she so quiet?"

Doretta whispered: "Of course she's fine. She's resting. Aunt Val's taking care of her. Mama'll be fine."

I gulped, then asked the question I'd been holding for so long: "You think maybe Aunt Val is Mama's kin? They look like kin, don't they? Same shape chin and eyes. Maybe Aunt Val's her own mama?"

Doretta's shoulders stiffened. "We don't need to worry about none of that now, do we?" Her chest rose in a deep sigh. "We don't have cause to wonder about things like that. Not now. Not ever."

She pressed her mouth to my cheek. "You just hush, Juliette. Hear me? We have plenty of work tomorrow."

We nestled our heads into the pillows and squeezed our eyes shut against the rays of the early sun creeping through the ruffled curtains in my room.

* * *

The weeks after the baby's birth were pricked out in my memory by the rapid rush of the coming winter. Ice slicked our front steps in the mornings and frost dappled the lawns of the college across the street. I was sure Helen brought the early cold that autumn.

Every Sunday afternoon, men met with Daddy Bob in our front parlor after church. They seemed to stay longer and longer each week. I heard their voices rising as the evenings darkened. I knew several of the men in those November gatherings: Mr. Wilson, my teacher's husband, a clutch of Bennett boys, and Mr. Johnson, a carpenter for the college. Sometimes Dr. Carter stayed to talk with Daddy Bob over dinner. The Sunday after Thanksgiving, all the Tuttle men, even their old grandpa, drove from their farm to spend the afternoon talking in our parlor. The Tuttles brought armloads of shotguns. They stowed several in our front closet and stood more long rifles behind the maroon curtains in the dining room.

The next day, I remember how excited I was when Mrs. Wilson told the class we were going home early. Doretta, not Mama, appeared at the gate of the schoolyard, waiting in the cluster of mothers. The women looked worried and distracted; a few fluttered fingers in front of their sagging mouths, some wiped their eyes. No one chattered or gossiped that day. Doretta hurried along Battle Street squeezing my hand, no dawdling to pick acorns allowed.

When we got home, the curtains were drawn at all the front windows. Though the pale sun still glowed, inside the house was dim and chilly when we entered. Daddy Bob stood in the darkened parlor. He pushed the door shut behind us, the loud report of wood against wood causing his eyes to widen. Even after sunset, Daddy Bob wouldn't let Doretta light a lamp in the dining room. We ate a cold supper with Mama in the silence and shadows of the cellar kitchen. But Daddy Bob stayed upstairs.

After supper, Mama returned to the parlor with Helen on her hip. She passed the baby to me and pointed to the settee. I perched there with the quiet child resting on my lap. Helen's eyes shone as she blinked and gazed around the room. Mama and Doretta pulled chairs toward the window. They sat hunched with elbows on knees, peering through the gap between the drapes. I startled when my father stepped into the room. I hadn't noticed him leave us. Daddy Bob stood at Mama's shoulder, looking over her head through the parted curtains. In his right hand, he gripped a shotgun.

We waited for an hour, no radio or lamps, only whispers. The racket began at eight with a blast of horns. From the settee I could see flickering lights as a parade of black cars crept along Battle Street. White men's voices rang out between the blare of the horns. Some hoots and raw hollers, no songs but plenty of whoops with laughter in between. I couldn't make out any words, but the shouts drummed into our parlor. Above the laughter, a gunshot blasted through the din. And then another. Helen stiffened in my arms. Her head wobbled as she turned her little face toward the window.

Another round of shots, like popcorn on a skillet. Mama and Doretta lowered their heads but continued looking through the curtains. Daddy

Bob straightened, then leaned closer to the window, his crisp shirt rippling over his shoulders. I held tight to the baby and poised my hand over her tiny mouth, but Helen kept silent.

Daddy Bob moved to the front door. I heard scrabbling noises on the stairs leading from the basement kitchen. Four strangers stepped through the doorway and into the parlor. After them came three Tuttles and Dr. Carter. A minute later, two of the Bennett boys, Mr. Wilson, and Reverend Daniels joined us.

Noises from the street grew louder. I heard iron pans clanking and cowbells tolling. Another round of shots. Someone in the parade rattled a tambourine and another beat a drum. As the procession drew near, I could make out some of the voices. I didn't recognize anyone, but Daddy Bob did.

"That's Billy Joe Prentiss in the lead. And George Hopkins limping out front too." His harsh voice wasn't a whisper, more a growl. Like a yard dog squaring for a fight.

"I'd know Old Man Winthrop's nasty croak anywhere," Tom Bennett said.

Dr. Carter said, "I don't care if they have hoods or not, they can't hide. I've known most of them good old boys since they were spring chickens."

"Cowards," Daddy Bob said. "Don't dare show their faces like honest men."

Mama nodded to me, then waved her hand. "Come here and hold the baby toward that window. I want her to see and remember this night."

I sat in the chair and lifted Helen to the glass, holding her upright in my left arm. She didn't squirm or kick. I could feel her little heart beating fast against my wrist. I propped her head with my right hand and made circles in her curly hair to keep her calm. We watched the jangling procession approach our house. The street lamps gleamed off the white hoods and robes of men who clung to the running boards. Others waved rifles from the dark recesses of the cars. At the front of the parade, four masked men in white capes carried flaming torches.

Behind me, our men slipped to the dining room. Each took a shotgun from the closet or behind the curtains. Daddy Bob opened the front door, then leaned against the screen as the men filed onto the porch. Stepping on the edges of their shoes to muffle the sound, they took positions along the edge of the porch.

I looked between the men to the street below. Moonlight coated the white stones that topped the low brick wall bordering the college campus. Dark figures rose from behind the wall, like smoke freezing solid. I saw heads and shoulders outlined against the bulk of the buildings in the distance. An arm's length separated each shadow, like the men on our porch. I craned my neck to count twenty-five men along the wall. The picket line stretched for two blocks on either side of the dividing walk that entered the campus. The moon glowed from the muzzles of shotguns clutched by each man. Their eyes flashed white in the gloom.

I squeezed the baby to my chest. "Mama, are they going to fight?" I whispered.

"Not unless we have to," she said. She smoothed a lock of hair behind her ear. Her eyes were cold and hard. "If it comes, we're ready."

We started at a thud behind us. Doretta strode into the parlor, long legs swinging as she moved. She'd pulled on her canvas hunting pants and tucked her dress into the waistband. Her hair was bunched into a wide-brimmed felt hat slouched over her face; I couldn't see her eyes. Only the set of her lips and her chin thrust out. She gripped a shotgun in her fist.

I held my breath, expecting Mama to object. But she nodded as Doretta stepped through the front door. She eased the screen shut and crossed to the edge of the porch, gun muzzle pointed toward the street. When Doretta took her place between Daddy Bob and Tom Bennett, she righted the weapon and balanced its stock next to her shoe. My father squared his shoulders, but kept his eyes on the cars in the street. I saw Tom's head swivel as she edged into line. A little smile bent his face. No one spoke.

In the street, the clanging and shouting stopped. The parade of autos halted in front of our house. Twelve cars, silent as a church on Friday morning. After a minute, I saw the white men's rifle barrels shrink inside dark windows. Then the panes cranked up. Inching slowly. The way an old turtle blinks his eye when you cross his path in the woods. Hoping you don't flip him over on his shell. Or invite him home for turtle soup.

Nobody on our porch moved as the car windows cranked shut. No one in the line across the street moved. An engine sputtered, then roared. Somebody tooted a horn. The parade of hooded men started down Battle Street again. Silent, except for the clatter of exhaust pipes and the tramp of boots. I watched the retreating torches shrink to the size of fireflies as the parade dipped down the hill toward the town square.

When the Klan procession disappeared into the night below our house, Daddy Bob and his line trooped into our parlor. The first frost of winter drifted in with them. Doretta peeled the slouch hat from her head and sank onto the settee. She patted her hair against her neck. I shivered, holding our baby sister close. I thought the men would be jubilant, cheering their success. But they were silent, like the fleeing parade of black cars.

After the men left, Doretta stood and Daddy Bob wrapped both arms around her, then kissed her brow. When he looked over her head at me and Mama, I thought I saw a glint of tears in his eyes.

I leaned into Mama's shoulder to whisper, "Will they come back?"

"Ku Klux, you never know with them. How they'll take it. What they'll do next," she said. Her jaw worked side to side. She breathed against my ear. "But you can be sure, they won't forget. And neither should you."

"I won't, Mama. Promise." I lifted Helen's chin toward the window for one last look. "And the baby won't neither."

* * *

Those white men in hoods didn't return to Battle Street that year. Or the next. Of course, we saw them in Hopkins's general store and the bank. At the movie theater and post office. Sipping Coca-Cola on a bench in front of the barber shop, chewing tobacco on the courthouse steps, repairing engines in the auto garage. We knew every one of the marchers and their wives too: Prentiss, Winthrop, Bailey, Heaton. Those Ku Kluxers were all over town. But we never said a word to them about their abandoned parade. And they said nothing to us.

The white people mostly stuck to their side of town after that night the parade went bust. They had enough sense to steer clear of ours. But we figured they hung on to those white sheets; their women kept those hoods laundered and pressed, ready to go. In August 1927, they had their big rally. Two hundred Klan boys gathered to burn a giant cross in Old Man Winthrop's cotton field.

Standing on the crest of our front porch that night, I saw the unnatural red glow in the eastern sky cast from that fiery cross. I thought I heard the crowd roar, hollow and dull like a moan. But it might have been wind kicking up for a late summer thunderstorm. I wondered if the Ku Kluxers might try another procession through our side of town after their cross collapsed into cinders. They didn't, so maybe some kind of lesson was learned after all.

That's what I remember from the autumn of 1925: Helen come into the world and the Ku Klux Klan on the march. After sharing picket duty with him on our porch, Doretta started walking out with Tom Bennett. She ended up marrying him, but not until 1963, after she buried two other husbands before she returned to poor old faithful Tom. Cancer took our Daddy Bob at Christmas 1950, just before you were born. Daddy Bob never got to meet you, but Helen came from Chicago for a visit in October of that year, so he knew you were on the way. I figured from his grin he was proud about it too: his baby having a baby. After Daddy Bob died, Mama held on for another twenty-five years. Stubborn like always, she passed kicking and raving in an old folks' rest home in Anniston. In all those years, I never did ask Helen if she remembered that Klan parade on Battle Street. Doesn't seem likely, does it?

That's enough of your questions now. You've kept me up too late as it is. I told you I want a good night's sleep before the services for Helen tomorrow morning. But I don't expect to get much rest tonight. Doretta's long legs and sharp elbows will dig into my back, her knees poking and prodding me the same as that night Helen was born. ∎

WE STARTED WITH MADNESS & ENDED IN CAR WASHES

Yesenia Montilla

—for Elma's Heart Circle & Nipsey

We are a rebellion
A cuckoo clock that never stops
We make warfare   daily
& if I could call us anything
I'd call us   poem

Yesterday I said madness
          & you said everything else
Cause we're our own language
Our own hands reaching
for something familiar
          in the dark

We were meant to be
our own little kingdom
with big mouths & smart
comments. We open wide
& it's a wormhole —

We suck in & spit out
We make plans & find trouble
We say I love you & we mean
                    thank you

I woke up wanting to say
one true thing: Friendship
is the only country whose
          sovereignty I recognize

People underestimate us
we're only shy   not unambitious

We are gonna make gazillions
off of   automated
    car washes
in Hunts Point & Riverdale

It's going to slap the madness
out of us, when we jet set
to the Riviera or St. Barts or
City Island — that dreamy place
                    off the coast of the Bronx—

I swoon at the sight of us
I rattle
My whole heart a dying dwarf
                till you —

EVERYTHING IS CRUMBLING
Yesenia Montilla

so I looked up my birth chart
I needed a reminder for why
I always wanna run away from
stability — being a Leo in sign &
rising can't compete with my
Gemini moon, how it becomes
bored at the slightest sense
of habitual dress up, how it fears
being a fraud & my Venus
how it resides in Cancer & its 7th
house of perpetual falling —
how I might die falling off cliffs,
down stairs, in love — how if
I look at someone & wish: be
mine, what I mean is: tell me
I'm worthy. How all I really want
is to be a Pisces moon like my
mother, whose madness is a
cursive M pinned to the soles
of her feet. How she steps off
chairs & buildings & trees &
never falls. How she floats —
a star dangling — a spore,
an albatross strewing
against a periwinkle blue —

THE COMEBACK
Sharyn Skeeter

Was that Darnell? The man at the back door under the Exit sign looked shorter than I remembered him. He was late. He strutted down the aisle waving, grinning, and greeting reporters on both sides as I heard them, mostly men, call out, "Hey, Duke A.!" A few reviewers, old high school buddies, leaned over others to shake his hand.

So, this man in skinny black chinos, a red-and-black tee, and a baggy black leather jacket was "Duke Anthony." He was no longer my cousin Darnell, Aunt Velma's boy, the scrawny teen I'd been awed by when I was a kid. I stopped staring and smiled, tentatively, as he slowly pranced to the front platform where I stood.

Good thing Velma didn't come. She would've had a fit if she saw "Duke Anthony" looking like that in a black-and-white scarf in June! And as he got closer to the front of the room, those multicolored high-tops squeaked on the shiny wood floor and seemed way too big for his feet.

But why did he bring his girlfriend? She, Makenna, was grinning behind him, feigning modesty like his tall shadow in her all-black jumpsuit and pulled-back braids. But as Duke Anthony passed them, the reporters—both men and women—were really craning their necks to see her. The rumor in the tabloids said that a few years ago she was such a disaster in her first role that she almost got thrown off the set. She went to Duke Anthony for help and he stepped up to coach her. Now she's "Makenna"—the one-name rising star, latest cover girl on every newsstand.

Frankly, I was pissed. I knew his flight from LA had arrived hours ago, so I'd hoped that he'd get here early. All I wanted was to enjoy a few minutes catching up on those five years I hadn't seen him. When I was little, Aunt Velma's apartment was all new to me. Those nights, he'd sit for hours on the couch where I slept, and he'd listen and tell me stories when I'd cry and whine about how I missed my parents. He was a good student and I looked up to him then, and years later, I was so proud to tell friends my "big brother" was a star.

A few months ago, he called to let Velma know he'd be here for the movie. She told him about my new-millennium gift to myself—this public relations agency that I was starting with my fiancé Tanner's help. Darnell wanted to be my first client. I was ecstatic! But here he was, taking his time, talking to friends who called him Duke A. as he walked toward me, late.

To bide time, I'd been going person-to-person, talking up his movie, *Two Guns*. Most of the press people were from neighborhood and regional publications, websites, and radio shows—not many from the big-name national media that I'd hoped for. By now, the photographers had eaten all the snacks that my assistant, Riya, had put out on the table near the door.

It was after work and the reporters were restless. I heard a young writer from a women's magazine ask another in the second row, "How long will this be? My baby's sitter is going into overtime."

The other said, "I don't know about that, but I told Johnny that I'd go out for a drink with him." She winked.

When Duke Anthony got to their row he said, "Hey, ladies!"

They stared, smiled weakly, then turned to each other to whisper.

I'd been worried that the TV entertainment news crew, at the side of the platform, might leave. They had another interview to do after this event and had squeezed in Duke Anthony only after Riya and I had phoned them more than a dozen times! So, before he arrived, to get their attention, I had to push up the schedule and show the *Two Guns* movie trailer before I'd planned to. I wished Duke Anthony would've said a few words to them before that.

This was his one shot for a comeback. Could be I was a fool to think he'd care more about being here on time for himself—maybe even for me. Or was it just that I was too "New York" and he'd acquired a more casual "LA" style?

When he finally got to the edge of the low platform, I gasped. In the spotlight, his face was gaunt with coal-black lines where he used to have full eyebrows that, I admit, as a teen I'd envied. A thick blanket of pasty tan makeup and dark contouring cream covered his skin. What had happened to his smooth, penny-brown complexion?

Makenna propped his arm as he stepped up to me. "Hey, Cuz!"

I gave them my best public relations smile. "Hey. It's been years, 'Duke A.'"

I wished he'd listened between my words, like he used to, so he'd understand that I wanted to catch up later. Instead, he said, "Yeah. You look good."

His eyes were straying around the room when he said that. I doubted it was sincere. After all, he had her, with her perfect dark oval face, holding his arm. Next to him, I suddenly felt self-conscious in my minimalist Armani pantsuit—my one splurge for my new business "uniform."

"Alika, this is Makenna. She's . . ."

"Glad to meet you." I would've liked to be more cordial, but I couldn't spend time with her.

I rushed him to a folding chair next to the sturdy oak podium that he had requested. He held the chair arms as he sat.

I turned my back to the audience, a buzzing mass of reporters and flashing camera lights, and whispered, "Look, Dar, uh Duke Anthony, we have to get this going. I don't know why you're late, but I only have this room for forty-five more minutes. I've already shown the trailer."

"Good. I told you my manager has the screening set for next week. Here and LA. This is big, Cuz!"

Hmmm. No apologies for lateness and the inconvenience he caused. I knew Velma had taught him better than that.

"Okay, they love you already. So, just be yourself."

"No problem."

I saw a few sweat beads leaking through the makeup on his forehead. I hoped his face would hold together under the lights.

As he looked around at the white walls, the two empty rows of seats in the back, and the high ceiling, I heard him mumble, "I thought she'd do better." I ignored that as I pointed Makenna to a reserved seat in the first audience row, next to Tanner. Duke Anthony glanced behind him at the posters for *Two Guns*, his comeback movie. He smiled at the glamour shots of himself as a cocky urban cowboy. He was strong, quite powerful, in those posters. I admired his direct look at the camera, even though it was posed just like every other publicity photo from his previous movies. He was what? Forty-one, almost forty-two? But you'd never know from that poster. He looked just like he did for his first movie at twenty-three.

He turned to me and quietly said, "Good job. I knew Cuz would earn her keep."

I took a deep breath. "Thanks for being my first client."

My notes shook in my hand as I walked to the podium. A clique of women from lifestyle magazines were talking and not paying attention to me. A few photographers inched their way up with their cameras in Makenna's face, then turned their lenses to Duke Anthony. At the back table, I saw Riya handing out press kits to stragglers.

This was the moment—the start of my own public relations business! I wished I had time to savor it, to really schmooze with everyone later, but I had to rush the program to make up for Darnell's, uh, Duke Anthony's lateness.

Courage, Alika, I told myself as I cleared my throat. A few who had been talking elbowed others to look up at me.

"Hello! To those of you who just arrived, I'm Alika Shea-Thornton.

Thanks for coming. This is what we've all been waiting for. Duke Anthony is back! You saw the trailer. You know he's blazing in *Two Guns!*"

I thought there might be some smiles, head nods, any nonverbal response. But nothing. These reporters had a seen-and-heard-it-all rigid patience about them. Dead silence.

"You've got the info you need from me in your kit. If you have any questions or want to schedule an interview, talk to me or Riya." I pointed to her. She held up and waved a press kit in the back.

"But, now, let's get right to it and hear from Duke Anthony."

I sat on the other side of the podium. Duke Anthony's wide smile was frozen on his face as he pushed himself on the chair arms to stand. Then he looked down and took a half step to the podium. A few cameras clicked as he paused, looking out at the press.

This surprised me. As Darnell, he was shy, very nervous at auditions for high school plays. But the Duke Anthony who I'd seen make a grand entrance this evening definitely knew how to work a room. I knew he'd done this before. Was he out of practice because of the eight years between movies? His pause, though it lasted only a few seconds, made my stomach churn. I saw Makenna silently mouthing what seemed to be "You can do it." That worked. He regained his posture as he took two more steps.

He gripped both sides of the podium. "Hey! I'm glad to be home, New York! I'm glad to see so many friends here." His voice began to waver. "Even some old friends . . ."

He looked at the reviewer in the second row with the bebop cap, the older man who I knew had trashed his last movie about eight years ago. That review hurt Duke Anthony so bad that he hadn't gotten a starring role until now—and only when his manager got some movie buddy of his to take pity on him. This was really his last chance. He had to take hold of this opportunity, or he'd be back to doing voiceovers and commercials. For that matter, if this event didn't work, I could be back to taking someone's orders as an assistant. I held my breath. I didn't want his old feuds to resurface. The reviewer smirked.

A heavyset middle-aged woman in a blue suit, a latecomer fan who must've snuck in the back row, stood up and yelled, "I love you, Duke Anthony!"

Makenna's eyes glared at Duke Anthony and became pinpricks as her head, braids flying, jerked toward the back. A younger woman near the aisle, hair in a side flip, giggled and said loudly, "Nice try," as the woman passed. The "love you" woman, humiliated, had sheepishly covered her face with her purse, then crawled over the laughing man next to her and skulked out the back door.

With that distraction, I didn't see why Tanner was pointing and running toward me on the platform. Makenna was half standing and panting. And some in the audience mumbled, "Oh my God . . ." In the next moment, I felt Duke Anthony leaning over me and saw him losing his grip on the podium. His legs wobbled, then straightened as he opened his mouth to speak. Instead, his chest rounded over the microphone. When his jacket rubbed it, the speakers blasted a loud buzz. The podium shook, but stayed upright. By reflex, I shot out my arms to stop his fall. But Tanner, a former halfback, was faster and, just before Duke Anthony could hit the floor, he caught him. For a quick moment I was stunned and still. Then I stood and pushed my chair closer to the podium. He was limp when Tanner gently sat him there.

Reporters and photographers, who had been slouchy in their seats, jumped up and crowded into the aisle to surround the platform. They were taking photos and videos, talking into recorders, and writing notes. I heard a man say, "I knew he must be on drugs," and a woman responded, "Yeah, hadda be to look like that."

I didn't want them circling us, but I tried to ignore them because I was more concerned about what had happened to my cousin Darnell. Riya pushed past the TV crew to shield Duke Anthony from their cameras, but the TV people were good at nudging their way in front of the others.

I was close to Darnell, who was mumbling gibberish about *Two Guns*. His sweaty, made-up face was grotesque—lots of smudged dark contouring and sparkly highlighting around his cheeks and half-open eyes. I glimpsed Makenna edging around the platform. One or two reporters jammed recorders toward her mouth. She turned away from them. A woman's voice said, "She thinks she's a diva!"

I called out, "Darnell, Darnell!" I wanted him back to his senses.

A reporter said, "Darnell?"

Another said, "That's his real name! Darnell Thornton. Everyone knows that. I went to high school with him—Performing Arts. He only got two decent roles before he graduated. Me, I was a star in senior year. Ha! Now, I'm writing about him."

"Yeah. Go figure!"

Tanner was kneeling in front of him, holding Duke Anthony's face. "C'mon, man, stay with me." I loved Tanner's calm strength—just what I needed now.

Duke Anthony opened his eyes and tried to sit up straight. Tanner let go and his hands were greasy with makeup. I gave him a tissue from my pocket.

I noticed Riya's curls gracefully moving back through the crowd. I waved her toward me. "Get an ambulance and move these people out."

"I'm on it." She disappeared, but the reporters stayed. I saw their heads bobbing as they tried to get a look at Duke Anthony.

Tanner and a strong black freelance photographer with white skin and a blond Afro were on either side of Duke Anthony, holding his arms and helping him sit up. Finally, he was more alert and sitting on his own. I bent down to hug his shoulders and noticed that the white dots on his scarf, now drooped across his lap, were skulls.

"I'm okay, Cuz. I just got a little dizzy. Too much hard work . . ."

Only then I realized my eyes were beginning to tear.

"Don't cry. Not for me. Alika, I know you can handle this . . . Breathe." His voice was soft, more like my cousin Darnell from the old days. So, I took a deep breath like I had when he was fourteen and I was nine and I was ashamed to tell Velma I'd failed a math test.

I heard muffled, excited voices near the elevator outside the room. Most of the chairs were empty, except for two men gathering their notes. I saw a small group of entertainment writers who were lurking behind the back row. Last week, I'd had copies of the movie posters printed on the covers of press kits. Half of those we'd given out this evening littered the floor. Just a few reporters and the blond-Afro photographer were still hanging around the platform. The TV news crew with a woman talking into a microphone were off to the side of the room. I pulled up a chair to shield Duke Anthony. He was sitting, with elbows leaning on his knees, looking lost. When I looked up, the TV crew was gone.

Tanner was moving around him, trying to protect him from cameras and keeping him upright. Tanner forced a smile toward me, "You got this."

I wanted to believe him. I wanted to salvage whatever I could of this event. My God, my first—maybe last—client! Yes, I had to make this right.

Riya led two ambulance workers, a young redhead and a stocky man with a gurney, down the center aisle toward us. Duke Anthony shook his head, "No, no . . . I don't need this." He raised his arm as if to push them away, but he was too weak to resist. The redhead stared at his face, then took his vitals as I told the man how he'd fallen. When they went to pick him up, Duke Anthony's shoulders collapsed. He relaxed and was silent, eyes tightly closed, as they lifted him onto the gurney.

Before I knew he was behind me, the blond-Afro photographer flashed his camera in Duke Anthony's face and backed up to the edge of the platform to shoot his whole body prone on the gurney. Tanner pushed him away, but he wasn't fast enough to stop the click of his camera.

The redhead told me, "We're taking him to Washington Heights Hospital. You wanna ride with him?"

I wanted to. Sure, I knew he couldn't help being sick, but I was angry at Duke Anthony. He blew it! His comeback and my business. But I was also very anxious about his condition and started following as they rolled him down the aisle. No, I didn't know how to feel about this man with the jigsaw puzzle of a made-up face.

Tanner grabbed my arm and said, "No. I'll take you. Let Makenna go with him."

I became aware that I hadn't seen Makenna since Duke Anthony had been placed on the gurney. But Tanner was right. I had to finish here. I watched as they wheeled out Darnell. He was trying to smile, but his top lip fluttered like a butterfly. He couldn't raise his arm to wave, so his hand teetered, back and forth, next to his hip. Makenna appeared in the hallway outside the door. She followed them into the elevator.

I stood straight and went to the podium. Five or six reporters were still milling about in the back, laughing, likely deciding which bar to go to. A woman from the second row saw me and nudged the guy next to her.

I felt queasy, but I had to talk. "Thank you for coming. I'll be in contact with a follow-up ASAP." I wanted to say more, but I couldn't. They were already walking out. I could see only a few were carrying press kits.

The blond-Afro photographer handed me his card. "I'm Brent. I'll see you there."

"Where?" But he saw Tanner glaring at him, and he ran out without answering as his camera swayed on a strap around his neck.

The room was empty. Riya had picked up press kits and put them in the box in our little cart. These were kits that had taken us days to compile.

She said, "Some of these are still good. I'll bring them to the office tomorrow."

"Yes . . . Riya. You did a good job."

She half smiled and left. Maybe she, too, was thinking that after tomorrow, we might not have an office.

When I thought of my cousin Darnell—Duke A., they said—sick and crumpled in the ambulance, my hands went cold. Tanner put his arm around my shoulders. "Let's go."

Outside, in the early summer sunset and warmth, the chatter of men and women, English and Spanish, the rush of black people in business suits, Puerto Rican students in jeans with backpacks, women in hijabs going into a grocery store, white teens jogging with earphones, others with shopping bags, talking with friends, going about their evening—the jumble of it was too frantic for me. Tanner jangled his keys as we walked down the block to his SUV. He helped me into the passenger seat and slammed the door. As he drove uptown to the hospital, I tilted back on the headrest and closed my eyes.

I needed quiet. Tanner said nothing. Was he thinking that he'd lost his investment in my business—Alika Shea-Thornton and Associates? I was afraid to ask. I'd wished so much for him to believe in me.

But, oh, Darnell, my cousin Darnell . . . though he was always more like my big brother. I remembered him as a shy, lonely boy who was good at playing make-believe. That's what got him into acting classes in high school. A teacher who respected his talent used to talk with Darnell after school. He got Darnell, fragile as he was, to begin trusting himself enough to start getting minor roles in school plays. He was working up the courage to do his first pro audition when he brought over two classmates—Tall Boy and Freckles—to rehearse for a scene study assignment. I'd finished my homework at the kitchen table and was eager to watch them.

"You really do live here?" Tall Boy, with the BO stink, asked Darnell. He was the one who said he got the subway from the Upper West Side. "I mean, like, I can't believe we're in a South Bronx project . . ."

Darnell cut his eyes at him and said, "Let's get this done."

Tall Boy looked around the living room, scared, as if he thought a mugger would pop out of the walls. When Aunt Velma appeared in the room after changing from her work clothes to a blue top and old jeans, both boys flinched at the same time. I covered my face and giggled.

"Would you boys like some snacks? I have cookies and chips." Aunt Velma was acting cheerful. She was always trying to encourage would-be friends for Darnell.

The other boy, Freckles, looked around the kitchen with the dirty breakfast dishes in the sink and said, "No, thanks."

"Soda? Milk? Water?"

"No, thanks. We're okay." Tall Boy sank into the sofa.

Aunt Velma's eyes showed the puffiness of workday fatigue. "Okay, enjoy yourselves." She went back into her bedroom, no doubt to nap.

I was glad that they didn't want to eat anything because I didn't want them hanging around for long. If they did, I'd miss *St. Elsewhere*. I wouldn't get to see that cute Denzel, who conjured up romantic fantasies in my preteen brain.

When Darnell turned to get his script out of his backpack, Freckles whispered to his friend, "This sure is low-rent, isn't it?"

"Must be why he's so skinny."

"Yeah, probably has peanut butter sandwiches for dinner."

They laughed with each other. I gritted my teeth. Too bad for them that we could hear everything they said. Darnell had the script in his hand already, but he didn't face them yet. I felt my cheeks getting warm, probably turning blotchy red.

Darnell took his time, looked at the script, then quietly put it away. When he pivoted toward them, his fists were fidgeting at his sides. All he said was, "Get out!"

Freckles stood up. "What? Why? We have to rehearse this by tomorrow." The fly on his khakis was unzipped. It must have been like that the whole time he rode the subway.

"I said, get out."

Tall Boy was wild-eyed. "What's with this freaking out? We just need to go through this once."

Freckles said, "But we came all the way here. We're the best actors in the class. We'll blow them away!"

"I'll say it one more time . . . Get out!"

Tall Boy said, "Okay, okay. We're done! Do your thing. We didn't want to come to this ratty place, anyway."

"What?" I couldn't keep quiet. "We don't have rats! You got them crawling in your head!"

"Shut up, Alika!" Darnell scared me as he walked closer to those two. Then he didn't move. They backed out the door. I heard them in the hall all agitated about how Darnell had gone crazy on them.

I went to close the door and, when I turned, Darnell was in the same spot in the living room, with tears in his eyes. I never saw him like that. Big brothers aren't supposed to have tears on their tee shirts. I felt the snarky way those boys viewed the project, Aunt Velma's old clothes, the chipped dirty dishes—and maybe everything in our lives—opened wounds I didn't know we both had. I felt like crying, too, but instead I hugged his waist. I felt his breathing get calmer and he jerked away from me to get a paper from his backpack.

"Maybe they think we're poor. So, what! I don't need them! I'll do this by myself!"

He shook the page in my face. It had *Network* on top. He blasted into the bathroom and started reading it in the mirror. I could only hear some of it, but what I could make out was ranting.

"'Since this show is the only thing I had going for me in my life, I have decided to kill myself.'"

I panicked. "Darnell?!" He didn't answer me, but I could see through the crack in the door that he was okay, still reading to himself in the mirror.

"'I ran out of bullshit.'"

I never heard him talk like that in Aunt Velma's place. I hugged myself.

"'Don't worry about the truth, I will put the words in your mouth.'"

He noticed me in the mirror and tried to close the door with the back of his hand, but it got stuck in a towel.

Aunt Velma rushed from her bedroom. Her bobbed hair was flattened on one side. "Boy, what are you doing in there?"

He said in his normal soft baritone voice, "I'm okay, Mama."

She went back to her bed and he continued.

"'We're not talking about eternal truth or absolute truth or ultimate truth, we're talking about impermanent, transient, human truth . . . you're at least capable of self-preservation.'"

He was quiet. I peeped in and saw him smiling in the mirror. He opened the door and I'd never forget how he looked straight at me.

"What d'you bet I'll be a star?"

I was just twelve, but when I saw his big grin, I was old enough to know he'd win that bet.

I felt my body slowing down, then I jolted with a hard break.

Tanner said, "We're here." ∎

INFLUENCES
Clifford Thompson

MING YANG FU, OR SEEKING WORDS AT AGE THIRTEEN
Clifford Thompson

1. BIRTHDAY

"I'm thirteen years old," I said aloud to myself, rising up on my elbows on my little bed, in my tiny room with its pale-yellow walls. Near the head of the bed, the window framed the view more familiar to me than the outside of my own house: the red A-frame across the street, sitting atop a grassy mound on the corner. Years earlier, when my brother—fourteen years older than I am—told me that Jesus was coming back one day, I had pictured Him walking quietly around that corner, alone and unceremoniously, with his long brown hair and beard, in his robe and slippers, arms raised in greeting. I wondered what he would say.

My mother sorted mail on the night shift at the post office. She walked in the front door downstairs at about the time I woke up and announced to myself that I was thirteen. Her mother, white-haired and all but deaf, turning eighty-two in exactly a week, had been up for hours, making herself butter-soaked toast in an aluminum pie plate in the broiler and loading great heaps of sugar into her coffee.

I went downstairs. The three of us sat around our dining room table. My grandmother, in a blue sleeveless housedress and one of the two or three cardigan sweaters she wore year-round, drank the last of the coffee she had perked, not hearing how loudly she slurped. My mother drank instant coffee. I ate cereal. My mother and I talked, intermittently, desultorily. Am I a bad writer if I admit that I have no idea what we talked about? The only one of those morning exchanges I remember is from the previous fall, when I explained to Ma, tears forming in my eyes, why I had a lump on my head. She listened with calm and detachment to this story, which ended with me unconscious. Ma was fifty-one years old, and her husband was dead; she was responsible for her aged mother and had been for decades, would be for the rest of my grandmother's life and all but the last few years of her own; and she pulled the night shift at the post office. As the general of our household, in the long slog of a battle that was her life, she seemed to view the problems of an enlisted man like me from a great height. That's not to say they weren't important to her. In the days after hearing my story, she gathered contact information for teachers at my old elementary school who would vouch for me if there should ever be a question of who was at fault, me or the boy I had gotten tangled up with. There was no question at all about that, and it was hardly the issue; but Ma was doing what she knew how to do. And at the breakfast table she gave me this, saying, despite all the evidence, "You're a pretty tough guy."

That, as I say, was the previous fall. The morning of my birthday—which I see from the internet was a Wednesday—I'm sure I got cards and presents from my mother and grandmother, because I did every year. I am also sure that when I left the table and got ready to go to school, my stomach was in a clench, because that's how it felt every morning.

This was March 1976, in Washington, DC, in an all-black section of what was then a mostly black city, when I was thirteen.

* * *

I left for school, walking up our block of red-brick semidetached houses. I crossed at the corner. At the opposite corner was Anthony Wilson's house. I went up the front steps.

Anthony was light skinned, with brown kinky hair. Though Anthony and I were never exactly friends, his path and mine intertwined at various points in our lives. Years earlier, beginning as seven-year-olds, we had attended the same summer day camp; he would tell jokes that made the rest of us cry with laughter, jokes so funny to us because they made absolutely no sense, as if—and this may have been the case—Anthony didn't know what a joke *was*, but simply imitated the form, like a person who doesn't know French speaking random syllables with a Parisian accent. A joke might go like this. Q: What did the bird bring back to the nest? A (spoken by Anthony with a broad smile and mischief in the knit of his eyebrows): Ketchup, and mustard, and . . . By the following summer, Anthony had gained an understanding of jokes but had lost something, too. We begged him to tell some of his jokes, whereupon he looked confused for a moment and then told one we all knew from TV. (Q: What's the best way to catch a squirrel? A: Climb a tree and act like a nut.)

My picking Anthony up on the way to school in the mornings had to have been our families' idea, a way for us to form a needed bond in that first year of junior high. Like Anthony's old jokes, this morning routine was all form and no content. We had little to say to each other, even when we were talking. Today I cannot recall a single thing we said as we walked; I could make up a representative conversation, but that's exactly what I would be doing. I do, though, remember one morning, because it so perfectly captured our relationship. I went to his door; he came out. For some reason, neither of us said "Hey" or "Morning" or whatever we usually said. Without a word, we went down to the sidewalk. And thus began our game: how far could we go without saying anything? All the way to school? And, in fact, we made it. At the front door of Kelly Miller Junior High School, Anthony headed off toward his homeroom, I toward mine. In that year's most eloquent communication between us, we had not exchanged a word.

2. SUMMER

My friend Trevor Sampson lived down the street. Trevor, who was my age, skinny like me, had come with his family from South America several years earlier; I didn't know enough, or it didn't occur to me, to ask which country they had come from, and to this day I don't know. Like me, Trevor had two older sisters and an older brother, but unlike my siblings, they were teenagers and still lived at home. I never heard the Sampson family speak a language other than English, which they spoke with an accent. Trevor himself had a few speech patterns that as far as I could tell were all his own. He would start many sentences, for example, with *soon*: "Soon, Cliff, you see that movie on TV last night?" The whole family did one peculiar thing I knew about. The way other families went to church, the Sampsons could be found every Labor Day, all day, in front of their TV, to watch the whole of Jerry Lewis's annual muscular dystrophy telethon. Trevor could have no guests on those days, and he could go no farther than the front porch, which is where he and I stood talking one Labor Day when, at one point, his mother stuck her head out the door; looking at Trevor, with a smile that radiated joy, and yet a quiet joy, suggesting humility before the inscrutable mysteries of goodness, she said, "They got twenty-one meelion."

Trevor and I went to different junior high schools and didn't always see much of each other during the school year. But summer had come, and after what I remember as a solid two weeks of dreaming that I was still at Kelly Miller—the way I imagine ex-cons dream that they're still in the joint, soldiers that they're still at war—I realized I was free. From sunup to sundown, while my mother slept before her shift at the post office and my grandmother alternately watched soaps and looked out the window, my only responsibility was to show up at home once in a while and feed myself. The rest of the time? I read my beloved superhero comic books and made up and drew my own. Trevor, with the tact common among us thirteen-year-olds, once told someone in my presence, "Soon, Cliff draw some terrible comics. But he keep tryin', though." I also rode my skateboard, so comfortable on it that I could read comic books at the same time.

And I hung out with Trevor. One day, outside, he spotted a girl who was new to the neighborhood and wanted to talk to her. I went with him. I have retained next to nothing about the girl. I mainly remember Trevor, who was leaning forward with his forearm across one thigh, so he must have had one foot on a front step of the house where the girl was sitting; and what he said interested me. In that time and place, there was much discussion of "talking to" girls—i.e., saying what was necessary to get to the next step. (What you said was your "rap.") I had no idea, none, of how this was done. I thought about girls a lot, but that was all I did. To me, getting somewhere with a girl was like standing in front of an enormous building complex and trying to locate, with no information, the room that had what you wanted. You could try to enter the complex and wander the halls, but you would look suspicious, and anything seemed better than that. All I knew to do was stand outside and gawk.

And so, when Trevor began "talking to" this girl, I was all ears, but what I heard told me nothing. While I stood just behind him, Trevor asked the girl her name, told her his; asked her how long she had lived here, where she'd been before that; asked her what school she would be going to, what grade she was in, etc. At some point the girl's eyes moved from Trevor to me; I moved closer to Trevor, as if for protection. Another question or two, and Trevor said, "See you later," and we walked away. The connection between the conversation I had just heard and having a girlfriend was like the connection between a roomful of guys with computers on Earth and a rocket landing on the moon: I could not make it out. The mystery of talking to girls remained a mystery.

* * *

The timing of my joining Boy Scouts of America's Troop 77 was such that I now wonder what was behind it. When my father died, in November 1974—I was eleven—my three friends in Lincoln Heights, the housing project behind my house, already belonged to the troop. Shortly afterward, at their urging, I started going with them to the weekly meetings, held in the basement of a Lutheran church in our neighborhood.

Had their mothers whispered to them that they should ask their suddenly fatherless friend along? (My friends, for various reasons, were fatherless themselves, which had a lot to do with why they lived in Lincoln Heights.) Our scoutmaster, the friendly, no-nonsense Mr. Moses, was a young black man with glasses and a moustache, a wife and toddler, and a surprising amount of gray hair—"from marriage and Vietnam," he told us once. Not counting the many boys who came to a meeting or two and then were never seen again (Trevor was one of those), about a baker's dozen of us could be counted on to show up every week.

Troop 77 had been on camping trips before—I remember pitching tents in the cold dark, my fingers frozen in place like my old GI Joe's well into the next day—but in August 1976 we went to Boy Scout Camp. Instead of being on our own deep in the Maryland woods, separated from the elements only by nylon tent walls, sleeping bags, and Mr. Moses's tough love, we were among other troops, all of them white, as were the Boy Scouts of America administrators in charge of us. Mr. Moses didn't go, which had something to do with the way things turned out.

Our troop got split into two campsites of six boys each. We slept two to a tent. My tentmate was Chris, who was nearly as light skinned as Anthony Wilson. Chris was bigger than me—everybody was—lean and well-muscled like an athlete; I have a memory, like a movie still, of Chris bare chested, chopping wood. I liked Chris, or I like the memory I have of him, because it is possible that I'm projecting backward, and I understand now, if I didn't then, the difference between gruffness and playfulness, on the one hand, and meanness on the other. I knew some mean boys when I was thirteen, but Chris was not one of them, not even when he said to me—an allusion to the fact that we in this campsite called ourselves the Bears—"You ain't no bear. You a cub." When he asked about one of the merit badges on the sleeve of my uniform, and I told him it was for "scholastic stuff," he said, "Aw, you punk." But it was Chris who, during long days when the six of us sat around the campsite like soldiers waiting to be sent to the front—and I will come to why we were doing that—it was Chris who came to where I was sitting in the tent reading a comic book and said to me gently, like a parent, "Why don't you come out and hang out for a while?"

"Don't make him put down that comic book," said Little Darryl, one of my Lincoln Heights friends. "That's his life."

He was telling the truth. To the extent that I was connected to life, to the world, superhero comics formed one of the few thin but strong threads. That had been particularly true since the previous summer, when I read *Origins of Marvel Comics*, by Stan Lee, detailing the creation of my favorite costumed heroes—Spider-Man, the Fantastic Four—and the human fears and insecurities they felt behind their masks. I felt I was them, without their masks or powers. And the world contained between the covers of those thin books was filled to bursting, overflowing, with the most wonderful words. (A couple of years later, when I used a word I'd learned from Marvel—"pummel"—in one of my own stories, one of my sisters, a graduate student, said she'd never heard it before.) There were the words the characters spoke, but even better were those in the narration at the tops of the panels, those wonderful, em dash- and ellipsis-filled musings that helped make sense of what I was seeing. ("Faster than mortal mind can comprehend . . . faster than the *speed of thought* itself . . . two gallant figures pierce the fabric of *infinity* as they hurtle towards . . .") When I wasn't reading Marvel comics, I was trying to create Marvel-like characters of my own. I had, to put it generously, a long way to go, but how I enjoyed the process, the struggle to get the drawings right, or what I thought was right, the joy of having the time, as I didn't in my regular life, to think of what to say.

If I had a favorite Marvel hero, it was probably the Silver Surfer, the gleaming bald alien who was trapped on Earth and both deplored and failed to understand human violence. He rode the skies on a surfboard, which was a little like my skateboard. He hated a fight, the Silver Surfer did, but if you picked one with him, you'd know you were in it. Oh, to be the Silver Surfer . . .

But about the reason we were just hanging out at the campsite:

On our first evening there, looking around that slightly slanted, grass-and-dirt-and-rock-covered clearing surrounded by trees, I took it upon myself to dispose of food waste left by whichever scouts had stayed there before us. I found what I thought was a good spot, amid some trees a little ways outside the clearing, and dumped it—not knowing what I was letting us all in for. A day or so later, some senior scouts came by our site to check on us, and this was when our single friendly interaction with others took place. One of the senior scouts was a pimply-faced sixteen-year-old whose name I have forgotten. Let's call him Jake. He and Chris, who was the strongest guy in our campsite, had a competition to see who could pump our heavy iron cooking grill over his head the greater number of times. I don't remember who won. I do remember that later that day, or the next day, some adult administrators came to inspect our site. Jake was with them. They nailed us for two infractions. One was that the food waste was too close to the site. Other guys in our troop, who apparently had not seen me dispose of the food, said it had to have been put there by the previous occupants. I said nothing. The other infraction was that the grill was on the ground and not on the stone stove, where it belonged. Jake said nothing. For those two things we were confined to our campsite.

(After the administrators left, there was talk among us, although not from me, of catching Jake alone and teaching him a lesson. No doubt fortunately for us, nothing came of that.) And here, I suppose, was my first experience—I don't expect ever to say I've had my last—with the unprovable suspicion that plagues every single black American. Would a white troop have been grounded for these infractions, or was our punishment a way to avoid dealing with half a dozen black boys? Here, too, was possibly my first experience with those racially charged situations, always different and always the same, in which the truth manages to be elusive for a few and clear as summer rain for many others. In this case, at least two people knew important things they chose not to say, or felt unable to say, or couldn't find the words for; and I suspect it is that way much of the time.

3. FALL

Dana West was Troop 77's senior patrol leader—the head scout. He was the oldest of my Lincoln Heights friends; the October that I was thirteen, he turned sixteen. The best thing you could call somebody, in that time and place, was "bad." Dana—handsome, lanky, on the light side, short brown hair—was bad. He had sex with girls, or said he did. ("I'm tired of bustin' virgins," he told me one time. I barely knew what he was talking about.) He knew how to fight, standing toe to toe with Mr. Moses when the two of them horsed around, even getting the better of him a couple of times, pouring on punches with those big fists of his while Mr. Moses turned his face sideways and covered it, laughing in amazement, "*Hoooooo . . .*"

And Dana tried to teach me to fight. Why he did is one of the great mysteries of my life. Or maybe the mystery is why I wonder. Why shouldn't Dana have cared enough about me to want to spend his time teaching me self-defense? I've been told a number of times in my life that I am hard to get to know, and I wonder if the reason is that I don't know why anyone would want to know me—I'm simply not that interesting—and I have an unease with people who make the effort, an unease stemming from distrust, especially if they seem different from or more interesting than me.

Dana, in some ways, was as different from me as it was possible to be, and yet I not only liked but trusted him, I think because I sensed one way that we were alike. There was a questing in him, a longing for an unnamable something that transcended his surroundings. And I think he sensed, because of my gentleness, detachment, and reputation for book smarts, that I held a key to that mysterious something. Dana would hang out in my basement or my backyard and unspool great stretches of talk, not knowing the meanings of all the words he used or even, some of the time, what he was talking about: observations about girls and boys, his very large family, assessments of our mutual friends based on their zodiac signs, pronouncements about blacks and whites. "I'ma tell you, boy," he would start out, and he would tell me a story—"I was walking downtown, and I seen these Africans get out a limousine, they was wearing white robes and headdresses and their skin was so smooth and *black*, man, and *beautiful*, it *glowed* it was so black . . . ." Some of what Dana said seems, in retrospect, like undigested chunks of philosophy and theories of history that came from Elijah Muhammad by way of Malcolm X and were disseminated far and wide to eager hearers, including a man Dana spent a lot of time with.

His name was Kenny. I don't know how old he was; he may have been thirty or forty-four. I don't know what he did for a living—the things you don't think to ask, or even wonder, when you're thirteen! I do know that he kept a lot of boys around him, a dozen or so of them present the one time I went with Dana to Kenny's apartment, about a twenty-minute walk in the autumn air from my house. There was talking and joking, there were games of dominoes and demonstrations of form in kung fu, a version of which was the main thing Kenny passed on to his young disciples.

And that is what Dana passed on to me in my basement. We would stand facing each other; he would aim one fist at me while the other returned, in rhythm, to his hip; and my arms, making circles in the air, would block his punches. Then we switched off. What a beating my forearms, those unmuscled sticks, took during those sessions. It didn't matter if I was blocking punches or throwing them—sixty or seventy times per minute my arms collided with Dana's, which were like heavily veined baseball bats. He told me not to massage my arms afterward or shake off the pain: "Absorb it. It makes you stronger." We practiced kicks; we practiced the alphabet, each letter a bodily position, one flowing into the next. Where was all this heading? To the point where, according to Dana, people would see me fight off somebody stupid enough to pick on me and say to themselves, "That nigger *know* some'm."

I struggle, now, to describe the effect all of this had on me. I would love to tell you about an instance when a bully from the previous year tried to pick on the new, Dana-trained me and found himself on the floor, dazed, with the imprint of my brown Wallabee on his cheek—but I would be writing fiction. The truth is that other boys, all of them bigger than me, would still casually pick on me. Once, in the hallway, a beefy kid named Ricardo thought it would be funny to bring his big blue three-ring notebook, thicker than the Yellow Pages and harder, down on the back of my head. I turned around and punched him in the stomach and chest as he laughed; I might as well have been hitting the side of the Chrysler Building. But I *did* hit back, and maybe, if there was an outer difference in me, that was it. Another time, a guy I was friendly with reached toward me, playfully, to take something of mine; to his surprise, and mine too, my foot knocked away his wrist. And my foot, defining its small, tight arc in the air, may have defined the parameters of the change in me. The world did not look at me and say to itself, "That nigger *know* some'm." I don't even know if *I* thought I knew anything. But there was *something* going on, even if only I could see it, even if I didn't have the words for it.

Whatever it was, I hadn't become a fighter. Once, on a sunny day when we were outside during a Boy Scout meeting, on the sloping lawn of the church where we met, a very stupid kid named Brian did something—I don't remember what, and I'm not sure I even knew at the time—that annoyed Dana. Dana told me to beat him up: "Take care of my light work" was how he put it. I didn't refuse, but neither did I do it. Later, at my house, Dana told me in an even tone that I had shown "too much softheartedness." I didn't argue, but neither did I think he was right. Assuming I could have beat Brian up, I saw no reason to.

That didn't prevent a graduation of sorts, a kind of ceremony in my basement that involved Dana's using the words "by the power vested in me" and presenting me with a gold-colored medallion—it showed two guys fighting—and giving me a new name: Ming Yang Fu.

When I told my mother that, she tried to stifle her laughter, but she couldn't quite.

4. BIRTHDAY

The irony, I suppose, is that one of the strongest threads connecting me to the world in those days, superhero comics, was so much about fighting. My favorite heroes—Thor, Spider-Man, the Silver Surfer—fought supervillains as well as one another. It would be easy to say, from the distance of forty-odd years, that those fights were metaphorical, that they were stand-ins for the difficulties of life, and that I saw them in that light even then; it would be easy, but a lie. I *liked* the fights. They were part of the excitement. But I can say that the fights were not nearly all that attracted me. There were the human failings of the characters, and there was also the power—it seemed powerful to me, as I was then—of Stan Lee's writing. And there was the other irony. The words that so often failed me in my daily life—failed me with girls, with friends, with my own mother, in situations in which silence equaled dishonesty—these words made up so much of what I embraced in comics.

That year I had an English teacher who gave us a list of vocabulary words. One of them was "mark." Her example of its usage: "It is not polite to mark the way people talk." When I said to her privately, "Isn't it 'mock'?" she said, "It's both." ("That is *so wrong*," one of my sisters said when I told her.) But my teacher was on the ball in other ways—one, anyhow. She assigned us *The Catcher in the Rye* and, unbeknownst to her, and for a long time unbeknownst to me, changed my world.

Here is where I was with my understanding of novels: I didn't get why Holden Caulfield was the name of the person speaking to me in a real voice—so real that I assumed he was an actual person—when the name on the cover was J. D. Salinger. I read the book slowly, oh so slowly, enraptured. That solid-purple cover with the yellow lettering: I sat with it nights at the counter in our tiny kitchen, after my mother had left for work and my grandmother had gone to bed; I read it in the tiny yellow bedroom where I opened this essay, the view of the A-frame across the street now dark and peaceful.

My birthday approached, my fourteenth. This was the one that, by unspoken agreement in our neighborhood, made you somebody. When I was eleven and Dana turned fourteen, he'd said to me in wonder, as if a song he'd written had gone to number one on the *Billboard* chart, "I'm fourteen, Cliff." The previous year, when my friend Big Darryl was acting superior, Little Darryl said, "That sweet fo'teen went to his head." I wanted to finish *Catcher* before I turned fourteen, ahead of my class's schedule, so I stayed up the night before my birthday until I did. There, talking to me in my bedroom, was a Marvel superhero without the superpowers, who said that he couldn't get into fights because he couldn't stand the thought of his fist in the other guy's face, whose story, it became clear as the last page approached, was not going to end in any way I was used to thinking of endings. Here were words without fights, or words that replaced fights, words that could be for me what fighting was in our neighborhood: a way of being in the world.

The next day, fourteen years old, after breakfast with Ma and Grandma, I went to school and told some kids, as they took their seats in the chair-desks in my English class, that I had finished reading the book. Not believing me, they asked me to prove it by telling them the last line. I recited, "Don't ever tell anybody anything. If you do, you start missing everybody." They looked at me, not knowing what to say. ■

THROW ME SOMETHIN' MISTA*
Mona Lisa Saloy

Throw me somethin' Mista
Throw me my pride in my step
Throw me my ancestors here, so we can *Cha Wa* & chat 'bout them,
    & now
Throw me my Motha, alive well before age 50 dancin' whole
Doin' dishes & trying to sing the Christmas song like
Nat King Cole *"Chestnuts roasting on an open fire . . . ."*
Throw me into a good Penny Party in the back yard when
Chunks of watermelon on a stick cold makes me forget
it Was 98 degrees in the shade
Throw me a tomorrow of equal humanity working together for a
Better life a better planet a better truth
Throw me into space, the
Galaxy glowing glad on God's Love
Picturing a peaceful earth from my left-eye view
Throw me a penal system eclipsed of profit &
Promoting rehabilitation not at the expense of voting rights
Throw me a new Constitution that eliminates the Electoral College
    now, whose need is Outdated by technology; they don't always
    vote with the people!
Throw me a real "for true" American Democracy where the people's
    vote counts

[*In New Orleans, parade-goer request for beads from float riders.]
[*Cha Wa:* Black Warrior (commonly ref. as Indian) Street Parade in Neighborhoods]
[Penny Party: a yard party where the entrance fee is by waist size.]

4 MY SISTER 2
Mona Lisa Saloy
Praise Song for Barbara Ann

Sometimes I call her BAP
Black American Princess
She the beautiful
Beating out Shirley Temple smiles at 5, attending Martinez Black
Creole pre-school speaking French Spanish skipping first grade, but
she recalls the turn.
When Daddy returned from WWII, a Sergeant, black-iron pot cook,
poet, Hungry to hug his first girl
Sis asked Daddy, "who are you?"
Threw her bread down on the gravel street in protest, and
Daddy fresh from seeing French kids eating rodents &
begging for food, demanded she pick up the bread, eat it.
Aries horns reared, she stood her in her pride, then
Daddy slapped her straight—"don't waste food!"

Because Mother sewed tropical seersucker suits by day, it was
Sis who walked me through girlhood, assuring me
I could keep swimming even when "jim crow" said no.
Stuck with me as audience, she do-whopped with other 7th Ward
Creole girls, danced at home under blue-light backyard parties. Sis
made sputniks out of halved-oranges & toothpicks with cheese per-
fectly cube cut at the ends, to Etta James, Fats Domino, or Bobby Blue
Bland slow drags with handsome Black Creole boys of every hue &
height under Mother's watchful eyes after Daddy strung lights from
fences for their fun after dark.

In her prom photo,
Sis is pretty as a young Dorothy Dandridge or Lena Horne &
Daddy afraid for her beauty,
still a heavy hand on her freedom.
Summers, we swam in water shows like Esther Williams,
she & I always centered in a heart made of the best swimmers in
Hardin Park each year with glued sequins on our swim caps to grand
applause from crowds around the city pool—
she the beauty,

me the athlete & geek.
Both of us inhale good books,
brain food for the senses & spirit.

One day, she announced she was leaving,
marrying a tall drink of hurricane, handsome too,
cut his '55 Chevy into a sports car called Lizzy with
painted black footprints the size of my 12-year-old fingertips on the
side mirror. She,
out of Daddy's house for the west coast,
left one jail for another.

Once Mother died, and Daddy drowned his grief in booze, broads,
drunken parties with strange men, there for the Jack Daniels, peering
into my bedroom once Daddy's face fell flat into the *Courtboullion* dinner I left for him; had to go, landed on my sister's doorstep with one
bag and a new coat I bought with savings from lifeguarding or selling
pleat-and-tuck pillows, hand sewed on Mother's Singer.

Stuck between scared & the next day, I cleaned, cooked their dinners,
cared for my nephew, washed & ironed their clothes, being useful and
avoiding a future. My Sister set me up for interviews with the activist
son, Larry Gossett, of her postal co-worker friend, Ms. Johnny, made
me go to college, so I went kicking & screaming, then took to it like a
catfish hugging river silt; by Grace, I did more.

Through four degrees, her hubby chided me,
"Negro, when you gonna get a real job?" All along the way, I sewed for big
guys—Garfield Heard, Big "Foots" Bob Lanier, Bob MacAdoo, Globe
Trotters, boy bands, and Sis sent me love boxes of beans, peas, stock-
ings, priceless presents. She said, go ahead; you do what I couldn't,
study.

Once a Ph.D., brother-in-law, tempered by fighting to stay in unions, to
earn rightful pay for his journeyman sheet-metal skills, and me working
for the R1, he shook his head;
I did alright, he admitted.

My sister outlived the love of her life, survives cancer for the second
time in over 30 years, has two new knees that holler in airport security
checks, a grown son, sweet friends, & we Jazz Fest each year in the
Crescent City.

These days, I call her *Execu-Sis*, who fundraises for the
Central District Senior Center, on a hill overlooking Lake Washington;
she Chairs their Board, escorts her elders to St. Therese for Sunday
service, Rides ferries in Puget Sound with her multicultural book club
of ladies, all *Sistas*.

Today, when the neighborhood owls call morning to light, before the
hum of interstate traffic rises, I have a dark cherry & soy smoothie, put
on the decaf, with chicory of course, plan to play something smooth by
Gregory Porter—"Painted on Canvas" one of our favs, & give thanks
for Sister love in my life.

AN AMERICAN RIGHT
Jerald Walker

There is Don Cornelius, fly as ever in a red velvet blazer with matching bow tie, four-inch platform shoes, his afro a magnificent dome. "Put your hands together," he's saying, "for the *mighty, mighty* Ojays!" I crank up the volume on my laptop before starting to dance, spinning and dipping like I'm a teenager back in the hood throwing down for some honeys and not fifty-six with a bad knee and short thinning hair I call an *after*-fro. Before long I've worked up a sweat and some good memories of growing up in a community vastly different from the ones I've known the last forty years, notable for their well-funded schools, farmers' markets, and lack of minorities. My wife was raised in such a community, and it's where we've raised our two sons. I'm the only member of our family, then, whose formative years were spent immersed in a culture so unbelievably awesome it compels me to reenact parts of it, though that's nothing, I concede, compared to how it inspired one white woman to adopt it as her own, even going the extra mile of wearing blackface.

Not a *literal* black face, I should stress, which I appreciate, since, in all of humankind, no one's is. But that fact hasn't stopped folks from continuing to reach for the shoe polish. They usually do it around Halloween because Halloween, to some privileged minds, is an acceptable occasion to be a Negro with an impossible complexion. Now and then they even claim to be *honoring* African Americans, but that's about as logical as had it been said of the original nineteenth-century minstrels, who I know, as an academic familiar with the topic, and as a person of common sense, would not have gone to such absurd lengths to distort their subjects' features if honoring had been the intent. Burnt cork would never have entered the equation. Nor the white or red lips. Nor the clownish clothes. Nor the shit-eating grins. Nor the bucked eyes, as if, audiences no doubt assumed, they were constantly taking in the sight of an unguarded watermelon, or of a relative on an auction block, or of, on the distant, unreachable horizon, freedom.

I hate these caricatures. Especially when they're perpetuated by public figures, such as, for example, Ted Danson, Howard Stern and Sarah Silverman. It bothers me nearly as much when the perpetrators are randos because randos sometimes end up being public figures, such as, for example, Governor Ralph Northam of Virginia, Governor Kay Ivey of Alabama, and Florida's secretary of state, Mike Ertel. Unlike entertainers, however, who at least can claim professional motives for blacking up, the motivation for randos is *at best* amusement, which is why, later in life, many of them would prefer to go to their graves without their dabbles in minstrelsy being widely known. But we live in a day and age where everything is, if not widely known, widely knowable. Particularly if you are among the most public of public figures, such as, for example, prime minister of Canada.

When Justin Trudeau's blackface photos emerged in 2019, he'd already established a reputation as an open-minded progressive, so I was willing to give him a pass, until he tried to explain himself. "The fact is," he said, "I didn't understand how hurtful this is to people who live with discrimination every single day." *That's nonsense*, I thought, and yet I wasn't surprised to hear it since feigning ignorance of racist behavior is directly out of the privilege playbook. Nevertheless, I gave Trudeau the benefit of the doubt, deciding the more likely scenario was that, as he dug his fingers into a fresh tin of Kiwi, he vacillated between two conflicting thoughts—*This will be a hit!* and *This is so wrong!*—although those thoughts, it could be argued, were actually in accord, as one of the photos shows him flanked by three fawning women and, three decades later, he was the subject of ridicule and scorn. In any event, he weathered the storm, which wasn't surprising either because powerful white men seeking, and receiving, second chances is a privilege too.

Rachel Anne Dolezal has not fared as well. But despite being neither male nor powerful, she at least might have avoided subsisting primarily on welfare, and her lucrative job offers could have extended beyond reality TV and porn, had her version of blackface been confined to a few hours, rather than thirteen years, and counting. She'd already been at it for eight in 2015 when a reporter, with a camera recording nearby, thrust a microphone before her and asked if she was black. The question appeared to stun her, and maybe, at that moment, if Justin Trudeau had had two thoughts, she had but one: *My life is ruined*. It was a life that included being president of the Spokane, Washington, chapter of the NAACP, an instructor of Africana studies at Eastern Washington University, and a police ombudsperson with a reputation as a well-regarded and effective civil rights advocate. Soon all that would be behind her, as behind her, figuratively speaking, as the reporter who watched wide-eyed when she fled without answering his question.

The answer was this: her parents were white and, when asked about their daughter's race, confirmed she was too. They were ashamed of and embarrassed by her, starting back when, as an undergraduate, she wore

dashikis and head wraps and permed and dyed her hair so that it resembled a curly brown afro when she wasn't wearing it in braids. She dated
black men, got impregnated by and married one, attended an HBCU
for graduate studies, and, in 2008, bridged the gap between her affinity
for blackness and her biological whiteness with tanning and makeup. She
darkened her skin to a color of just enough ethnic ambiguity that she
could have been any number of things, really, with African American, as
is often the case in such instances, being the default. At first, when new
friends and acquaintances sought to confirm this impression, she gave
rambling, convoluted responses about strongly identifying with black
culture and being enlisted in the struggle, but in time that approach gave
way to a deception just short of lying, whereby she stated her mother
was white. Sometimes the white parent was her father. Eventually the
inquiries ceased, which may have ultimately led to her undoing because
she lowered her guard and, in the moment of truth with the reporter,
faltered. By the time she had regained her footing enough to refer to
herself as "transblack," it would be too late for many, and, for others,
too ludicrous.

But some people found it neither. These were the people who believe
that race and culture, like gender, can be and often are fluid. People
who support the concept of self-identification. And people like one of
Dolezal's former colleagues at the NAACP who said that her real or per-
ceived race was not the issue, but rather what good she was doing for the
black community. She must have found great comfort in his words, as they
were in stark contrast to others being hurled at her like brass-knuckled
fists. "Blackface remains racist," said one critic, "no matter how down
with the cause a white person is." Another called her "the undisputed
heavyweight champion of cultural appropriation."

Cultural appropriation, generally defined as the taking of another's
property or culture without permission and often for monetary gain, was,
of course, at the core of minstrelsy's origins, so there is no denying the
poisoned soil from which the phrase grew. But there is also no denying
that the phrase has come to mean "cultural prohibition," which is to say
that only certain people can do certain things with impunity. For adapting
blues, country and gospel, Elvis is considered a prime violator, but so too,
for having the audacity as a person of Puerto Rican descent to blend
jazz, soul and hip-hop, is Bruno Mars. Other offenders include Miley
Cyrus, Eminem, Justin Timberlake, Post Malone and, as much for her
music as her fashion, Madonna. Madonna, true to her nature, pushed
back. "I'm inspired and I'm referencing other cultures," she has said.
"That is my right as an artist." Change *artist* to *American* and, in essence,
she's channeling Ralph Ellison.

"It is here," Ellison wrote in 1978,

> on the level of culture, that the diverse elements of our various backgrounds, our heterogeneous pasts, have indeed come together, "melted," and undergone metamorphosis. It is here, if we would but recognize it, that elements of the many available tastes, traditions, ways of life, and values that make up the total culture have been ceaselessly appropriated and made their own—consciously, unselfconsciously, or imperialistically—by groups and individuals to whose own backgrounds and traditions they are historically alien. Indeed, it was through this process of cultural appropriation (and misappropriation) that Englishmen, Europeans, Africans, and Asians *became* Americans.

Cultural metamorphoses, then, including those aided by ultraviolet rays and Maybelline, are as American as apple pie, though I suspect even Ellison would have felt there was something slightly amiss by the one undergone by Dolezal. Why, after all, if to her mind she had truly *become* black, didn't she stand her ground, à la Madonna, when challenged by the reporter? But to be clear: assuming for argument's sake that she'd answered in the affirmative and thrust a bronzed fist into the air, she still would have received hostile blowback, just as Tiger Woods did when he, in recognition of his assorted bloodline, self-identified as "Cablinasian." Beliefs of race in this country are too simplistic to accept that level of nuance without a fight, and yet, because it is only in that level of nuance where racism stands to be defeated, the fight must be taken on; this, it seems to me, is the moral of Dolezal's story. Her failure to articulate it from the start, however, and in behaving like someone caught in the act of committing a diabolical con, resulted in such a loss of credibility that later, when she presented her "trans" defense, the person I thought of, by way of comparison, was not Laverne Cox but Tootsie.

But what I find entirely credible, largely due to Dolezal's upbringing, is her professed love of black culture, and I believe that, unlike nineteenth-century minstrels, or their Halloween-going descendants, her motive for darkening her skin *was* to honor African Americans. When she was in her teens, for instance, her parents adopted four black kids and she sought to build their self-esteem and counter the racism they endured in their rural Montana town by teaching them black history. "A funny thing happened," she said of that process, "I began to feel even more connected to it myself." Connected enough that at college she joined the black student association. She even asked to be one of its officers, which was met with skepticism by some of the members. "I delivered an overly earnest speech explaining how passionate I was about black culture," she later explained, "how I'd always felt a connection with blackness, and about how deeply I cared about my siblings' future." The speech worked. She was approved for the position she sought, which represented her informal induction into the black community, from which, fifteen years later, she would be informally expelled. That outcome, as she described it, was "very painful," and, knowing something of what it means to be a part of and then apart from the black community, I find that credible too.

And yet "very painful" isn't how I describe my circumstances, as I have not, formally or informally, been expelled from anything. No one questions my race. By virtue of my complexion, no less my birth certificate, my indulging in black culture is approved. What I feel, then, from my outpost of white suburbia, is the intense ache of nostalgia. And when it seizes me, I often soothe it with a little old-school boogying, as I'm soothing it again now, though this time I'm not throwing down for some imaginary honeys but rather a single real one. My wife is laughing at my moves, as usual, so I'm not sure she takes me seriously when I mention an idea for a party. It'll be a house party, I explain, like the ones I attended back in the hood, only this time, given our community's demographics, the attendees will be white. I'll serve them all the classics of my youth, I say: collard greens, sweet potatoes, fried chicken, corn bread, stewed okra, and, for dessert, a rum cake so rummy, as was my mother's legendary version, that it'll fail to fully rise. And I'll play R&B oldies on a loop, so I anticipate there'll be a great deal of singing and, later, after the meal has digested, and possibly with the aid of a good port, a *Soul Train* line too. Maybe I'll host this party once a month. And maybe my neighbors will come to think of it as a safe space where they can, as is their American right, be awesome. ■

. . . STAYED ON FREEDOM[1]
Jan Willis

I.

As I write this, in 2020, we in these United States sit in the midst of three crises: one caused by the new and frightening coronavirus; another, the economic disaster that has resulted the world over from it, as businesses, banks, and factories have been forced to shutter their doors; and still another in the form of the ongoing, though now more apparent, racism and police brutality that has been the stuff of this country's existence since its creation. We are witnessing, some perhaps for the first time, the intertwining and interconnectedness of these various phenomena all together.

Amidst these overlapping crises, I have been thinking lately a lot about "freedom." Especially about what freedom might feel like for black people on this continent, after centuries of never actually knowing it here.

"We hold these truths to be self-evident . . . that all men are created equal . . ."[2] Lofty words to be sure, but words spoken by white men who—even as those very words were spoken—kept black bodies enslaved in order to bring them, the white folk, profit. We sit amidst a grave paradox here, in a country that proclaims freedom for all but was founded on the genocide of Native Americans and the theft of their lands on the one hand, and on the forced labor of captured and enslaved Africans on the other. Once viewed only as chattel, degraded, denigrated, and denied full humanity, black people have for centuries continued to be viewed here as being less than human and as "only fit to be slaves" by white men who see no shame nor moral imperative to view us otherwise. When will

---

1   This phrase forms part of the revised gospel song "Woke Up This Morning with My Mind Stayed on Jesus." The young Freedom Singers of the civil rights movement (Bernice Johnson Reagon and others) changed the wording to ". . . My Mind Stayed on Freedom." In this version, it became a staple of the movement, sung at many marches.

2   The words beginning the second paragraph of the U.S. Declaration of Independence, signed July 4, 1776.

we be viewed by them as free men and women? When will we be able to view *ourselves* as free human beings?

James Baldwin famously said, "Not everything that is faced can be changed; but nothing can be changed until it is faced."[3] White Americans must face their great "original sin"[4] against people of color (red, brown, and black), a sin of their own, white, creation. We must together—as a country of full-fledged *citizens*—recognize and speak this truth. The truth that puts a lie to the fairy tale of American democracy for all. It is our only way to salvation, to a true multiracial democracy.

In a 1964 essay titled "The White Problem," Baldwin identified the "lie" that white Americans told themselves in order to keep black people slaves here:

> The people who settled the country had a fatal flaw. They could recognize a man when they saw one. They knew he wasn't . . . anything *else* but a man; but since they were Christian, and since they had already decided that they came here to establish a free country, the only way to justify the role this chattel was playing in one's life was to say that he *was not* a man. For if he wasn't, then no crime had been committed. That lie is the basis of our present trouble.[5]

---

3   This quote comes from the unfinished book Baldwin was writing when he died. Its focus was on the lives and times of three civil rights icons, Medgar Evers, Martin Luther King, Jr., and Malcolm X. Raoul Peck made the quote a central theme of his documentary on Baldwin, *I Am Not Your Negro*.

4   This characterization of slavery was advanced by James Madison, one of the nation's "founding fathers" and its fourth president. But one description of Madison's ambivalence (Paris Amanda Spies-Gans, "James Madison," The Princeton & Slavery Project, https://slavery.princeton.edu.) states the following: Madison's antislavery thinking seems to have been strongest during the 1780s—at the height of Revolutionary politics. But by the early 1800s, when in a position to truly impact policy, he failed to follow through on these views. In February 1801 Madison Sr. died, leaving Montpelier and more than one hundred slaves to James Madison, as his eldest son. The following week, Thomas Jefferson became President of the United States and appointed Madison as his Secretary of State. Madison managed Montpelier from afar, yet took no concrete steps toward freeing his slaves or changing the plantation system. Upon becoming the fourth President of the United States in 1809, Madison brought slaves to serve him in the White House.

5   Cited in Glaude Jr., *Begin Again*, 9.

W. E. B. Du Bois had argued in his 1903 work, *The Souls of Black Folk*, especially in its chapter 2 (titled "Of the Dawn of Freedom"), that regardless of the governmental freedoms supposedly granted to the newly freed man following the Civil War, the Negro remained enslaved through more modern measures. The Freedmen's Bureau had been closed long before its work was actually done. And, while no longer literally chained to their masters on plantations, Negroes remained un-free and segregated in the United States. Du Bois therefore concluded the chapter by saying that "the problem of the Twentieth Century is [and we might say, still remains] the problem of the color-line." I think that, deep down, what we might say today (some 115 years after Du Bois first commented on this) is that we black folks are still waiting for our *full-fledged freedom* in these United States of America. We still wonder what that freedom might *feel* like. We still *yearn* for it. We sing mournfully in our churches for it, wondering aloud, "How long, oh Lord, how long?" This yearning is the same, I believe, as the longing expressed by the young rapper J. Cole, in his 2014 rap "Be Free" (which he dedicated to Michael Brown and Eric Garner).[6] The rap's refrain says:

All we want to do is be free.
All we want to do is take the chains off.
All we want to do is break the chains off.
All we want to do is be free.

The chains, finally, were "taken off" after 250 years of slavery, *once—* but only for a brief moment—following the Civil War. And immediately thereafter, for twelve to thirteen years, "African Americans" showed themselves to be *ready* for freedom. After all, as the civil rights song said, their minds had been "stayed on freedom"! And during the period known as "Reconstruction," this country witnessed a veritable overnight transformation—as blacks ran for, and VOTED for, various public offices, and built and ran schools and churches, and rebuilt their families. Blacks took their freedom and hurried to grab citizenship, which, alone, could continue to evidence and to ensure their freedom.

But seeing blacks in businesses and schools and positions once only reserved for whites was too much for some hateful whites, who began almost immediately to craft new forms of enslavement and new controls over black bodies, *more modern measures.* As Carol Anderson has said, they

---

6   J. Cole performed this rap on a segment of the *Late Show with David Letterman* in 2016. It is available on YouTube at https://www.youtube.com/watch?v=qQZc8SH6EFk.

began their project to "reconstruct Reconstruction."[7]

They moved quickly to reinterpret, reinvent, and totally revise the actual history of the Civil War, dubbing it their grand "Lost Cause." They began a campaign of segregation, and of terror . . . the kind of terror we saw demonstrated by those policemen who murdered George Floyd before our very eyes. They instituted laws to segregate, mark, humiliate, and re-enslave us. They founded organizations like the Klan and built prisons to rehouse us. And other Americans, other free men, did not see it, nor care to see it.

In a speech delivered in 1926 called "Criteria of Negro Art," Du Bois asked:

> What do we want? What is the thing we are after? As it was phrased last night it had a certain truth: We want to be Americans, full-fledged Americans, with all the rights of other American citizens. But is that all? Do we want simply to be Americans? Once in a while through all of us there flashes some clairvoyance, some clear idea, of what America really is. We who are dark can see America in a way that white Americans cannot. And seeing our country thus, are we satisfied with its present goals and ideals?[8]

The implication of his last question, I believe, is that perhaps, "we" ("Negroes" or blacks)—because of our unique vantage point and history here—might be able to describe or to say more about what America could, or ought to, be. Dr. King's idea of the Beloved Community might be such a vision. For what is it that we truly want? We want to be treated like any other American; we want to *feel free*, as free as any other American. But is there more?

Here—and in keeping with the theme of art—I cannot pass over a 2020 gem of a book that was "curated" by Natasha Marin, called *Black Imagination*.[9] Marin, together with a few other black women, "planned an exhibition that would de-center whiteness and provide space for healing and validation. [They] agreed to collect sound from black folks of all kinds, and craving nuance over stereotype, sought out black children, black youth, LGBTQ+ black folks, unsheltered black folks, incarcerated black folks, neurodivergent black folks, as well as differently-abled

---

7   Carol Anderson, *White Rage; the Unspoken Truth of Our Racial Divide* (New York: Bloomsbury, 2016), 7–38.

8   Du Bois's speech was later published in *The Crisis* 32 (October 1926): 290–297.

9   Marin, *Black Imagination*.

black folks. . . . Using field recorders, [the team] spent months collecting responses to three prompts: What is your origin story? How do you heal yourself? Describe/imagine a world where you are *loved, safe*, and *valued*."[10] Many of the responses are astounding works of art. Here are just three examples:

1. "I am healthy, whole, and black at the same time."[11]

2. "When I wake up there is someone there who loves me. When I leave my home the people living on my street know my name, know my parents' name, and claim me as their own, drop by with soup when I am sick and small gifts during holidays. And I do the same for them. We break bread together. We laugh and dance and work and build together. Wherever I go I am known and I know others. We greet each other with smiles and hugs. Our expressions are always genuine. We don't hide resentments between clenched teeth or anger in clenched fists. We say the words that need saying. We speak and listen and forgive and understand. We are peaceful in our hearts and actions and our peace is never built on the sacrifice of another's peace. Our community is not built on the suffering of others. We live in balance, never taking more than we need, never needing so much we can't sustain ourselves. And each of us are honored and valued and respected as equal members of a collective irrespective of age, ability, ethnicity, gender, or any other political descriptor. We bring all of who we are."[12]

3. "Close your eyes—
   Make the white
   gaze disappear."[13]

---

10   Ibid., 11.
11   Ibid., 9.
12   Ibid., 31.
13   Ibid., 15.

Yes, yes. To be sure. The "forty acres and a mule"[14] once promised to newly freed former slaves would certainly have helped us to make a dent in the economic inequities caused by the centuries-long one-sided cruelty of slavery, that most "peculiar institution."[15] We had indeed labored *without pay* for 250 years, under lash and unspeakable torture. It might have gotten us onto a path of economic equity to have a modicum of land and a means to till it. But can money, or "back pay," ever truly "repay" such brutality? Such degradation? Such trauma? Such soul-crushing pain and barbarity? Reparations, yes, perhaps. But something more is needed. Something much more valuable.

II. WE AFRICAN AMERICANS HAD BEEN "FREED" —BUT WITH CONDITIONS.

On January 1 of 1863, President Abraham Lincoln's Emancipation Proclamation was declared. It stated:

> That on the first day of January, in the year of our Lord one thousand eight hundred and sixty-three, all persons held as slaves within any State or designated part of a State, the people whereof shall then be in rebellion against the United States, shall be then, thenceforward, and *forever free*.

Lincoln had proposed the proclamation the year before, on September 22, 1862, in what became known as the preliminary Emancipation Proclamation. He had made it clear to the Confederate states, in public, that if they did not return to the Union by January 1, 1863, he would issue a proclamation freeing slaves in those rebellious territories. So, we must note that the "Emancipation Proclamation" did NOT offer freedom to *all* enslaved folk. Rather, as a warning to the Confederacy, and in order to recruit former slaves from those states to

14 "Forty acres and a mule" was a phrase echoed throughout the South in the aftermath of the Civil War, asserting the right of newly freed African American to redistributed lands—particularly those plantations confiscated by U.S. troops during the war—as compensation for unpaid labor during slavery. Many historians trace the phrase to a specific order issued by General William Tecumseh Sherman as Special Field Orders Number 15.

15 The use of the expression "peculiar institution"—"peculiar" here means "special," possibly with a positive implication—to refer to Southern slavery began in 1830 with leading Southern politician John C. Calhoun and became widespread.

join the Union ranks, it promised freedom to those slaves still living in the so-called Confederate states.

The ten states in rebellion as of September 22, 1862, had no intention of returning to the Union, and on January 1, 1863, Lincoln signed the final Emancipation Proclamation, which had, by then, several changes, including a provision that allowed freed slaves to fight in the Union army. In the four states within the Union where slavery *remained legal*, nothing changed for black slaves.

Owing to recent events, especially following the brutal killing of George Floyd in May, many white Americans have just learned about Juneteenth.[16] June 19, 1865, is the date when African Americans celebrate "freedom." It is the date when all slaves within the former Confederacy finally learned of Lincoln's Proclamation.

Throughout my childhood, celebrating the Fourth of July meant barbecues and family picnics. We knew that July 4, 1776, marked the revolutionary, democratic break from England and the declaration of a new form of governance for America, democracy. But it carried no depth of feeling for most of us, because we were still enslaved here then. And we would continue to be.

One could say that we agreed with Frederick Douglass on this matter. The great black abolitionist had given a speech about it in 1852 called "What to the Slave is the Fourth of July?" and we had read and recited it in elementary school:

> Am I to argue that it is wrong to make men brutes, to rob them of their liberty, to work them without wages, to keep them igno-rant of their relations to their fellow men, to beat them with sticks, to flay their flesh with the lash, to load their limbs with irons, to hunt them with dogs, to sell them at auction, to sunder their families, to knock out their teeth, to burn their flesh, to starve them into obedience and submission to their masters? . . . No, I will not . . .
>
> What, to the American slave, is your 4th of July? I answer: a day that reveals to him, more than all other days in the year, the gross injustice and cruelty to which he is the constant victim. To him, your celebration is a sham; your boasted liberty, an unholy license; your national greatness, swelling vanity; your sounds of rejoicing are empty and heartless; your denunciation of tyrants,

---

16   The name "Juneteenth" is a combination of the words "June" and "nineteenth," which is the date in 1865 when this powerful moment in African American history took place.

brass fronted impudence; your shouts of liberty and equality, hollow mockery; your prayers and hymns, your sermons and thanksgivings, with all your religious parade and solemnity, are, to him, mere bombast, fraud, deception, impiety and hypocrisy—a thin veil to cover up crimes which would disgrace a nation of savages. There is not a nation on the earth guilty of practices more shocking and bloody than are the people of the United States, at this very hour. . . . For revolting barbarity and shameless hypocrisy, America reigns without a rival.[17]

My grandparents and the other blacks that I knew also celebrated Juneteenth, the date when the (former) slaves in Texas finally received the message that President Lincoln had proclaimed the "freedom proclamation." That irony was not lost on us. On Juneteenth we always thought of the poor slaves who had labored on under the brutal lash—for two and a half years *after* Lincoln had declared them "freed!"—their slave owners too immoral, and too cruel, to let them know it.

After the freedom proclamation, former slaves had to garner the strength to reinvigorate themselves and to reconstitute their fractured families once again. It was another lie that black folks didn't value family, part of the excuses and justifications proffered for treating them as subhuman chattel. If black people had not treasured their family and kin, and their community—such as it was in the slave quarters—and even though its bonds could be easily broken by the mere whims of a slave owner, we would *not have survived* the harshness and trauma of slavery. But we did survive—because we built kin connections and life-sustaining communities. And we found ways to be human and sometimes, even, to be happy. We had lives, and we found sources of resilience that carried us through our pain. As the young performance artist Joshua Bennett joyously declares in a line of his celebratory poem "Say It, Sing It If the Spirit Leads (After Vievee Francis),"[18] a poem he wrote in 2016 to celebrate Black History Month:

I exist in excess of my anguish!

I observed the post–Civil War reconstituting of black family ties as

17   John W. Blassingame, ed., *The Frederick Douglass Papers: Series One: Speeches, Debates, and Interviews, 1847–1854* (New Haven: Yale University Press, 1982). Cited in Ralph F. Young, *Dissent in America*, 124.

18   Watch and listen to Joshua Bennett perform "Say It, Sing It" on YouTube at https://www.youtube.com/watch?v=R3vpEd4Ce7g.

I worked on my own family's history and genealogy. The project required that I visit county courthouses throughout the South, gathering information about my family's slave ancestry. I wrote about the experience of doing such work:

> "W-h-e-r-e'-re you f-r-o-m?" That question, with all its lilting, accusatory, white Southern drawl, was invariably the very first thing that greeted me whenever I entered a county probate office and asked to be directed to the records room. In at least twenty different Southern counties—throughout rural Alabama, Georgia, and South Carolina—there was not a single variance of that one question. I often wondered, was it my Northern accent? Or the fact that I looked them directly in the eyes? I had little doubt, however, about the meaning of their response. The different clerks were all saying the same thing; each was asking where I'd gone, how I'd lost the sense of "my place."[19]

But I persisted with the work. It was too important. I determined not to let these uninformed individuals stop me.

The work was also difficult for my heart and soul. As I also wrote,

> To begin with, though U. S. census materials have been available since 1790, blacks were not mentioned by name until the census of 1870. This was so because prior to 1870, blacks in this country were mostly the property of slave owners, and as such they were considered to be non-persons. Thus, rather than find names of possible kin, I found only tallies of slaves, listed by their age, sex, color (that is, "B" for Black, or "M" for Mulatto), or specific infirmity ("blind," "idiot"). There were some exceptions. For example, some blacks were free people of color and so were listed as such, and by name. . . . And if a slave somehow lived past her or his 100th birthday, that slave was listed by name, even on the earlier materials.[20]

Wading through reams of census materials for the year 1870, the first year when former slaves were listed with both a first name and a surname, I saw former slaves renaming themselves when first they could. Rather than keep the surnames of their former "owners," they gave themselves new surnames: some, of the country's presidents—"Lincoln"

19   Willis, *Dreaming Me*, 265.
20   Ibid., 272.

and "Washington" were common. Some named themselves after their heart's longing for recognition. I watched as they renamed themselves with the surnames "Self," "Person," and "Worthy." And my heart broke, again and again.

If the Emancipation Proclamation had suggested freedom for once-enslaved beings, the Thirteenth Amendment (to the 1789 Constitution) voiced it, explicitly: No more slavery! Slavery no longer exists in the United States! But the amendment, which passed in December of 1865, did not quite say that, not exactly. There was an "exception" clause.

The Thirteenth Amendment to the U.S. Constitution was well crafted. It provided that "neither slavery nor involuntary servitude, *except as a punishment for crime* whereof the party shall have been duly convicted, shall exist within the United States, or any place subject to their jurisdiction." Almost inevitably, this exception meant that recently enslaved blacks became immediately targeted for prisons. How else does one continue the practice of free labor? In these United States, there are no "un-thinking" decisions when it comes to racial equality, or not.

There are, in fact, three amendments to the Constitution that bear directly upon blacks. Together, they are known as the Civil War Amendments. These three continue to dramatically impact black people's lives today. The Thirteenth Amendment was designed, it is said, to ensure equality for recently emancipated slaves. It banned slavery and involuntary servitude (except in the case of punishment for a crime). The Fourteenth Amendment (ratified in 1868) allegedly "granted citizenship" to all persons born or naturalized in the U.S. and, importantly, guaranteed all citizens "equal protection of the laws." And the Fifteenth Amendment (ratified in 1870) granted African American men the right to vote, declaring that the "right of citizens of the United States to vote shall not be denied or abridged by the United States or by any state on account of race, color, or previous condition of servitude." (White and black women, as we know, would have to wait another five decades.)

And that was that, *or so it seemed.* Blacks henceforth were granted "freedom" from servitude—except if convicted of a crime—*citizenship* and *equal protection under the law* and *the right to vote.*[21] One wants to shout, *Hallelujah!* The Civil War Amendments were indeed the "Big Three" and all three of them *are necessary* if we are to be, in truth, "free" human beings here in America. But *who among us can truthfully say that* any *of these*

---

21 Despite the Fifteenth Amendment, by the late 1870s, discriminatory practices were already being used to prevent blacks from exercising their right to vote, especially in the South.

rights and freedoms still hold for blacks in the U.S. of 2020? Is there any truth or backbone to any them?

I am a child of the Jim Crow South and also of the early marches for civil rights. I have vivid memories of men carrying signs that said "I Am a Man" (in response to decades and centuries of being called, regardless of their age, knowledge or skill, only "boy") and signs saying "I Am Somebody," when that should have been already evident. Today, some sixty years later, the signs say "Black Lives Matter."

In 1963, as a fifteen-year-old tenth grader, I marched with Dr. King and others in the Birmingham civil rights campaign. During those weeks in April and May, we children were fire-hosed by the Birmingham fire department and the police commissioner, Eugene "Bull" Connor, sicced his dogs on some of us. But we continued to march, and we filled his jails. And, in the end, the Birmingham City Council conceded and agreed to desegregate some public accommodations, increase job opportunities for blacks, and provide amnesty to those arrested. A massive sigh of relief and joy went up from Birmingham's blacks. As I would later write about those heady events:

> But white segregationists could not stomach the agreement. On May 11, a bomb exploded at the home of Dr. King's brother. A second blast shattered Dr. King's own headquarters at the Gaston Motel. Some blacks rioted in response. Two hundred and fifty state troopers were sent downtown to keep the peace. White racists' maliciousness continued to smolder. Eventually, the eyes of the nation would be brought once again back to Birmingham when, on September 15 of that same year, four little black girls were killed in the bombing of the Sixteenth Street Baptist Church, and Birmingham came to be known as "Bombing ham."[22]

III. EVEN WITH CONDITIONS, THERE IS BACKLASH

Backlash. There is always backlash. For every step forward in the march toward freedom, there seem to be two steps back. These vengeful reactions are not un-thinking decisions either. They are calculated decisions made at the highest levels of our government. Carol Anderson's superb book *White Rage* chronicles many of these governmental and policy backlashes. A summary of the book lays this out plainly:

---

22   Willis, *Dreaming Me*, 67.

Anderson makes clear that since 1865 and the passage of the Thirteenth Amendment, every time African Americans have made advances toward full participation in our democracy, white reaction—usually in the courts and legislatures—has fueled a deliberate and relentless rollback of their gains. The end of the Civil War and Reconstruction was greeted with Black Codes and Jim Crow. The Great Migration north was physically opposed in many Sothern states, and blacks often found conditions in the North to be no better. The Supreme Court's landmark *1954 Brown v. Board of Education* decision was met with the shutting down of public schools throughout the South while taxpayer dollars financed segregated white private schools. The Civil Rights Act of 1964 and Voting Rights Act of 1965 triggered a coded but powerful response—the so-called Southern Strategy and the War on Drugs that disenfranchised and imprisoned millions of African Americans. The election of Barack Obama, and the promise it heralded of healing our racial divide, precipitated instead a rash of voter suppression laws in Southern and swing states, while the Supreme Court's decision in *Shelby County v. Holder* gutted a key provision of the Voting Rights Act.[23]

I say again that each of these responses was calculated. And those who were not black, and so did not feel the stings and jabs of these responses, did nothing to stop them, or to right the so-obvious wrongs. And so, the backlashes were enacted, in silence.

We might want to shout, *What kind of "freedom" comes with "conditions"?* But this is, apparently, how our forefathers thought of it. And how some, today, still think of it: *We gave them their freedom. What more do they want?* A description of the earliest Civil War Amendment (the Thirteenth) says the following:

On February 10, 1864, [Judiciary Committee chairman Lyman] Trumbull reported the amendment out of committee and full Senate debate began. Fears of race-mixing and social upheaval—issues that figured prominently in the later House debate—were largely absent. Rather, senators argued over the constitutionality of uncompensated emancipation, the nature of federalism, and the propriety of adopting the first constitutional amendment in 60 years. A few radicals sought *ways to empower the freedmen with civil and economic rights*, but most senators agreed that abolition alone

---

23   See overview on the inside flap of *White Rage*'s jacket.

was the goal. "We give the [black man] *no right except his freedom*," explained Missouri senator John Henderson. "[We] leave the rest to the states."[24]

Henderson no doubt knew that "freedom" without a path to economic, educational, and political equity was no freedom at all.

We know it today. Yet, our government continues to play such politics with our black lives. It allows still for unfair housing policies like "redlining" and "blockbusting." It allows still for for-profit prisons to dot rural areas, growing, not lessening, the prison industrial complex, which sees the possibility of "billions behind bars,"[25] to say nothing of the continuance of free labor. It allows for substandard schools in inner cities where black and brown bodies live. It allows for polling places to be dismantled, making voting more inaccessible for black- and brown- and red-skinned folk. It allows for institutions intended to safeguard the rights of life, liberty, and the pursuit of happiness for black people to be crippled to the point of nonexistence, to be trampled before our eyes. Today, during the COVID-19 pandemic, we see who are "essential workers," whom we have always depended on and yet have been unwilling to pay. Today we see who dies in record, and unequal, numbers because of how we have forced them to live in unhealthy environments without our even noticing that those areas are also precisely the same places that become "food deserts" through our negligence, the same places where we allow lead-polluted water and where we build our environmentally ztoxic plants.

We keep repeating the *facts* that we have long known; but no one else seems to be listening: For example, for all its talk about "freedom," the United States is a callously punitive nation. The U.S. has the largest prison population in the world and the highest per-capita incarceration rate. "The prison population has increased from 300,000 in the early 1970s to 2.3 million people today. There are nearly six million people on probation or on parole. One in every fifteen people born in the

---

24   See https://www.senate.gov/artandhistory/history/minute/Senate_Passes_the_ Thirteenth_Amendment.htm.

25   "'Billions Behind Bars: Inside America's Prison Industry,' a CNBC original documentary, goes behind the razor wires to investigate the profits and inner workings of the multibillion-dollar corrections industry in the U.S." (CNBC, "CNBC's 'Billions Behind Bars: Inside America's Prison Industry' Will Premiere Tuesday, October 18th," news release, September 19, 2011, https://www.cnbc. com/id/44552028.)

United States in 2001 is expected to go to jail or prison; *one in every three black male babies* born in this century is expected to be incarcerated."[26] Black and brown women fare no better in the U.S. prison systems, their numbers of incarceration being far higher than those for white women. Class and race meet at the intersection of justice. If one looks solely at drug offenses, for example, one can see that there seem clearly to be two different justice systems in place, with the "poor man's drug," crack, usually drawing sentences far longer than "rich man's drugs" like cocaine. The prison and legal systems lay bare the fact that it is far better to be rich and guilty, than poor and innocent. As Bryan Stevenson has said, "The opposite of poverty is not wealth; the opposite of poverty is justice."[27]

Thanks to three strident and wise young women—Alicia Garza, Patrisse Khan-Cullors,[28] and Opal Tometi—the Black Lives Matter movement was founded in 2013 in the wake of the "innocent" verdict handed down in the case of the murder of Trayvon Martin. The movement focused on black and brown men. But black and brown *women and little girls* are just as likely to suffer police brutality in America. We know this because of the corollary movement founded in December of 2014 called #SayHerName. The description of this organization can be found on its website. In part, it reads:

> Launched in December 2014 by the African American Policy Forum (AAPF) and Center for Intersectionality and Social Policy Studies (CISPS), the #SayHerName campaign brings awareness to the often invisible names and stories of Black women and girls who have been victimized by racist police violence, and provides support to their families.
>
> Black women and girls as young as 7 and as old as 93 have been killed by the police, though we rarely hear their names.[29]

We know that true justice has not been meted out because young black women—like Sandra Bland and Breonna Taylor—keep being brutally killed by the police and no one is being held accountable.

---

26 Stevenson, *Just Mercy*, 15.
27 Ibid., 18.
28 Of this dynamic trio, one has written a stirring memoir. See Khan-Cullors and bandele, *When They Call You a Terrorist*.
29 See https://aapf.org/sayhername.

And yet, as Baldwin wrote in 1966 in his famed letter to his nephew, "it is not permissible that the authors of devastation should also be innocent. It is the *innocence which constitutes the crime.*"[30]

I watched today (August 27, 2020) as Doc Rivers, a literal giant of a man, the six-foot-four black head coach of the Milwaukee Bucks basketball team, with tears in his eyes—just after his team had won in the first night of the NBA 2020 playoffs, but other teams had said they planned to boycott the remaining games because of the police killing of Jacob Blake in Kenosha, Wisconsin—made a pleading, emotional statement:

> It's *amazing* to me *why* we keep loving this country, and this country doesn't love us back.

We are at an inflection point. But we have been here before.

Today, the eloquence, insight and incisiveness of Eddie Glaude Jr. challenges us pointedly:

> The videos of George Floyd and Rayshard Brooks dying have combined with the vulnerability caused by COVID-19 and the feeling that the country is broken to bring us all to the brink of madness and, apparently, to the precipice of significant change. An odd admixture, but an understandable consequence of our troubled times. We now face a moral reckoning: Americans have to decide whether this country will truly be a multiracial democracy or whether to merely tinker around the edges of our problems once again and remain decidedly racist and unequal.[31]

Representative John Lewis, in his last letter to us, said that Emmett Till was his George Floyd; that Till's death had sparked his determination to get involved and to seek change in this country. I can honestly say that I did not think that, after the civil rights movement of the 1960s, there would be need for a Black Lives Matter movement some sixty years later. But I was wrong.

In January of 2009, I, along with millions of others, beamed with pride and almost unbelievable joy as the duly elected Barack Hussein Obama took the platform at his first inauguration for the Presidency of the United States. The Voting Rights Act had not yet been completely gutted by the U.S. Supreme Court. Many people seemed to be rethinking

---

30   Baldwin's "Letter to My Nephew on the One Hundredth Anniversary of the Emancipation" in *The Fire Next Time*, 5–6.

31   Glaude Jr., "The Country That Refused to Change," 82.

the need for so many prisons. It appeared that the promise, the deep values, and the moral ideals of what America could be were, at last, actually dawning. It was as if a mighty weight had been lifted from us and we could *all* breathe.

But it was not just Obama. For me, it was the moment when Aretha Franklin came to the podium and approached the microphone. It was when she, in her one-and-only unmatched style, solemnly and magisterially crooned out,

> My country, 'tis of thee,
> Sweet land of liberty,
> Of thee I sing;
> Land where my fathers died,
> Land of the pilgrims' pride
> From every mountainside,
> Let freedom ring[32]

. . . that I felt, *at last, free*, that those words had meaning for *me*; that this was my country too, and that I "belonged" here because I had earned it, and I had at long last been seen. I felt, for the first time in my life on this continent free; a citizen of this country with all the rights and duties that pertain to it. That this country held, indeed, the promise to be a land of "sweet liberty" for all.

That spirit of freedom engendered by the 2008 American election, while a joyous one all over the world, has not proven to be lasting. After eight years of watching and listening to a thoughtful and articulate black man in the White House, we have seen the vicious backlashes and reprisals. We have seen the ugly specter of the worst inclinations of small minds, hatred and greed, rise up again in America with venomous and vicious fury.

We simply cannot allow this latest backlash to stand. We must seize this moment to bend the moral arc toward true justice and equality for all. And we must do so together. As Representative John Lewis told us: "Democracy is not a state [of being]; it is an *act*."[33] If we do not *act now*, we don't know whether we will get another chance to be free. ∎

---

32 See Franklin sing at the 2009 Inauguration of President Obama on YouTube at https://www.youtube.com/watch?v=QW7n8hklwsk.

33 Lewis, "Together, You Can Redeem the Soul of Our Nation."

SELECTED BIBLIOGRAPHY

Anderson, Carol. *White Rage; the Unspoken Truth of Our Racial Divide*. New York: Bloomsbury, 2020.

Baldwin, James. *The Fire Next Time*. New York: Vintage International, 1993. First Published 1963 by Dial Press (New York).

Glaude, Jr., Eddie. *Begin Again: James Baldwin's America and Its Urgent Lessons for Our Own*. New York: Crown, 2020.

———. "The Country That Refused to Change." *Time*, July 6–13, 2020.

Khan-Cullors, Patrisse, and asha bandele. *When They Call You a Terrorist: A Black Lives Matter Memoir*. New York: St. Martin's Press, 2017.

Lewis, John. "Together, You Can Redeem the Soul of Our Nation." *New York Times*, July 30, 2020. https://www.nytimes.com/2020/07/30/opinion/john-lewis-civil-rights-america.html.

Marin, Natasha. *Black Imagination: Black Voices on Black Futures*. San Francisco: McSweeney's, 2020.

Stevenson, Bryan. *Just Mercy: A Story of Justice and Redemption*. New York: Spiegel & Grau, 2014.

Willis, Jan. *Dreaming Me: Black, Baptist, and Buddhist*. Somerville, MA: Wisdom Publications, 2008.

Young, Ralph F., ed. *Dissent in America: Voices That Shaped a Nation*. New York: Pearson-Longman, 2008.

NOTES ON CONTRIBUTORS

A Chicago native, **JEFFERY RENARD ALLEN** is the author of five books, most recently the novel *Song of the Shank*. Allen has received numerous accolades for his work, including a Whiting Award, a Guggenheim fellowship, a residency at the Bellagio Center, and fellowships at the Center for Scholars and Writers, the Johannesburg Institute for Advanced Studies, and the Schomburg Center for Research in Black Culture. His collection of stories *Fat Time* will be published in 2022. Founder and editor of the online magazine *Taint Taint Taint*, he is at work on several projects, including the critical study *The Rhythm of the Hot Dog: Music as Narrative*, the memoir *Mother Wit*, and the novel *Hour of the Seeds*. He makes his home in Johannesburg. Find out more about him at www.authorjefferyrenardallen.com

New York Times bestselling Afrofuturism pioneer **STEVEN BARNES** has published over thirty novels, including the NAACP Image Award winning *In the Night of the Heat*, written with his wife and partner, American Book Award-winning novelist Tananarive Due. Born and raised in Los Angeles, he has also written for television's *The Twilight Zone, Outer Limits, Stargate SG-1, Andromeda* and more. His next book, written with National Book Award winner Charles Johnson, is a graphic novel using EC comic style storytelling to explore Buddhism's path to enlightenment, and will be published by Abrams Comic Arts/Megascope in 2022.

ARTHUR BURGHARDT is formerly a professional actor secretly writing for fifty years. These poems herein will mark gratefully for him, at seventy-three, the very first time he is published in a prestigious periodical and mantled as poet. He considers his work epic narrative poetry; observation and diegesis of the disastrous 20th century is a major part of his poetic autobiography in odes & short poems.

A 2019 Guggenheim fellow, **CYRUS CASSELLS** has won the National Poetry Series, a Lambda Literary Award, and a Lannan Literary Award. His 2018 volume *The Gospel according to Wild Indigo* was a finalist for the NAACP Image Award. *Still Life with Children: Selected Poems of Francesc Parcerisas*, translated by Cassells from the Catalan, received the Texas

Institute of Letters' Soeurette Diehl Fraser Award for Best Translated Book of 2018 and 2019. His eighth book of poems, *The World That the Shooter Left Us,* is due from Four Way Books in March 2022. He has recently completed a first novel, *My Gingerbread Shakespeare,* and is currently midway through a second novel, *The Going of the Inland Soul to Sea,* set in late 19th and early 20th century Hawaii, the first book in a planned trilogy about epidemics and pandemics. He is a tenured full professor of English at Texas State University.

LOUIS CHUDE-SOKEI teaches at Boston University and directs the African American Studies Program. His academic work includes the award-winning *The Last Darky: Bert Williams, Black on Black Minstrelsy and the African Diaspora* (2005) and *The Sound of Culture: Diaspora and Black Technopoetics* (2015) and his public work has appeared in a range of national and international venues. His memoir, *Floating in a Most Peculiar Way,* was published by Houghton Mifflin Harcourt in 2021. He is the Editor in Chief of *The Black Scholar,* one of the oldest and leading journals of Black Studies in America, and the founder of the sonic art and archival project, *Echolocution.*

AARON COLEMAN is the author of *Threat Come Close* (Four Way Books, 2018), winner of the Great Lakes Colleges Association New Writers Award, and *St. Trigger* (Button, 2016), selected by Adrian Matejka for the Button Poetry Chapbook Prize. Aaron is the recipient of fellowships from the National Endowment for the Arts, the J. William Fulbright Program, the Cave Canem Foundation, and the American Literary Translators Association. He has lived and worked with youth in locations including Spain, South Africa, Chicago, St. Louis, and Kalamazoo. His poems and essays have appeared in publications including *Boston Review, Callaloo, The New York Times,* the Poetry Society of America, and the Academy of American Poets' *Poem-a-Day* series. Aaron is currently a PhD Candidate in Comparative Literature at Washington University in St. Louis, where his research focuses on translation's role in vivifying relationships between Afrodescendant writers across the African diaspora.

celeste doaks is an award-winning poet, editor, and journalist. She is the author of *Cornrows and Cornfields* (2015), and editor of the poetry anthology *Not Without Our Laughter* (2017). Her chapbook, *American Herstory* (2019) was the first-place winner in Backbone Press's 2018 chapbook contest; it contains poems about Michelle Obama and the art she chose for the White House walls. Her poems, essays and reviews have appeared in multiple on-line and print publications including *Ms. Magazine, Time Out*

New York, The Village Voice, The Rumpus, The Millions, Huffington Post, Chicago Quarterly Review, and *Asheville Poetry Review* among others. Currently, she teaches creative writing at Stevenson University and writes a monthly book recommendation column at *B'more Art* magazine called *Litscope.* Her new works-in-progress include her second full length poetry collection and a hybrid music biography and personal memoir. In her *very* spare time, she tends to her husband and budding plant collection.

RITA DOVE was born in Akron, Ohio, in 1952. She is the author of a novel, short stories, the drama *The Darker Face of the Earth,* as well as ten books of poetry, including *Thomas and Beulah,* winner of the 1987 Pulitzer Prize, and *Sonata Mulattica,* a poetic tribute to 19th century Afro-European violin prodigy George Bridgetower; her eleventh poetry collection, *Playlist for the Apocalypse,* is forthcoming this year from W.W. Norton. Her numerous honors include an NAACP Image Award (for *Collected Poems 1974-2004*), the Heinz Award in the Arts and Humanities, and the Academy of American Poets' Wallace Stevens Award. She was U.S. Poet Laureate from 1993 to 1995 and is the only poet to have received both the National Humanities Medal (from President Clinton in 1996) and the National Medal of Arts (from President Obama in 2011). She edited *Best American Poetry 2000* and *The Penguin Anthology of 20th-Century American Poetry* and has written weekly poetry columns for *The Washington Post* and *The New York Times.* A member of the American Academy of Arts and Sciences and the American Academy of Arts and Letters, she is Henry Hoyns Professor of Creative Writing at the University of Virginia, where she has been teaching since 1989.

RACHEL ELIZA GRIFFITHS is a poet, novelist, and photographer. Her most recent hybrid collection of poetry and photography, *Seeing the Body* (W.W. Norton 2020), was nominated for the 2021 NAACP Image Award in Outstanding Literary Work (Poetry). Griffiths' visual and literary work has appeared widely, including in *The New York Times, The New Yorker, The Paris Review, Los Angeles Review of Books, Best American Poetry (2020, 2021), Poets & Writers, Mosaic, Kenyon Review,* and many others. Griffiths is the recipient of fellowships from the Robert Rauschenberg Foundation, Cave Canem, Kimbilio, and Yaddo. Her debut novel, *Promise,* is forthcoming from Random House. She lives in New York City.

Throughout his writing career, **PETER J. HARRIS'** cultural work has respected and celebrated the intimate lives of Black men. He has published essays, poetry and fiction since the 1970s, and in 2010 he founded The Black Man of Happiness Project, a creative, intellectual and artistic exploration of Black men and joy. Harris writes the monthly blog *WREAKING HAPPINESS: A Joyful Living Journal.* His book of personal essays, *The Black Man of Happiness: In Pursuit of My 'Unalienable Right,'* won a 2015 American Book Award. The Pollination Project, in awarding him two grants for the See You Campaign on Instagram @seeyou247, called him "among a select group of individuals who are using their gifts to create positive change in the world," and featured him in a *Profiles in Compassion* video profile. Harris is a 2018 Los Angeles COLA Fellow in literary arts and a Fellow of the Los Angeles Institute for the Humanities at USC. His work about manhood and masculinity has been published in several anthologies: *The Black Body,* edited by Meri Danquah (2009); *What Makes a Man: Twenty-two Writers Imagine the Future,* edited by Rebecca Walker (2004); *Tenderheaded: A Comb-Bending Collection of Hair Stories,* edited by Pamela Johnson and Juliette Harris (2001); *Black Men Speaking,* edited by Charles Johnson and John McCluskey, Jr. (1997); *Fathersongs: Testimonies by African-American Sons and Daughters,* edited by Gloria Wade-Gayles (1997); and *I Hear a Symphony: African Americans Celebrate Love,* edited by Paula L. Woods and Felix H. Liddell (1994).

A Chicago-based performance artist and published poet and writer, **LE VAN D. HAWKINS'** prose has appeared in such publications as *Lunch Ticket* literary journal, *EDNA, Bleed Literary Blog, LA Times, LA Weekly, Santa Fe Reporter* (NM), *Sacramento News and Review* (CA) and *Children of the Dream: Our Own Stories of Growing Up Black in America* (Simon & Schuster). He is the winner of the 2019 Great River Writers Retreat Contest. His poetry has appeared in publications such as *Spillway 10, Voices from Leimert Park, Best of Austin International Poetry Festival,* and *City of Los Angeles African Heritage Month Cultural Guide.* In Chicago, he has read and performed at John and Nancy Hughes Theater, Filet of Solo Festival, Don't Be Ridiculous Series at Steppenwolf Theatre, the Homolatte Reading series, Outspoken series at Sidetracks, This Much is True Chicago, Links Hall, RhinoFest, and The Center On Halsted. Previously of Los Angeles, he has appeared at USC, UCLA Hammer Museum, Disney Hall Redcat Theater, Highways Performance Space, Beyond Baroque Literary Center, and the World Stage. A recipient of several fellowships including the MacDowell, Le Van received his BFA from the Goodman School of Drama of the Art Institute of Chicago and his MFA from Antioch University-LA. Currently, he is working on *What Men Do,* a memoir.

TSEHAYE G. HÉBERT, MFAW (she/her/hers) is a citizen playwright (Alliance Kendeda National Graduate Playwright Award; American College Theatre Festival; Voices Rising Fellow, Vermont Studio Center; Chicago

State University, Playwright-In-Residence; The Guild Literary Complex, 30 Writers to Watch; Midwest Black Playwrights Project; Native Voices and Visions, Louisiana State University; RhinoFest; Finalists Cultural DC/SourceFest, Frank McCourt Memoir Contest, Sundance Theatre Lab), whose devotion to craft, inclusion and access brings her unique voice to the fore with hybrid, quirky stories of Black American life. Fueled by a family of creatives, the writer's imagination ultimately led the Northwestern University alum to complete the MFAW at the School of the Art Institute where she wrote *The Chicago Quartet*. This series of stage works crosses genres and epochs and is an intimate look at history, its invention and reinvention, in the writer's hands. One might find Holy Mother Bishop Consuela York, Ida B. Wells, Lucy Parsons and Benji Wilson in this Dramatists Guild member's work. Hébert volunteers with ETA Creative Arts Foundation, ADA 25 Advancing Leadership, and Chicago Cultural Accessibility Consortium, among others.

DAVID HENDERSON was connected to the Black Arts Movement through the Umbra Workshop, where he served as an editor of their magazine and editor of the three Umbra anthologies. *De Mayor of Harlem* and *Neo-California* are his best-known books of poetry. He has read a selection of his poetry for the permanent archives of the Library of Congress. Author of the lyrics to Sun Ra's composition "Love in Outer Space," he has also recorded with the saxophonists and composers Ornette Coleman and David Murray and the cornetist and composer Butch Morris. Author of the biography *'Scuse Me While I Kiss the Sky: Jimi Hendrix: Voodoo Child*, he wrote and produced an award-winning two-hour documentary on the African American Beat poet Bob Kaufman for National Public Radio and Pacifica Radio, which inspired a critically acclaimed film, *And When I Die I Won't Stay Dead*, directed by Billy Woodberry. He was a poet-in-residence at The City College of New York, has taught in CUNY's SEEK Program and has been a visiting professor at the University of California, Berkeley; UC San Diego; the State University of New York at Stony Brook; and Wesleyan University. Most recently he became the first Fellow of the Lost and Found Poetics Initiative out of the Center for the Humanities at CUNY's Graduate Center, New York.

E. HUGHES is an MFA+MA candidate in poetry at Northwestern University. Her poems have been published in *Poet Lore*, *The Offing*, and *Wildness Magazine*—among others. In 2017, she was nominated for a Pushcart Prize. Hughes has been a participant in the Tin House summer and winter workshops, the Zora Neale Hurston/Richard Wright Foundation workshop, as well as the Palm Beach Poetry Festival. Hughes' work broadly explores, in lyric, the minutiae of intercommunal and systemic violence and the ways one endures the aftermath of history. Originally from San Jose, California, Hughes lives in Chicago with her partner, hound dog, and calico cat.

DR. CHARLES JOHNSON, University of Washington (Seattle) professor emeritus and the author of twenty-five books, is a novelist, philosopher, essayist, literary scholar, short-story writer, cartoonist and illustrator, an author of children's literature, and a screen-and-teleplay writer. A MacArthur fellow, Johnson has received a 2002 American Academy of Arts and Letters Award for Literature, a 1990 National Book Award for his novel *Middle Passage*, a 1985 Writers Guild award for his PBS teleplay "Booker," the 2016 W.E.B. Du Bois Award at the National Black Writers Conference, and many other awards. The Charles Johnson Society at the American Literature Association was founded in 2003. In February 2020, Lifeline Theater in Chicago debuted its play adaptation of *Middle Passage*. Dr. Johnson's most recent publications are *The Way of the Writer: Reflections on the Art and Craft of Storytelling*, his fourth short story collection, *Night Hawks*, which was nominated for a 2019 Washington State Book Award, and *GRAND: A Grandparent's Wisdom for a Happy Life*. With Steven Barnes, he is co-author of the forthcoming graphic novel, *The Eightfold Path*. Johnson is one of five people on posters created in 2019 by the American Philosophical Association (APA) to encourage diversity in the field of philosophy.

JAMIEL LAW is an illustrator, problem-solver and creative thinker. He was born and raised in Sarasota, Florida, where he was exposed to the arts and the cultures behind them. His client list includes *The New York Times, The New Yorker, Medium, NBC News, Slate, The Washington Post, The Atlantic, Bravery Magazine, Equal Justice Initiative,* and *The Guardian*.

CLARENCE MAJOR is the author of sixteen collections of poetry, including *From Now On: New and Selected Poems,* and two collections of short stories. He is also the author of the novels *Dirty Bird Blues, Painted Turtle: Woman with Guitar, Such Was The Season* and eight other novels. He is a painter and distinguished professor emeritus at the University of California, Davis. Among his many honors and awards are a National Book Award Bronze Medal, a Western States Book Award, a "Lifetime Achievement Award for Excellence in the Fine Arts" from the Congressional Black Caucus Foundation, the PEN-Oakland Reginald Lockett Lifetime Achievement Award in Literature, a Fulbright Fellowship, and a National Council on the Arts Fellowship.

JOHN MCCLUSKEY, JR. is Professor Emeritus of African American and African Diaspora Studies at Indiana University-Bloomington where he taught fiction writing and literature. He is the author of two novels, *Look What They Done to My Song* and *Mr. America's Last Season Blues.* His short fiction has appeared in numerous journals and collections including *Ploughshares, Southern Review, Ancestral House: The Black Short Story in the Americas and Europe, Best American Short Stories,* and *Calling the Wind.* As a founding co-editor, he is an Editor Emeritus of the "Blacks in Diaspora" series at Indiana University Press, a project that published some fifty titles in the humanities and social sciences. Currently he is an associate editor at the journal *Callaloo* and at work on a series of historical and contemporary short stories.

E. ETHELBERT MILLER is a writer and literary activist. He is the author of two memoirs and several books of poetry including *The Collected Poems of E. Ethelbert Miller,* a comprehensive collection that represents over forty years of his work. For seventeen years Miller served as the editor of *Poet Lore,* the oldest poetry magazine published in the United States. He hosts the WPFW morning radio show *On the Margin with E. Ethelbert Miller* and hosts and produces *The Scholars* on UDC-TV, which received a 2020 Telly Award. Most recently, Miller received a grant from the D.C. Commission on the Arts and Humanities and a congressional award from Congressman Jamie Raskin in recognition of his literary activism. His latest book, *If God Invented Baseball,* published by City Point Press, was awarded the 2019 Literary Award for poetry by the Black Caucus of the American Library Association. Miller has two forthcoming books: *When Your Wife Has Tommy John Surgery and Other Baseball Stories* and *the little book of e.*

YESENIA MONTILLA is an Afro-Latina poet & a daughter of immigrants. She received her MFA from Drew University in Poetry & Poetry in translation. She is a CantoMundo graduate fellow and a 2020 NYFA fellow. Her work has been published in Academy of American Poets *Poem-a-Day, Prairie Schooner, Gulf Coast* and *Best American Poetry 2020.* Her first collection *The Pink Box* was published by Willow Books and was longlisted for a PEN award. Her second collection, *Muse Found in a Colonized Body,* is forthcoming from Four Way Books in 2022. She lives in Harlem, New York.

DAVID NICHOLSON's story, "that's why darkies were born," is part of a collection, tentatively titled "*dysaesthesia Aethiopica.*" He is working on a family history/memoir, *The Simonses of S Street: The Story of an American Family,* which begins with a slave who bought his freedom in 1819 and ends after World War II. A former editor and reviewer for *The Washington*

Post Book World, Nicholson is the author of a collection of stories, *Flying Home: Seven Stories of the Secret City*. He lives just outside of Washington, D.C., with his wife and college-age son.

DELIA C. PITTS is the author of contemporary noir mysteries including *Lost and Found in Harlem* and *Pauper and Prince in Harlem*. The fifth entry in this private eye series, *Murder My Past*, was published in February 2021. Her short story "The Killer," published in *Chicago Quarterly Review* #31, was selected for inclusion in *Best American Mystery and Suspense 2021*. Born and raised in Chicago, Pitts began her writing journey as a copy boy for the Chicago *Sun-Times*. After earning a PhD in history from the University of Chicago, she served as a U.S. diplomat in West Africa and Mexico. She then worked as a senior administrator in universities in Texas and New Jersey. She lives with her husband in central New Jersey. For more information, visit her website, www.deliapitts.com and follow her on Twitter at @blacktop1950 and on Instagram at @deliapitts50.

MONA LISA SALOY, PhD, is an award-winning author & folklorist, educator, and scholar of Creole culture in articles, documentaries, and poems about Black New Orleans before and after Katrina. Currently Conrad N. Hilton Endowed Professor of English at Dillard University, Dr. Saloy has documented Creole culture in sidewalk songs, jump-rope rhymes, and clap-hand games to discuss the importance of play. She writes on the significance of the Black Beat poets, especially Bob Kaufman, and on the African American Toasting Tradition, Black & Creole talk, and on life and keeping Creole after the devastation of Hurricane Katrina. A poet, her first book, *Red Beans & Ricely Yours*, won the T.S. Eliot Prize and the PEN/Oakland Josephine Miles Award. Her collection of poems, *Second Line Home*, captures day-to-day New Orleans speech, family dynamics, celebrates New Orleans, and gives insight into the unique culture the world loves. Saloy's screenplay for the documentary *Easter Rock* premiered in Paris, the *Ethnograph* Film Festival & at the National Museum of African American History and Culture. She's lectured on Black Creole Culture at the Smithsonian, Purdue University, and the University of Washington. Her documentary, *Bleu Orleans*, is on Black Creole Culture. She is an editorial reviewer for *Meridians: Feminism, race, transnationalism*.

SHARYN SKEETER was fiction, poetry, and book review editor at *Essence* magazine and editor in chief at *Black Elegance* magazine. She taught journalism, writing, and black American literature at Emerson College, the University of Bridgeport, and Three Rivers, Norwalk, and

Gateway community colleges. Skeeter's poetry and articles have been published in magazines, journals, and anthologies, including *In Search of Color Everywhere* (ed. E. Ethelbert Miller) and *Our Black Sons Matter* (ed. George Yancy). Her debut novel *Dancing with Langston* received the 2019 Gold Foreword Reviews INDIES Book of the Year Award (multicultural adult fiction). She has given readings and participated in literary events in the United States, India, and Singapore. She is on the Board at ACT Theatre in Seattle. "The Comeback" is an excerpt from her second novel-in-progress, working title *Crossing Darnell's Mirror*.

CLIFFORD THOMPSON is the author of *What It Is: Race, Family, and One Thinking Black Man's Blues* (2019), published by Other Press and selected by *Time* magazine as one of the "Most Anticipated Books" of the season. Thompson received a Whiting Writers' Award for nonfiction in 2013 for *Love for Sale and Other Essays*, published by Autumn House Press, which also brought out his memoir *Twin of Blackness* (2015). His personal essays and writings on books, film, jazz, and American identity have appeared in publications including *The Best American Essays 2018*, *The Washington Post*, *The Wall Street Journal*, *The Village Voice*, *The Times Literary Supplement*, *The Threepenny Review*, *Commonweal*, *Cineaste*, and *The Los Angeles Review of Books*. He is the author of a novel, *Signifying Nothing*. For over a dozen years Thompson served as the editor of *Current Biography*, and he teaches creative nonfiction writing at the Bennington Writing Seminars, New York University, and Sarah Lawrence College. He lives in Brooklyn. A painter, Thompson is a member of New York's Blue Mountain Gallery. His first graphic novel, *Big Man and the Little Men*, is due out from Other Press in Fall 2022.

Along with two memoirs, *Street Shadows* and *The World in Flames*, **JERALD WALKER** is the author of *How to Make a Slave and Other Essays,* a 2020 nonfiction Finalist for the National Book Award. His work has appeared in publications such as *The Harvard Review, Creative Nonfiction, The Iowa Review,* and *Mother Jones,* and it has been widely anthologized, including five times in *The Best American Essays* series. He has received fellowships from the National Endowment for the Arts and the James A. Michener Foundation, and is a Professor of Creative Writing and African American Literature at Emerson College.

JAN WILLIS (BA and MA in Philosophy from Cornell University; PhD in Indic and Buddhist Studies from Columbia University) is currently Professor of Religion Emerita at Wesleyan University in Middletown, Connecticut, and Visiting Professor of Religion at Agnes Scott College in Decatur, Georgia. She has studied with Tibetan Buddhists in India, Nepal, Switzerland, and the U.S. for five decades, and has taught courses in Buddhism for over forty-five years. She is the author of *The Diamond Light: An Introduction to Tibetan Buddhist Meditation* (1972), *On Knowing Reality: The Tattvartha Chapter of Asanga's Bodhisattvabhumi* (1979), *Enlightened Beings: Life Stories from the Ganden Oral Tradition* (1995); and the editor of *Feminine Ground: Essays on Women and Tibet* (1989). Additionally, Willis has published numerous articles and essays on various topics in Buddhism—Buddhist meditation, hagiography, women and Buddhism, and Buddhism and race. In 2001 her memoir *Dreaming Me: An African American Woman's Spiritual Journey* was published. It was re-issued in 2008 by Wisdom Publications as *Dreaming Me: Black, Baptist, and Buddhist—One Woman's Spiritual Journey.* In December of 2000, *TIME* magazine named Willis one of six "spiritual innovators for the new millennium." In 2003, she was a recipient of Wesleyan University's Binswanger Prize for Excellence in Teaching. *Newsweek* magazine's "Spirituality in America" issue in 2005 included a profile of Willis and, in its May 2007 edition, *Ebony* magazine named Willis one of its "Power 150" most influential African Americans. In April of 2020, her latest book, *Dharma Matters: Women, Race and Tantra; Collected Essays by Jan Willis*, was published.

Best Books of 2018
"A stunning debut memoir..."
KIRKUS REVIEWS

Best Book—Indie Nonfiction 2018
CHICAGO WRITERS ASSOCIATION

Literature of the African Diaspora

From

SWAN
ISLE
PRESS

Malambo
Lucía Charún-Illescas
Translated by Emmanuel Harris II

2004 *Foreword* magazine's Gold Book of the Year

"*Malambo* calls into question hegemonic assumptions about Spanish American history by underscoring the role that African-descended people played in shaping that history."—*PALARA*

"Charún-Illecas presents a welcome alternative view of the origin of her home continent."—*Belletrista*

Cloth $28.00

Over the Waves and Other Stories /
Sobre las olas y otros cuentos
A Bilingual Edition
Inés María Martiatu

Translated by Emmanuel Harris II with a Postscript by Tànit Fernández de la Reguera

Appearing for the first time outside of Cuba, this collection of short stories provides an intimate and critical view of Afro-Cuba. Martiatu's stories—presented here in the original Spanish, with facing-page English translations—span postcolonial Cuba of the early twentieth century to contemporary life in the streets of Havana.

Cloth $28.00

Now in Paperback

Shadows of Your Black Memory
Donato Ndongo

Translated and with a Postscript by Michael Ugarte

"An enthralling text."—*Atlanta Books Examiner*

"*Shadows of Your Black Memory* is a sensual, impressionistic, seemingly autobiographical novel about a young boy growing up on the mainland of what was then the colony of Spanish Guinea."
—*Words Without Borders*

Paper $20.00

Distributed by the University of Chicago Press   www.press.uchicago.edu

Let's just write!

An Uncommon Writers Conference

MARCH 19-20, 2022

WARWICK ALLERTON HOTEL DOWNTOWN CHICAGO

Join us for two days for an in-person event,

LET'S JUST WRITE! AN UNCOMMON WRITERS CONFERENCE

- More than 20 amazing presenters and panelists
- Book signings
- Two breakfasts, one lunch, dinner with special author interview
- Manuscript consultations
- Publishers panel
- Networking/New friends

and more...

Brought to you by

chicago **writers** association

chicagowrites.org/conference

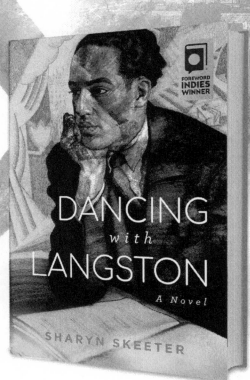

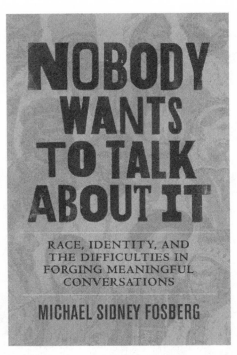

NOBODY WANTS TO TALK ABOUT IT

RACE, IDENTITY, AND THE DIFFICULTIES IN FORGING MEANINGFUL CONVERSATIONS

MICHAEL SIDNEY FOSBERG

FOR THE PAST FIFTEEN YEARS, MICHAEL FOSBERG HAS PERFORMED an autobiographical one-man play at middle & high schools, colleges, corporations, government agencies and community organizations across the country. The play chronicles the journey to find his biological father and discovering his family's African-American roots. Having been raised thinking he was White, this sudden discovery of his Black roots had implications beyond simply his own identity. By performing both Black & White characters, intentionally incorporating suggestive racial stereotypes, candidly examining passing, covering, White privilege and code switching, he challenges audiences to openly discuss these issues while also acknowledging their common bonds.

In both his show and memoir, *INCOGNITO: An American Odyssey of Race and Self-Discovery*, published in 2011, he purposefully sets a course to engage people in meaningful conversations about how we see ourselves and others, and the ways in which we do and don't talk about race & identity. In *Nobody Wants to Talk About It*, Michael shares stories of his travels across the country to provoke conversations about race & identity. His 15+ years of fostering constructive dialogue lead him to craft seven helpful tools to navigate difficult conversations around issues of race and identity. The book also includes the script of his one-man play Incognito, suggestions for creating space for meaningful dialogue, resource materials and more.

Available at **www.incognitotheplay.com**

MUNRO CAMPAGNA
ARTIST REPRESENTATIVES

410 S. Michigan Ave. Suite 439
Chicago, IL 60605
+1 312 335 8925

steve@munrocampagna.com
www.munrocampagna.com

Illustrator
Clint Hansen

Portrait of
Amanda Gorman

handcrafted by hedda

HeddaLubin.com   Green Briar Jewelry.com

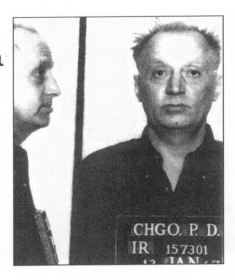

CRDT
CERQUA RIVERA DANCE THEATRE

"These are historic times that call for bravery and leadership. Being quiet is not an option for this company."
– Cofounder and Artistic Director Wilfredo Rivera

Cerqua Rivera Dance Theatre uses dance and music to nourish the mind and the soul. The company unites artists and audiences to explore themes that shape our community.
more on Facebook, Instagram, and www.cerquarivera.org

SUNDAY SALON CHICAGO
IS A READING SERIES
THAT TAKES PLACE EVERY OTHER MONTH

NAMED ONE OF CHICAGO'S BEST LITERARY ORGANIZATIONS
BY NEWCITY

THE SALON SERIES HAS BROUGHT WORD POWER TO
NEW YORK CITY, NAIROBI, MIAMI AND CHICAGO
MAKING OUR BEST LOCAL AND NATIONAL WRITERS AVAILABLE
TO A LARGER COMMUNITY
FOR OVER 10 YEARS

WE MEET AT
THE REVELER*
3403 N Damen Ave. in Chicago
FROM 7PM TO 8PM ON THE LAST SUNDAY OF EVERY OTHER MONTH

EAT, DRINK YOUR FAVORITE DRINKS, MAKE NEW FRIENDS
AND ENJOY EXCELLENT READINGS WITH US!

OUR EVENTS ARE ALWAYS FREE

Find us at https://sundaysalon-chicago.com
https://www.facebook.com/Sunday.Salon.Chicago/

*Because restaurants and bars in Chicago are closed due to Coronavirus
beginning January 2021, we will have virtual events
until restaurants and bars can operate to full capacity.
Please check our website or Facebook page for registration information.

"An important and groundbreaking collection, bringing together important voices and biographical context illustrating four decades of Black perspectives on everything from daily life to the civil rights movement. Some of the strips will make your jaw drop with the way they bring to life a particular period in history, some of them will make you shake your head with the poignant realization of how little has changed, and some of them will just make you laugh."

—Eve L. Ewing, sociologist and Marvel Comics writer

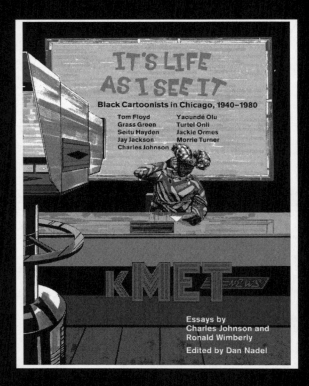

This anthology is a companion to the Museum of Contemporary Art Chicago's exhibition *Chicago Comics: 1960 to Now*.

Available June 1, 2021
www.nyrb.com/comics

An Ecotourism Nightmare

DEATH IN CENTRAL AMERICA

JACK HAFFERKAMP

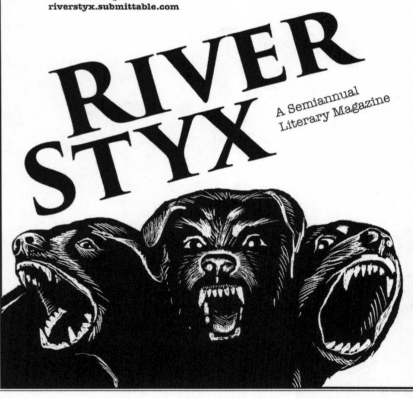

Made in the USA
Columbia, SC
02 June 2021